TRAILB.

Pioneering Alaska's Iditarod

By Rod Perry

"**Gold!** . . . *Sixty-eight rich men on the steamer Portland. STACKS OF YELLOW METAL!*" screams morning headlines of the Seattle Post-Intelligencer. A continent primed to catch gold fever is inflamed. The great rush to the fabled Klondike is on! Dawson booms to become the largest Canadian city west of Winnipeg!

"**Gold!** . . . *Incredible discovery at Anvil Creek! 'Three Lucky Swedes' strike it rich! Gold in the very beach sand! Gold back on the Third Beach Line!*" The turn-of-the-century cries flash around the globe. Teeming swarms of gold-crazed humanity stampede to the Nome beaches. Almost instantly, the "City of the Golden Sands" explodes into being. Within three years between 20,000 and 30,000 people inhabit the Seward Peninsula.

"**Gold!** . . . *Felix Pedro makes rich find sixteen miles northeast of Barnette's Post!*" . . ."*Gold on Ester Dome and other nearby locations. The entire mining district appears to be underlain with the wondrous stuff. We're rich!*" Discovery of one of the world's greatest gold-producing districts ignites a great stampede. The city of Fairbanks quickly becomes the lustrous center of Alaska's heartland.

"**Gold!!!** . . . **John Beaton and Henry Dikeman strike gold on Christmas Day!**" One last time the clarion cry rings forth, this time echoing out of the remote, unknown upper Iditarod River country. The last great gold rush on the North American Continent is on! Briefly, Iditarod becomes Alaska's biggest city!

To serve the great human influx and the mining industry, vast numbers of men, and amounts of mail, supplies, building materials and equipment must be brought in. Most come by water during the usual four or five ice-free months. Once the Bering Seacoast becomes ice locked, however, the only means of moving people, mail and freight in and out is over winter trails, mostly by dog team.

An important part of the story of the fabulous gold rushes of the North is the story of that transportation over the trail. Without winter movement, their discovery and development would have unfolded much differently.

During the harsh, sub-arctic winter, the towering bastions and deadly glaciers of the greatest mountains on the continent bar the way to interior gold for a thousand miles along the ice-free shipping waters around Alaska's southern coast. Only five rifts—just five cracks in the mountain fortress—provide useful corridors for moving men, freight and mail into the heartland mining districts. The last one found, over Rainy Pass, is the most remote and most primitive, taking travelers and their loads through some of the wildest country and most majestic scenery on the continent on their way to the gold fields of Iditarod and Nome.

Rod Perry writes *TRAILBREAKERS* in two volumes. The first chronicles the history of how the gold rush trail came to be. The second is the history of how the modern Iditarod Race was founded.

TRAILBREAKERS, Volume I chronicles the rich history of daring men and dynamic events that force the lock and break of the silence of the unknown North. Gold rush leads to gold rush, trail leads to trail, until it culminates in the last, glorious, hell-bent-for-leather gold rush and the final great gold rush trail in North America.

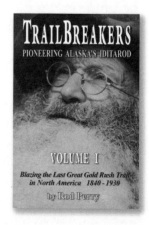

TRAILBREAKERS
PIONEERING ALASKA'S IDITAROD

VOLUME I

Blazing the Last Great Gold Rush Trail in North America 1840 - 1930

by Rod Perry

Trailbreakers, Volume I is the most-complete, most-accurate telling of how the fabled Iditarod Trail came to be. As it relates the 1840–1930 progression of events establishing the "Last Great Gold Rush Trail in North America," the book educates and corrects long-standing myths and misinformation that have grown up. It interests and entertains, filled as it is with humorous anecdotes and colorful gold rush tales. Anyone acquainted with Rod Perry as a raconteur knows he couldn't write history any other way.

TRAILBREAKERS, Volume II is the story of the founding of *"The Last Great Race on Earth®."* By Rod Perry, a race pioneer who ran the first Iditarod Race, it is the most in-depth telling of how today's Iditarod Trail Sled Dog Race came to be.

This volume:

- Includes never-before-told revelations surrounding the establishment of the event by an old insider.

- Blows away long-held myths and errors that have become imbedded in race lore.

- Draws from the only complete set of radio reports of the founding 1973 event.

- Tells little-known, incredible adventures and surprising details that were part and parcel of the wild and crazy, barely organized, absurd, glorious, trail-breaking running of first Iditarod Trail Sled Dog Race.

Books by Rod Perry may be purchased at
www.rodperry.com

TRAILBREAKERS
Pioneering Alaska's Iditarod

Volume I

Blazing the Last Great Gold Rush Trail in North America 1840 – 1930

By Rod Perry

TRAILBREAKERS
Pioneering Alaska's Iditarod
Blazing the Last Great Gold Rush Trail in North America
Volume I

ISBN 9780982373002

Library of Congress Control Number: 2009926082

364 p

Early exploration history—Alaska and Yukon Territory

Early history of prospecting, discovery, gold rushes—Alaska and Yukon Territory

History of discovery, use, development of transportation corridors to gold strikes—Alaska and Yukon Territory

Gold rush era dog team use—Alaska and Yukon Territory

Gold rush era stories—Alaska and Yukon Territory

Design and Layout: Sundog Media, Anchorage, Alaska, www.sundogmedia.com
Cover: Daniel Quick

First Edition 2009

Dedication

———❖———

OUR POPULATION—probably in Alaska more than
elsewhere—has individuals who, to use the words of the
late Territorial Governor of Alaska Ernest Gruening, "are
not wholly reconciled to the benefits of civilization—those
who, while enjoying civilization's creature comforts, still hold
a nostalgic longing for a vanished era in which men pitted
themselves against nature's hazards and still yearn for the
risks and challenges of an unspoiled wilderness."

That Gruening's words describe me may be attributed to
the influence of my parents, both of whom were born shortly
after the turn of the last century. My late mother, Eva Perry,
grew up in a sod house on a land claim in the New Mexico
Territory when Pancho Villa was raiding nearby. Gilbert
Perry, my late father, spent his early life on a homestead and
trapline in the foothills of the Canadian Rockies where his
family's closest neighbors and trapping partners were Native
Canadians still living a semi-nomadic lifestyle. This book is
dedicated to the memory of my parents.

To Ben,

Hold tight to the sled!

Rod Perry   July 1, 2009

i

TRAILBREAKERS

Acknowledgements

I ENTHUSIASTICALLY THANK the following contributors
to *Trailbreakers*:

Foremost, my Creator and Lord, Jesus Christ who inspired
me to write and blessed me with talent to spin a tale.

Larry and Pam Kaniut, my Alaska friends of longest standing,
who, for more than thirty years, continued to believe I should
write and never eased up on their urging.

Ingrid Sundstrom Lundegaard, whose expertise with words
reflects a lifetime of professional editing .

Daniel L. Quick, one of my oldest, truest friends, author
of *The Kenai Canoe Trails: Alaska's Premier Hiking and
Canoeing System*, creator of the *Trailbreakers* cover.

Alan Perry, my brother, artist, partner in many adventures,
Iditarod pioneer in his own right, and creator of the maps
that are so instrumental in orienting the reader.

Chad and Jessie Chilstrom, friends and supporters
extraordinaire whose untiring patience and cyber talents
were desperately needed by an author just emerging—not
very readily—from the Stone Age.

Bob and Karen Byron, Rick and Jane Erikson, Clovis
and Denise Marechal, Robert and Sandy Doran, Steve, Gwen
and Lindsay Hufford, Fred Perry, Richard and Velma Perry,

TRAILBREAKERS

Speed and Evelyn Rasmussen, Irene DeLauney, Cliff Sisson, Richard and Lillian Person, Patty Parker, Ken Davis and Dr. Frank and Sandi Moore for support that enabled production of *Trailbreakers*.

Kevin Keeler, Iditarod National Historic Trail Administrator, BLM Anchorage Field Office, who provided invaluable historical resources.

Dr. J.P. Waller, a God-sent friend, professor of creative writing at Wayland Baptist University and University of Alaska at Anchorage who generously gave of his time and considerable talent to mentor and encourage me, pre-edit the work, supply changes in phraseology far beyond mere editing and suggest creation of the "voices" and other literary devices which so inject life-blood and orientation to this history.

My children, Jordan, Ethan, Levi, Laura, and Gabriel, who stir my heart to leave them a legacy. Lovingly, they assisted in the work and lent listening ears to my testing of wording and passages.

Finally, my gratitude embraces the love of my life, my wonderful wife, Karen, whose faith, patience and encouragement allow me to lose myself in far-off realms of sentences and paragraphs as well as broader visions beyond this book.

Table of Contents

---◆---

Table of Maps

About the Author

Fat Albert and Rod Perry, "Nome or Buss"

ROD PERRY HAS RIDDEN and nursed from the udder
of a moose, eats Eskimo delicacies such as *oshok* (walrus
flipper buried in the frozen ground for a year to ferment,)
worked on a moose research project, made the motion
picture *Sourdough*, the most widely viewed feature ever
filmed in Alaska, and competed in the wild-and-crazy,
loosely-organized, first Iditarod Trail Sled Dog Race. To read
more about this Iditarod pioneer, turn to page 348.

Introduction

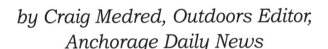

by Craig Medred, Outdoors Editor,
Anchorage Daily News

FOR AS LONG AS THERE HAS BEEN fur, gold, game and
adventure to be found, Alaska has fueled dreams and crushed
them. The land has made a few rich. It has sent far more
home penniless and beaten. And it has forged in some others
a strange fascination, a love almost, of what the north is,
what it was, and what it yet might be. Rod Perry is of these.

There is old joke among them: "I'm a sourdough. Sour on
the country, but without the dough to get out." The joke is not
heard so much these days. The civilized parts of Alaska have
become as politely Americanized as Seattle or Minneapolis.
But the joke was once heard quite often, usually uttered by
people you couldn't have paid enough to leave the country.
Alaska grows on these people even as it pounds the snot
out of them.

Perry knows of this. He is among that small group who
once dreamed of winning the Iditarod Trail Sled Dog Race,
though he'd probably deny that. Every Iditarod wannabe does.

The truth is different. Deep down, they all harbor the
fantasy that somehow it might happen, that somehow by some
freak accident they could win. It is a fantasy as old as Alaska.

The whalers, the trappers and especially the gold miners
all flooded the country chasing the dream they would be the
one to strike it rich, and they all knew full well how bad the
odds were stacked against them.

When you read *Trailbreakers,* you almost have to wonder
if the supposed lust to profit off the bounty of the land wasn't

more just an excuse for the adventure than anything else.

Too much of what so many did in those early years is like a grizzly bear excavating an entire mountain side in a futile effort to catch a tiny ground squirrel. Until you've witnessed this sort of behavior, or better yet lived it, it can be hard to fathom. Perry has lived some of it and well understands. He has sweated and grunted his way around Alaska. Anyone who does that develops a deep appreciation for the reality over the fiction.

As he notes: "Some modern writers claim that with the Nome Gold Rush beginning in 1898, and even more so with the 1906-1907 coming of mining to the Inland Empire, that mushers immediately commenced whizzing back and forth over the way through Rainy Pass.

"That could not be farther from the truth. Such writing demonstrates an absence of understanding of long-distance, wilderness dog team travel and Iditarod trail history. Unknowing writers just repeat what has been written by other unknowing writers, and so it goes back and back and back. To one who knows the subject, the constant errors in newspapers, magazines, books, brochures, tourist information, television and the internet stand out like the proverbial sore thumb."

It is time someone set the record straight. *Trailbreakers* is a good first step, though much remains to be done. Too much of what is written about what goes on along the Iditarod Trail to this day is written by people clueless of what it is actually like out there. Perry is at the opposite end of that spectrum.

As a chronicler of the sweat, the struggles and the sheer bullheadedness of Alaska history, he is excellent.

This probably isn't so much a book about adventure, as it is a book about men who were by God determined to get from point A to point B for reasons often known only to themselves.

Their journeys became an adventure.

And the amazing thing is that people like this still exist in Alaska today. They are the best of the place and yet remain, at times, the hardest to understand.

Time changes everything and it changes nothing.

Prologue

GOLD! WE KNOW IT LIES IN the structure of the western mountain chain through the Americas from the Southern Andes up through our Rockies. We've dug it out of California, mined it from the Rocky Mountain West. The lure of yellow riches has compelled us to these placers and lodes of British Columbia's Frasier, Caribou and Cassiar. Why stop here, the most driven gold-hunters reason, gazing ever northward.

But among even among the most aggressive of the wandering breed's boldest searchers, the great, unknown North chills the heart; few seem willing to test it. The vast, silent expanses are mostly a foreboding mystery. All that has seeped out from scant reports of the few explorers is that it is a harsh, unforgiving land of limitless distances, great rivers, deadly rapids and looming, foreboding mountains towering range beyond range, the whole country lying in wait to swallow even the bravest and best. It remains almost unknown to even its English and Russian owners. They have hardly probed it.

Now Russia sells Alaska to the United States. The entire northwest subcontinent is thrown open to exploration and its wealth made available to personal acquisition. Yet just the tiniest vanguard, only the most visionary and daring of the breed, set forth, turning their backs upon the last, wild fringes of the northern frontier, disappearing toward the distant Arctic Ocean. They will penetrate the unknown and probe it for gold, or, perhaps, perish in the attempt.

Great mountain ranges almost completely seal off the way into the country, especially the way in from the Southeastern Alaska and Gulf of Alaska seacoasts. By great good luck, having only the barest, most fragmentary ideas of the geographical lay of northwestern North America, the forerunners gamble on a surprising, roundabout route that takes them almost to the polar sea, the better part of a thousand miles farther than the way most would try. But those thousand miles bring them through the back door into the heart of the gold country, taking them completely *around* the Northern Rockies, fortunately saving them perhaps years of frustrated searching had they instead tried to find the few, thin breaks leading *through* the mountains from the southern, seaward side.

They find intriguing traces of gold, vindicating their expectations. As well, their discoveries kindle bright fires of hope among the most intrepid of their brethren to the south who are first to learn of the vanguard's success along the great and wonderful river they tell of.

The coastal mountain fortress yields but slight, hard-to-detect chinks in its armor. However, from inside information gleaned in bits and pieces from the native inhabitants, the earliest gold-hunters find those cracks. The country is entered and prospected. Small gold discoveries lead to the richest strikes on earth and the greatest, most glorious gold rushes the world has ever known.

Efficient transportation by water is developed, but is useful only during the brief, four-to-five-month summer shipping season. Most of the year arctic temperatures seize the North, squeezing down or completely cutting off transportation and communication to the outside. Gold country is separated from the industrialized world, choking development.

Winter passageways must be found and developed if men, supplies and mail are to be moved in and out of the golden heartland and the country is to grow.

An Old Album Speaks

———◆———

Rod Perry: *As a young boy growing up in Oregon, I got to know Al and Alma Preston, a generation older than my father and mother, yet close friends. How close? When I was a baby, they appealed to my parents: "Would you consider giving Rod to us? You'd still be able to watch him grow up and you're young enough to have more children." While the idea was naturally unthinkable to my folks, they felt honored.*

When I was about eight years old I became aware that whenever the weekly broadcasts of Sergeant Preston of the Royal Canadian Mounted Police and his great lead dog, King, hit the airways, Al and Alma would glue themselves to their radio. From the speakers Preston's urgent cry would sound out, "On, King, on you great husky!" Ne'er-do-wells shuddered to hear the Sergeant's banal proclamation, "You're under arrest in the name of the crown! This case is closed." Years later, I understood that the attraction had nothing to do with the coincidence of a shared name; from those episodes the old couple received their weekly fix of reminiscence.

Later, I was to learn that Alma had eloped a few years after the great gold rushes with her first husband, Merrill Leonhardt, and shipped north to Seward, Alaska. There they were employed by "Colonel" Harry Revell, to whom the U.S. Postal Service had awarded the contract to run Seward-to-Nome mail over the Iditarod Trail. Working in Revell's dog-team transport business, Alma met many of the legendary dog drivers who covered the trails of Alaska and the Yukon. Perhaps realizing she was participating in history, she

7

Alma in Seward

snapped pictures documenting her work—invaluable snapshots that she later assembled into a treasured album.

Merrill Leonhardt died in the devastating, worldwide influenza epidemic of 1918. Some years later, Alma fell in love with and married Al Preston, a miner from the Nome end of the Iditarod Trail. And so, as I came to know them, they would mesmerize my family with gold-rush era anecdotes and tales of the old trail drawn from experience at both ends of the Iditarod.

Over time, as Al and Alma drew close to death, they offered everything they had to my parents. Almost everything. I was given the ancient album. There, inside the front cover and next to her memorabilia, Alma had lovingly affixed my portrait, taken when I was but six months old.

Today, a century after Alma began snapping her pictures of the "Colonel," his dogs, sleds, shelter cabins and dog barns, Alaska Railroad construction and the drivers and teams hauling U.S. Mail coming through, and a half century after she first took me on a guided tour through her Iditarod photo record, I remember. Now, once more I open the old brown cover. Thumbing slowly through and savoring aging images, the pages of the old album take me back yet once more to yesteryear. I fight to curb the emotions and choke back the lump in my throat as voices and images from a never-to-be repeated, glorious age I wish I, too, had seen, overtake my reverie.

Again, as I listen anew, the memory of her becomes so real that I smell the aromas that inevitably wafted from her kitchen, and I again hear not only her low, raspy, voice but other voices brought to life through her well-told reminiscences. Drifting, I can listen to the give and take, ebb and flow of conversation... always I detect Alma's voice through the mix of the others. Her special way of speaking comes back as clearly as if she now sat near me patiently answering another of my persistent questions.

"Alma, how did the Iditarod gold rush and the Iditarod Trail come to be? The rush and trail couldn't have just *materialized at once. Mr. Beaton and Mr. Dikeman did not just find gold at Iditarod out of the blue. The Iditarod Trail wasn't already there, was it? How did the Iditarod Strike and the Trail come to be?"*

Foreword

—◆—

Alma Preston: "Rod, people are always asking me about Alaska, the great gold rushes and the Iditarod Trail. Of course there is a lot I can talk about with them but for quite a bit of it, I tell them, I can talk and talk, but if they don't get a pretty good grasp of the geography, they have no way to understand what I'm trying to explain.

"Privately, Rod, I sometimes wonder to myself as I answer their questions, 'Why am I going to the trouble, Sir? Without at least a rudimentary idea of the lay of the land, oceans, rivers, mountains and passes, I'm just beating my lips together for nothing; you won't get it anyway.'

"But I like them and enjoy talking about Alaska, the old trail and my wonderful sled dogs so I try to do the best I can. If they look interested enough, sometimes I get a paper and pencil and sketch.

"Really, Rod, if people want to comprehend the Iditarod, I'll tell you this. No one can come close to understanding the history of the Iditarod in any depth as far as getting into the foundation of how it came to be, the background of how it all started, unless they understand the coastline and its mountains from clear down about Ketchikan or Wrangell all the way up and around to Cook Inlet. And the passes, *especially* the passes."

—◆—

MOST TURN-OF-THE-CENTURY Yukon Territory and Alaska gold finds were effectively served by water during the summer seasons, being located either in country drained by the Yukon

11

River or on the Seward Peninsula, which extends into the Bering Sea north of the Yukon mouth. But the Bering Sea's winter ice pack stopped ocean vessels far south of the mouth of the Yukon. At the same time, though, the North Pacific Ocean along the Southeastern and South Central Alaska coastline remained free of ice, so winter shipping readily plied those waters.

The obstacle to travel and transport between the southern ice-free bays and the northern interior lay in the daunting fortress of mountain ranges thrown up between the sea and the gold fields: the towering crags and huge glaciers of the great Coast, Saint Elias, Chugach and Alaska Ranges. These are not your garden-variety, weathered-down Appalachian Mountains, nor do these peaks attain their heights after a head start of rising from an already elevated plateau like the Colorado Rockies. No, these ranges not only include North America's highest mountains, but many rear their jagged summits far into the sky after rising virtually from the sea bed of the continental shelf, a thousand feet below sea level.

The cataclysmic shocks of geologic past that upthrust the earth's crust into such heights rent great clefts between them, rifts that, through the nearest range, present views of even more ominous mountains behind, and beyond them others, and others, mountain crowding mountain, precipice jostling precipice, rearing higher and higher, graying out into the uttermost distance, offering no hint of relief, only discouragement that pressed upon the hearts of even the brave. Instead of grassy valleys and gentle waterways, these interstices between the ragged bastions are filled with treacherous rivers of mile deep ice split with deadly, shifting crevasses—many so deep as to be effectively termed bottomless—many gaping, but some hidden under thin coverings that wait to give way under the slightest footfall.

Anyone who would set forth to dare this harsh, inhospitable barrier had better be long on wilderness skills, endurance, heroic courage and daring.

For a thousand miles, this menacing coastal fortress glowers down upon the Inside Passage and Gulf of Alaska waters and guards the interior and northern gold fields. A look at the map of the Alaskan coastline reveals that once you turn your back on the Stikine River, which begins in interior British Columbia, then cleaves through the Coast Range to empty into the Pacific near Wrangell in Southeastern Alaska, north and west the frowning mountains, ice caps and glaciers yield only eight such useable, ice-free breaks leading from the sea into the interior, only five of which played important gold rush roles. A great part of the story of the opening of the North and of winter transportation between saltwater and the gold fields could aptly be titled *A Tale of Five Passes*.

If only the early gold-seekers could find and broach the barricade through those narrow notches, and if later developers could only tame them with their trails, roads or railroads, then almost all of the vast heartland of the entire northwest Yukon Territory-Alaska subcontinent would be open to them, the entire 327,000-square-mile drainage of the Yukon Basin, a basin two thousand miles long and several hundred miles wide.

Not only would that vast heartland be opened, it would be available. In winter, although the everlasting subarctic cold hangs over the North like a cruel penalty, it would also transform the Yukon Basin into a perfect platform for dog team travel. Frozen stream courses gift travelers with not only a clear path, but a gradient that is, practically speaking, level. In addition to the length of the Yukon (the trunk river), the lengths of its tributaries, the forks and branches of those tributaries, their feeder streams and the creeks that in turn fed them are virtually uncountable. These magnanimously handed early explorers—and those who would follow— thousands upon thousands of miles of white ribbons awaiting the stamp of snowshoes, the footfall of working huskies and the glide of runners carrying men, supplies and communications.

Alma Preston: "And Rod, that was not all. Once mushers had progressed all the way down to the Yukon mouth and had left behind the vast inland network of potential winter trails, they could travel the sea ice and shoreline margin south to the Alaska Peninsula or north to the Seward Peninsula (where Nome would spring up) farther north to Kotzebue Sound and yet farther to the whaling station at Point Barrow. Beyond that northernmost outpost on Alaska's arctic coast, the way was clear all the way to the Pole and beyond—if they could just get through the coastal mountain barrier to access it all.

"Rod, it was just incredible, a gift from a Creator who must hold a special love for prospectors. In summer, a portage of but 32 miles from saltwater would deliver simple access to the second-longest navigable waterway in North America. It was floatable for some 2,200 miles top to bottom. That sequence, top to bottom, is the operative idea. Remember, the going wage for labor was only about two dollars a day. Gold-seekers did not have to access the river from its mouth upstream. That would have necessitated use of a steamboat costing thousands. No, it took almost no other resources than their own strength, wilderness skills and the will to succeed. If men could just get through from the sea into the upper drainage of the Yukon they could fashion crude boats and cruder rafts from native materials and the power of the river would take them as far as they wished to drift.

"So if they could only find and break through the mountain barricade they could access the golden heartland's trails and waterways regardless of season."

The first of the eight rifts through the mountains beyond Wrangell—up the canyon of the swift Taku River near Juneau—was tried during gold rush times but was largely discarded. Gold-seekers regarded it as a barely doable, but largely impractical route to reach the interior lake system draining into the upper Yukon River.

A triumvirate of passes—the second, third and forth breaks north of the Stikine—issue from the head of Lynn Canal, some 100 miles north of Juneau. The southernmost of these three is the White Pass, separating saltwater by only 40 overland miles from Lake Bennett which drains into the Yukon River. The great attraction to the White Pass was first, that the grade was ballyhooed as a simple, steady grade to the summit suitable not merely as pack trail but offering possibilities for a wagon road. Second, once gold-seekers had hauled their gear and supplies to Yukon headwaters, they could let the river take over and do the work, floating their mountainous loads the final 550-or-so miles to the diggings.

Though this gap looked deceptively easy at its beginnings at Skagway, several miles inland the way grew into The Path from Hell. Quagmires, boulder fields and precipices along the fiendish trail killed horses by so many thousands in the days of 1897–98 that it earned world fame as The Dead Horse Trail.

However, up the side of the valley that at first appraisal appeared the least probable, the White Pass did offer possibilities for carving out a workable gradient. By taking creative engineering genius and superhuman effort to their extreme limits, the craggy, cliff-ridden side narrowly allowed a marvel of a railroad to be blasted through into the Upper Yukon. So immediate was the industrial and political pressure to force this supply line through that road builders started during the very height of the Klondike Gold Rush frenzy and pushed rail over the summit within a year. Trains transported passengers and hauled freight and mail by the hundreds of tons to where it could be boated downriver, turning the towns of Whitehorse and Dawson, Yukon Territory into transportation hubs that fed not only the immediate Klondike and other nearby Upper Yukon discoveries, but the distant strikes of Fairbanks and even Nome, almost 2,000 miles west.

The fabled Chilkoot Pass (the middle of the three Lynn Canal passes) courses parallel to the White Pass' and but a few miles north of it. Like that of the neighboring White Pass, the Chilkoot's great appeal was a short portage followed by a long float. Across its lofty summit, a mere 32 trail miles from ocean waters, lay Lake Lindeman which connected by a short waterway to Lake Bennett and the Yukon. However, those 32 miles would become fabled as the earth's Cruelest Thirty-Two Miles. The summit was so elevated and the climb at the final pitch so steep that it stymied crossing not only with beasts of burden, but even hand-drawn sleds could not be used beyond a certain point. Strong, hardy men were reduced to having to break down their freight into light packs and make scores of repetitive, spirit-breaking ascents to the crest. This most-famous of gold rush passes was the most heavily trodden route to the gold fields of the upper Yukon but, as soon as builders established the nearby railroad over White Pass, use of the Chilkoot ceased.

Not far west of the Chilkoot Pass, beginning near the present town of Haines, the glaring mountains begrudgingly yield the third of the Lynn Canal triumvirate, the Chilkat Pass.

While the White and Chilkoot Passes carried stampeders by the tens of thousands, the Dalton Trail which coursed the Chilkat route received but a fraction of that traffic. The former two held the allure of a beginning short overland passage to where wind and current would take over the work. However, the Chilkat Pass began with some 250 miles of overland travel which absolutely necessitated the expensive use of large pack trains to haul gold-seekers and their freight. The Dalton Trail met the Yukon far downriver from where the White and Chilkoot Passes reached its headwaters. Dalton Trail users, starting their float so much closer to Dawson, could take but reduced advantage of river power. Decades later, the quality of the route would be proven as a highway corridor. The builders of the scenic Haines Cutoff would use much of it to connect the Alaska Highway to the town of Haines on Lynn Canal.

Beyond the Chilkat Pass, the craigs and peaks of the Fairweather and St. Elias Ranges rear from two-mile-high ice to rend the clouds and bar the way for fully 350 miles farther north and west. The way is unbreached along the shelterless coast until the mighty Copper River irresistibly forces its way from the interior through to the sea. Alas, the roiling swiftness and steep banks of the lower river thwarted upstream poling and lining (towing by ropes walked upstream along the river edge.) Additionally, following the river upstream took stampeders to a location too far away from the gold fields. The Copper did not offer a practical route to the gold mining centers.

Shipping must travel another hundred miles northwest of the Copper River to anchor at the beginning of the next ice-free break, the sixth up the coast from Wrangell. There, at the east side of Prince William Sound, the harbor of Valdez marks the saltwater terminus of a route through the Chugach and Alaska Ranges. This route saw heavy use first as a dog-team and pack-train trail, then as a road for horse-drawn sleighs, sledges and wagons, and finally as the roadbed for the Richardson Highway serving Fairbanks. Many decades later, the corridor would be chosen to carry the Trans Alaska Oil Pipeline. While a sleigh, sledge or wagon could not haul mail and freight by the *hundreds* of tons as could the White Pass and Yukon railroad, they could at least bring it by the *ton* into Fairbanks. Because Fairbanks was closer to Nome by hundreds of miles than Dawson, much of Nome's winter traffic switched to this Valdez-Fairbanks Trail once it became useable.

As the coastline turns southwest, the port of Seward on Resurrection Bay (about 200 miles by water from Valdez) provided a jumping-off point for a route across the Kenai Peninsula, around Turnagain Arm, across mouths of the Knik and Matanuska Rivers, up the Susitna and Chulitna River Valleys and through the Alaska Range by way of

Broad Pass and the Nenana River Canon to Fairbanks. Unlike the aforementioned passes, this Seward-to-Fairbanks-via-Broad-Pass route was not used by stampeders to rush to a new gold strike. Following well after the great Fairbanks gold discovery, builders planned and constructed it solely as a railroad route designed to open up and develop the territory. Everyone understood that growth of the country would continue to be inhibited until Fairbanks gained what Whitehorse and Dawson had when the White Pass and Yukon Route breached the mountain barrier. That is, it needed crucial year-round, high-volume transport, connecting ocean shipping to the economic and political center in the Interior.

A half century after the Alaska Railroad began carrying freight in and out of the Interior, the George Parks Highway would be laid running parallel to the rails. With northern Alaska's only lasting railroad and a major highway over it, this seventh pass would eventually carry more traffic and tonnage than all of the other passes combined.

There is another pass—one that offered the eighth and final supply and travel route, a distant way to reach the far northwestern gold fields, a last slip through the thousand-odd miles of mountains and ice up the coast from Wrangell. The assent to its summit climbs through some of the most majestic mountain scenery in the world. It crosses the great Alaska Range not far from the mightiest mountain on the North American continent—20,320-foot-tall Mount McKinley, which rises higher from its base elevation than any other mountain in the world. This spectacular pass is named Rainy Pass. The trail established over it provides the subject for this book: the Iditarod.

Rod Perry: *I was fortunate to be among the first five dog drivers of the modern era to crest Rainy Pass, the more circuitous side route through Ptarmigan Pass having been taken instead on the first four Iditarod Trail Sled Dog Races.*

Pausing at the summit after a long jog uphill behind the sled, I stood awed by the transcendent view. If you, too, are by some design or chance fortunate enough to find yourself on that crest at brightest midday and drinking in the vistas as I did, you will lean back to gaze high at shimmering mountainsides slanting steeply over you—too brilliant to permit a long stare. Looking down, the deep, shadowed canyon of the fabled Dalzell lies ahead. Perhaps you will, as I did amidst that surpassing grandeur, lapse into an inner grandiloquence as you inadequately attempt to express your impressions, as well as reflect on how it would take a jaded and callous person indeed not to be struck by the magnificence of the creation and humbled before its omnipotent, magnanimous creator.

The approach to Rainy Pass is long, very long. Traffic in the earliest days of the route's use had to first snowshoe and dog team about 250 miles—a laborious trip of 10 to 20 days depending upon whether the way was broken or not—before reaching even the beginning of the lowest foothills.

Though the railroad was not completed until the 1920s, more than two decades after the Fairbanks Rush, construction began from the Seward end much earlier. Therefore, for some years before trains began winter service, its roadbed blessed foot travelers and dog teams by providing them a trail out of Seward toward various diggings around Cook Inlet country.

Dog team and foot travel simply kept a well-packed thoroughfare beaten in between the rails and even beyond the rails where crews clearing the route and preparing the road bed worked well ahead of those installing ties and rail. So, as construction progressed northward, Rainy Pass-bound travelers were able to take increasing advantage of the easy grade. Finally, when winter train service began to reach Anchorage, 120 miles from Seward, and then onward to Wasilla, at mile 160, these points became the successive trail heads, significantly shortening the total distance and making trail use more attractive.

Near the present site of Wasilla the trail left the rail route and split off to the northwest toward the pass. It lead across the rolling lowlands and gradually ascended the successive valleys of the Susitna, Yentna and Skwentna Rivers. A steeper climb beginning at the Happy River finally gained the summit of Rainy Pass.

For years following the Nome Rush there glimmered a hope among Nomites who were aware of explorer's reports of the remote pass. They were intrigued by possibilities that the little-known way might offer a suitable shortcut from ice-free saltwater to Nome. However, because of its length through remote, uninhabited country and fears of insufficient use there was a great question about whether building such a trail could be justified. Need, which as the years went by declined as Nome's population dwindled to one-tenth of its gold-rush numbers, appeared to be offset by the probable difficulty and expense of trail building and upkeep.

Rod Perry: *Ah, Alma's voice. But playing through my memory I can hear another as familiar and affectionate, but deeper, with an edge to it.*

Al Preston: "I can tell you quite a lot about the state of affairs as we thought about our trail situation up in Nome in the early years, Rod. About the time of the Nome Rush, the government explored Rainy Pass country. A few years later congress created the Alaska Road Commission as a branch of the U.S. Army. Of course the ARC office in Nome had copies of the explorer's report and maps. When we Nomites found out about the pass someone came up with the idea of a trail through there to shorten up our way to winter shipping somewhere down on the Gulf. The idea caught on, circulated around town and from then on almost all of us held a glimmer of hope that some day, some way such a trail could be put in. The cabin I rented in Nome belonged to an ARC employee who was a pretty close friend. Since the Commission was in charge of trail work, the idea of a Rainy Pass trail was something I got into in depth more than most.

"It's great to have dreams because they lead you to creativity. But a lot of those dreamers I rubbed shoulders with in Nome weren't being very realistic. It wasn't all rosy. There were some big obstacles apparently blocking the way. Well, if not exactly blocking, at least they were enough to raise serious doubts. For one, if we were right in guessing where it might go, it looked like the trail would lead through maybe 400 or 500 miles of the most desolate wilderness. It had hardly been visited since Russian times but from what the Commission could learn, in the whole length it was only inhabited with a couple or three native villages.

"Next, there was a great question about whether that route would ever get a small fraction of the traffic it would need to make it worth putting in and keeping up. If the Road Commission had existed while Nome was booming with 20,000 or 30,000, and Turnagain Arm on Cook Inlet still had maybe two or three thousand mining down there, the government would have probably ordered that trail put in without a second's hesitation. But by the time the ARC came into being and the explorers' reports became known, nine out of ten stampeders had pulled up stakes, our Nome population was down to only about one-tenth of its peak and Turnagain Arm mining had tapered off.

"Because it was such a long, long haul over the established way from Nome to Valdez, and it appeared the distance between Nome and someplace like Seward must be hundreds of miles shorter, that comparison of miles, alone, took over almost everyone's thinking. As if there were no other factors to consider than a distance differential.

"But face it; winter travel and mail delivery were already working just fine the way they were through Dawson and

Fairbanks because they had their smoothly-working links to saltwater. And those trails were so loaded with settlement and resources. It was plain to the Road Commission that the Valdez Trail and especially the Yukon River Trail with all of the roadhouses, trading posts, villages, missions, wood cutting stations, settlers' cabins and fish camps studding the way, there were shelters aplenty. And then, steamboats by the dozens that were running back and forth all summer could stock every place along the Yukon so easily and comparatively inexpensively.

"Then there were the factors that made it easy on the drivers. To hand them easy feed, on the Yukon River route salmon by the millions swam right up to the cutting tables and drying racks. And to make the going good, there was such constant traffic the trail was always being rebroken. If a really big snow fell or an extra strong wind drifted the trail in deep, everyone just waited for the mail team to come through because the carriers had to go: they were bound by their schedule. And if the mail driver thought it was *really* tough, to conserve his own team he could hire a big, fresh team from a nearby riverside village to plow through and break it out.

"You compare all of that with the emptiness and remoteness of the Rainy Pass route and wonder how you'd come close enough to duplicating the Valdez-to-Fairbanks and Yukon Trails' resources to be able to take enough of the business away from them to make such a Rainy Pass trail feasible. That would be so monumental: you can see how slim the chances were for the new trail.

"As much as the idea of a shorter way intrigued you, you had to face this question: Who in tarnation was going to travel it? Would anyone build, supply and man so much as the simplest roadhouse if all that comes through once in awhile is some poor, dang, crazy mail carrier that's hungry enough to take a contract when it means wallowing through deep, unbroken snow all the way because he's the only traffic? A roadhouse business can't run on thin air, now, can it? And how's a shorter trail going to benefit Nome if it takes longer to cover the distance slogging over the mountains on snowshoes breaking trail alone, than over the old, smoothly functioning way where you cover the well-broken, level, river miles at a nice brisk trot?

"You had to look at it this way: the long distance way through Fairbanks was indeed time-consuming and expensive, no argument. But the way the government looked at it, the cost was being spread out in incremental installments shouldered by individuals and businesses, use by use, if that makes sense. In a nutshell, it was expensive, but still affordable.

"That meant, to those making the trail-building decisions and controlling the purse-strings, that allocating a sizeable lump of government funding to cut through what trail-builders would likely find out there—the great standing forests, downed timber and dense brush—plus construction work to bridge numerous small streams, erect thousands of trail markers and build shelter cabins, then afterwards maintain the hundreds of miles of an entirely new (in some ways duplicative) trail system, Rod, all of that apparently looked like funding an unnecessary upgrade, if not a luxury."

———◆————◆——

But then the situation began to change. Several minor gold rushes to a little-traveled area located midway along this proposed trail route tipped the scales enough in the minds of government road builders to initiate an investigative expedition in the winter of 1908. Alas, the reconnaissance only bore out their former trepidations. Though the way did indeed appear to provide a good route, they deemed it too expensive to build and keep up.

As Al Preston pointed out, road builders saw that building and maintaining the trail would not be the only expense. Most of the route between Seward and the Yukon led through off-the-beaten-path country virtually devoid of habitation.

It offered almost no support to travelers. Therefore, a roadhouse and supply system would have to be built, supplied and run at government expense or at least subsidized. The thin population bases of Seward and Cook Inlet on the southern end, the minor importance of the midway gold strikes and the dwindling population of Nome predicted few travelers besides the mail carriers. With traffic so sparse, a roadhouse venture would hardly attract entrepreneurs. Authorities decided to keep to the status quo and continue using the river routes to Dawson and Fairbanks.

The northwestern-most break through the mountains over Rainy Pass would never have seen much more than an occasional trickle of use had it not been for a blockbuster occurrence: From one of Alaska's most remote, little-prospected regions, the almost unknown upper Iditarod River, the cry once more rang out, **"Gold!"**

The location of the last great strike of the gold rush era happened to be not far to the west and about midway along the proposed Seward-to-Nome mail route!

The last, old-fashioned, hell-bent-for-leather gold rush in North America was on. When that final, glorious stampede burst upon the scene and Iditarod quickly grew to become, briefly, Alaska's largest city, the thousands of the gold town's dwellers desperately needed winter transportation routes. Suddenly road builders had rationale aplenty dropped in their laps to go to the effort and expense of putting in the trail over Rainy Pass. Would-be entrepreneurs, dollar signs dancing in their eyes at the thought of heavy traffic, chomped at the bit to establish waypoint roadhouse businesses.

Of the five hard beaten cracks through the almost impregnable armor of the great, thousand-mile mountain fortress north and west of Wrangell, only this last trail to the northwest—the Iditarod Trail—would never be replaced with a railroad or highway. Traversing swampy quagmires and sodden, tussock-ridden muskegs and crossing so many waterways, it was suitable for travel only in winter's frozen state. Even with all of the traffic it received at its zenith, the Iditarod afforded Nome only a long, rugged path allowing foot travel and difficult passenger, mail, and freight delivery by dog team.

As a trail it began, as a trail it lived gloriously, and when the gold petered out and the rush was over, as a trail it died.

Rod Perry: *That no road was ever built over the route and that the country it traverses remained largely raw wilderness would preserve its primitive character and its colorful, romantic gold-rush luster through the decades of abandonment as if the trail had an appointment with destiny.*

To the trail's romantic allure may be attributed one of the main reasons the Iditarod would one day live again. A half century after heavy trail use died out, in a man-and-team-against-the-wilderness setting, the old path would experience a glorious rebirth. From its long slumber it would awake once more to hear the barely audible hiss of runners and the creaking of sled joints, it would feel the staccato footfall and listen to the panting of trotting huskies. The world's longest, most grueling sled dog race, termed "The Last Great Race on Earth®" would be held over its spectacular course, capturing international imagination.

But I forget myself at times and stray, as this is all so alive to me. Back to the Iditarod Trail's founding . . . .

To fully comprehend the evolution of Nome's winter transportation situation a few years after the turn of the 20th century, one must understand how the earliest traders and prospectors began almost 35 years earlier to force the Yukon's lock and pry open the northern interior. Then one must comprehend the mining and prospecting booms and the resulting population explosions of Dawson, Yukon Territory

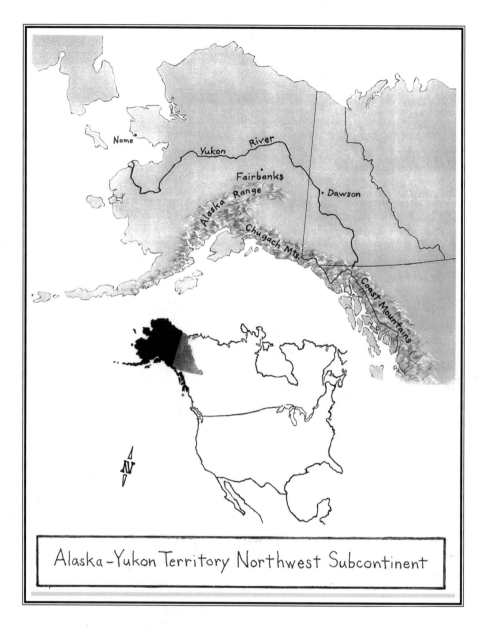

Alaska-Yukon Territory Northwest Subcontinent

and Fairbanks—and the supply systems that developed
to serve them.

Why is such comprehension necessary? Because early on,
Nome's winter travel and mail and freight supply was so
interwoven with and dependant upon those transportation

systems developed to serve the fabled Klondike strike of the upper Yukon River in Yukon Territory, Canada, and the fabulously rich Fairbanks strike in the valley of Alaska's Tanana River.

Though Nome was dependant upon the transportation systems of those other towns and the Seward-to-Nome Mail Trail feasibility reconnaissance of 1908 delivered a discouraging report, Nomites continued to dream of a trail of their own. The Iditarod Trail, as it came to be called, grew out of those dreams. Because the Iditarod was Nome's, and Nome was so tightly linked by trail use to Dawson and Fairbanks, the story of the Iditarod Trail is inextricably joined to the rich and fabled history of gold discovery along the upper Yukon River and Fairbanks.

Rod Perry: *I once spent a week hunting with a man about whom another of the hunters in camp commented, "If all you need to know is the time and you ask Harley, he'll give you a dissertation about the evolution of telling time and a detailed explanation of how the clock was constructed!"*

The reader of this work which explores the history of the gold-rush-era Iditarod Trail may wonder, upon finding so much space devoted to early exploration of the upper Yukon and the ensuing gold rushes it produced, if perhaps this tome were written by Harley himself. To the unknowledgeable who wish to remain that way or to those types who demand to cut to the chase, it may seem much too unnecessarily roundabout to begin the Iditarod story so long ago and far away as the chronology of developments that took place many decades before the Iditarod Strike and over 2,000 miles from Nome.

However, the patient, inquisitive reader may better understand Nome's early winter transportation desires and realities by examining the overall transportation picture leading up to the Iditarod Trail's establishment, because the three great, blockbuster gold rushes of the North—the Klondike, Nome and Fairbanks—were so intermeshed not only by the routes that all three communities shared, but also by many of the same people who flowed over those common routes from one strike to another.

Following the 1867 purchase of Alaska from Russia, America's interest in her new acquisition faded. In 1880, fewer whites populated the territory than under Russian dominion. The post-Civil War years saw the nation swept up in a period of great industrial development. Vast regions that previously had been reachable only by wagon became available to development and commerce as transcontinental railroads opened the west. That simply flooded investors and developers with so much opportunity right at home they had little reason to look farther—especially into remote, unfamiliar regions that were widely disparaged as the desolate Frozen North. Therefore, Alaska lay dormant for three decades, virtually forgotten by the American public and its government.

The great geologist, explorer and historian Alfred Hulse Brooks, for whom Alaska's Brooks Range is named, observed that the real development of Alaska began in 1896, not with anything that happened in Alaska, but with the discovery of Klondike gold in the adjacent Canadian Yukon. The hordes who thronged into the largely unknown North usually found it necessary to cross some part of Alaska to reach the strike, acquainting Americans to the possession they had almost totally ignored since its purchase three decades before from Russia. With the Klondike Gold Rush grabbing headlines and capturing national attention, America's last frontier began to occupy a new and important place in the country's collective mind.

Moreover, Brooks argued that the discovery of gold at many Alaska locations was the direct result of a spill-over from the vast horde of gold-seekers who had first flooded into the Klondike.

Additionally, other strikes may be attributed to explorations by prospectors who were driven in their search by the sheer excitement and potential of awaiting riches first widely generated by the fabulous Canadian discovery. The 1908 Iditarod strike was the last major strike in the chain of discoveries that began with the Klondike.

———— • —— • ————

Alma Preston: "Alfred Brooks stopped overnight at our place at Mile 34 and another time had a long layover with us waiting out a storm after we moved our operation up to Mile 54. Later, he corresponded with my former father-in-law. Though he was a giant as a geologist, explorer and historian, he was so friendly and down-to-earth. You look at the tremendous hardships he endured on his explorations. Maybe that's what kept him so close to the earth and humble. How many people would sit down around the barrel stove and talk with you for hours—and on your level—who have one of the greatest mountain ranges on the continent named after them? Rod, even though you knew you were listening to someone who was very educated, sounding like a professor, he was just so warm and open around my former, late husband, Merrill, his dad and me.

"Now if you're really interested in understanding from the ground up the evolution of how the Iditarod Trail came to be, listen carefully to what Alfred Brooks told us."

———— • —— • ————

Rod Perry: *From the back of my mind I can draw up a picture of the great explorer as I imagined him then from Alma's description, larger than life in intellect, accomplishments and renown, a veritable immortal, yet sitting there around the barrel stove, stocking feet propped up on a stove-door-size chunk of spruce in the round, in choke-bored Malones, suspenders down off his shoulders, shirted in a wool long-john top with several buttons undone at the neck, chair leaned back, hands clasped behind his neck, enjoying a break from the trail and a long visit with the Leonhardts.*

Alfred Hulse Brooks: "I don't think anyone would argue with me that this is fact: If it had not been for the lure of the Klondike gold, the mineral wealth over here on the Alaska side would have stayed in the ground dormant for many years, and Alaska would have remained a land of mystery to most Americans. They'd have just kept denigrating it as Seward's Icebox. With the huge rush to the Canadian Yukon, that population explosion absolutely necessitated the establishment of lines of transportation. How could a population of 30,000 get by, let alone flourish, had they not built a bustling riverboat system and constructed, first trails and later wagon roads and eventually railroads? All of it was brought about by Klondike gold. So although these deposits belonged to Canada, Alaska benefited directly by their mining development.

"When the worldwide excitement caught up untold thousands of people it carried them northward into a virtually unknown land. It was trail-less and roadless. The coastline was so treacherous, because it was not only rock-bound, it lacked charts and other navigation guides. Gold-hunters packed across wild passes and boated down swift rivers where the next bend might reveal an upcoming cataract. To make it worse, the new territory was almost totally lacking government or laws. I will tell you that it was then—and not until then—that it dawned on our nation's leaders, its press and our people, of the utter criminal folly of the United States' attitude of neglect toward its northernmost possession. With the Klondike raising awareness, Army posts were now established in Alaska. Laws were enacted. U.S. marshals were appointed, and commissioners. To begin its enormous task of detailed charting of the coast line, Congress finally funded the Coast Survey. It was like the nation was trying to admit their error of remaining blind for so long to the richness of the territory and make amends for the long neglect.

"I worked with the United States Geological Survey once they were ordered to begin exploring and studying Alaska's mineral resources. Washington became convinced of the need for a careful investigation of the fisheries, forests and lands suitable for agriculture. One would indeed have to be blind not to see that Alaska's modern history truly begins with the Klondike discovery in the Canadian Yukon."

Alma Preston: "Brooks was ahead of his time. Rod, let's go over to the old folks home, I want you to meet an old friend of Al's from Nome. Anton Radovitch went in over the Chilkoot in '94. He's one of many who hit all four of the big rushes up North, the Klondike, Nome, Fairbanks and Iditarod, not to mention a number of the smaller ones. That gives him quite an encompassing perspective. He's spent most of his adult life standing day after day working so many cold streams by summer, and so many winters thawing his way down to bedrock and drifting deep in frozen ground following pay streaks that he's just gnarled with arthritis. But he's a perky old character and he loves visitors, especially if they come to talk about the old days. Of course, not many do down here so far from the North. They don't value what those old eyes of his have seen. If some writer wanted to plumb the depths of the history stored away in that ancient, gray head they'd have the material for quite a book on their hands. On the way home, Rod, I need to stop by the corner grocery up on Flag Street. You can pack my shopping bag for me."

Anton Radovitch: Yessiree! Like a lot of others, I just seemed to miss it on the big stampedes. Got there a little late. Or rolled the dice and staked the wrong ground. Actually did better at some of the lesser discoveries. But let's say you're some wretched shovel stiff on the Klondike like me just slaving to further the interests some lucky El Dorado king who had happened to hit it big. One day you get an early tip from a guy who's just come up from someplace you never heard of he calls "Nome." More'n a thousand miles away. What's a thousand miles when you're young and eager? You'd be a fool not to go. Nothing ventured, nothing gained.

"Worst can happen is you get a month's worth of exercise. When you roll in, if nothing good's left to stake, well, you've seen some new country. And you don't come out of the stampede any worse off than you were. You're back swinging a pick and wrestlin' wash boulders out of a sluice box for another lucky so and so. If that happened you'd be ready to do it again. The big strikes came one after another about every two years at first. Got to where I'd just keep everything ready to throw an outfit together and be gone in a couple hours, brand new shoes on my runners for slick going. Always had it in my mind where I'd go to buy a couple of good dogs on a moment's notice, either to pack in summer or tow the hand sled in winter.

"I tell you true, if you didn't come into the country before the big Klondike Rush, you probably wouldn't have a clear, complete picture. Wouldn't have much of an idea of how the country was opened. How a few set it up for the rest of the miners to come in, stay, prospect and mine. How that made it possible for the big Bonanza discovery on the Klondike. How the Klondike produced Nome and Fairbanks and how those two led to Iditarod.

"I've seen many times that out bushwhacking in country you don't know, that sometimes you look over and see where you want to get to but you can't go straight there. Often the best path across is the longest way around. You really want to understand how the Iditarod came to be? Start 60 years before and a couple thousand miles to the east."

———————

Rod Perry: *I sit looking out my window at the snow-burdened spruce and reflect on those words old Anton*

Radovitch spoke almost 50 years before, "Often the best way across is the longest way around." Turn-of-the-century Nomites, desiring a short, direct connection to winter shipping but not understanding the topography and surface character of the landscape between Seward and Nome, might have wondered, and even impatiently chafed that the seemingly possible short trail directly to Seward was not put in. After all, the straight-line distance was known to be fewer than 600 miles. Likewise, an impatient reader of this history may wish that I would take a short, direct line to more quickly gain its destination—the Iditarod—just sticking to the bare-bones, nuts-and-bolts of Iditarod Trail history and not heading down what they might consider side trails of peripheral information.

Knowledgeable trail-builders back in the day as well as today's knowing historians understand that neither the trail, if it is to be passable, nor the history of the trail, if it is to be informative, can take an arrow-straight line. Just as the old, historic Iditarod Trail took many twists and turns on its way to Nome, sometimes necessarily deviating many degrees from its general northwest direction to complete its course, and just as the modern Iditarod Sled Dog Race Trail deviates from the old route for various sound reasons, adding greatly to the richness of the spectacle, (such as to bring numerous native villages into the event) so this history takes twists and turns and side trails I deem essential to bring the reader to his Nome. And just as the trail does not start at Iditarod, but has to begin hundreds of miles far back to the southeast, this telling of the history must start much earlier in time than the gold strike at Iditarod, and start with events a thousand miles away to the southeast that led up to it. Unlike followers of the trail in gold-rush days or the competitors in the modern race, readers of this book will find its long, roundabout path will not make them trail-weary. The complete, meandering story is too rich, informative, adventurous, and sometimes rollicking.

I encourage you to don your parka, pull on your mukluks, jump onto my sled and travel with me start to finish, taking in

Alma Ready to Head Out

all of the interesting and informative twists and turns of the entire trail and enjoy learning about the evolution of gold-rush transportation. The result at trail's end is that you will step off the runner tails knowing more about the interesting old trail than you ever guessed existed.

Chapter 1

First the Trapper, Then the Prospector

Alma Preston: "OK, Rod, if we're going to help people really understand how the old Iditarod Trail came to be, you simply must begin by tracing the way the first gold-hunters came into the country and how the succeeding gold rushes unfolded. Of course, in a land locked in ice most of the year, the transportation needs of the different gold towns demanded winter trails. All over the Yukon and Alaska, the progression of gold discoveries and evolution of trails were interrelated.

"Yes, you've got to go way back. How far, you ask? See this old man in the picture harnessing one of the Colonel's swing dogs? He was my late husband's dad. I sure loved Dad Leonhardt. Well, Dad knew Moses Mercier who had been in charge of Fort Yukon from the days Alaska Commercial took it over after the U.S. government ran the Hudson's Bay Company out. Moses had served as agent for the Bay Company and made the transition, not just from one company to the next, but from Russian to American ownership of Alaska.

"Whereas almost all of the Bay Company management, from agents and factors on up, were Scotsmen, most of the common laborers, the voyageurs and dog men, were French or French Metis. Moses Mercier was a French Canuck, originally from Montreal who beat the stereotype and occupied the position of agent—probably because he had a good education. Actually, an outstanding education— part of it formal, part of it because he had a wonderful library and had adopted a lifetime habit of reading in a chair by the fire during many winter hours spent at remote posts.

"He was quite a philosopher and a real student of history, especially history of the fur trade. He'd get so excited while talking about it with Dad, his eyes would fairly dance. He knew a lot about prospecting history, too. Just as much, Dad just loved to pump the old agent for stories. Dad was a keen listener with almost a photographic memory; he just soaked it up. The two really were real peas in a pod and to say they were quite a pair to draw to was the understatement of understatements! Raconteurs? I've never heard their equal. Hearing Dad Leonhardt quote Mercier while imitating his Montreal French Canuck accent was like listening to Mercier himself and listening to Mercier was like listening to a polished lecturer—with a twist.

"I think Mr. Mercier had lived so much in books that his words flowed like you were reading one. Now, I must say, Rod, that he had such a very distinctive way of expressing himself. He spoke impeccable English, so even with the accent you knew he thought in the language, but then, when he was really rolling along, from out of the blue he'd pop in these quick, French phrases. It was sort of Mercier, the French Canuck, interjecting commentary on what Mercier, the Englishman, had just said.

"It's really hard to figure whether he was just losing himself in the telling and slipping back into his old tongue (I don't think so, he had too much command of the spoken word), if he thought the expressions added spice or punch to his story, perhaps toying with the mixture as some sort of story-telling device for his private enjoyment, or yet again, whether he liked to see the effect on his listener, particularly on Dad. For whatever reason, it sure gave Dad, the true master at imitating the old agent's French accent, a great tool for making his dramatizations of Mercier's stories come even more alive, with humor. Dad could never sit down while doing Mercier and he did him so well that it wasn't hard to imagine that you were listening to the animated, energetic old Frenchman himself, pacing the floor right before you in the

36

Leonhardt Family

very room, expressing himself with his hands and waving arms. They were every bit as captivating as his voice."

———◆———

Moses Mercier: "As European immigrants pushed their way westward across North America, men of steel spirit bent on discovery ventured far in front of even the vanguard of settlers. Their goal? *Les bonnes affaires!* To harvest and extract the abundance of the continent. Of all of those rich natural resources there for the taking, the quest for two— fur and gold—lured men the farthest in advance.

"The two enterprises affected the frontier differently. By nature, trapping was a rather solitary undertaking, benefiting from the country remaining wild and undeveloped. On the other hand, once gold and other minerals were found, they had to be mined. Mining required manpower and industry, which brought development and settlement.

"The advance guard was invariably the fur trapper. The trapper had always ranged ahead, but when hats manufactured from the felted fur of the beaver set off a fashion craze in the early 1800s, soaring demand and rocketing prices triggered an explosion in the North American fur trade beyond any other in history. *C'est vrai!* That birthed the wildest, most daring, most competent frontiersmen the nation has ever seen, the colorful Rocky Mountain fur trappers, the Mountain Men. *Magnifique!* As noteworthy as the most famous woodsmen of the eastern frontier had been— such as the likes of Daniel Boone, Simon Kenton, George Rogers Clark and Louis Wetzel—their 1700's probes and forays through the Appalachians went, at most, a couple of hundred miles west of the settled frontier. By comparison, the distance covered by some of the expeditions of the Mountain Men measured in the thousands of miles. Jim Bridger, Tom Fitzpatrick, Jed Smith, Kit Carson and their contemporaries rode, explored, fought and trapped their way from the Mississippi to the Pacific. *De tel homes courageux!* They would have gone farther west had they not run out of continent.

"Long before Bridger and Fitzpatrick, even almost a century before Boone and Kenton gained fame, the great Hudson's Bay Company had begun its relentless quest for furs north across the international boundary line. Across Rupert's Land, Canada, they formed the wedge of advancing British Civilization, systematically driving their interests west until they reached the Great River North, the Mackenzie. Eventually, from their well-established Mackenzie River posts they looked even farther west toward the Russian-Alaska boundary.

"In 1847, Alexander Murray ventured through an arctic gap in the northern continuation of the Rocky Mountains *pour exploiter*—to poach—upon the preserves of the Russian Bear, floating out of Northwest Territories down the Porcupine River into Alaska. He quietly established a Hudson's Bay Company (HBC) post, Fort Youcon (as Fort Yukon was known in the mid-1800s), at the confluence of the Porcupine and Yukon Rivers. At first, *comme ceci, comme cela*—the Bay Company did not know if the larger stream was the great river that explorers had reported emptying into the Bering Sea from Alaska's far west coast, or the Colville River that their own people had found during exploration west of the Mackenzie delta 10 years before.

"What they felt sure of was that they had gone far enough west to be trespassing on Russian soil. *Mon Sa alors!* Many in the company knew that the incredibly swift and far-reaching 'moccasin telegraph' between native peoples of the river would reveal their presence to Alaska's owners. But Fort Youcon lay way out at the extreme fingertip reach, separated from the strong-arm might of the Russian American Company seated in Sitka by thousands of river and sea miles and from the Czar seated on his throne half a world away. Should they be caught by the uneducated tenders of the minor RAC outposts, they reasoned that they could feign *étant ignorant* and there would be no great repercussions. The lucrative trade would be worth it as long as it lasted.

"Although HBC exploration and cartography had been responsible for filling in much of the space on early maps of the remote north, the company carefully guarded what they knew about northeastern Alaska, withholding all information about this country so far to the west of where they were supposed to be. And although during their almost 200 years in Canada they had spared no effort when it came to advancing into new regions in pursuit of fur, the company halted at their farthest west location, maintaining a buffer of several hundred miles to avert confrontation with the Russians trading downstream. It was, as we say, *très sage!*

"In 1864 the Overland Telegraph scientists would visit Fort Youcon, as had Robert Kennicott some years earlier, and would feel certain that the Bay Company was operating far west of British territory. But they were U. S. citizens visiting foreign soil and as guests had no vested interest or authority to conduct a definitive survey to confirm their suspicions.

"The HBC continued to trade and feign ignorance. One of their men, James Anderson, carefully worded a communiqué to his superiors that the HBC 'might not be particularly anxious about clearing up the doubt that exists regarding the position of this fort.'

"Russian America was a land of magnificent distances and dramatic solitudes that had seen little known, formal exploration. It was a *region sauvage.* During Russian dominion—as well as the earliest United States ownership which would begin in 1867—the almost universal opinion among Americans and Canadians was that Alaska and the Yukon was a vast wilderness wasteland, remote, empty, unexplored, uncharted, and largely undesirable. The Russian American Company had tentatively probed the Interior, sending expeditions up some of the major watersheds, most notably the Copper, Kuskokwim and Yukon Rivers. Indeed, some of the very earliest American and Canadian explorers into the upper Yukon reported viewing the remains of buildings featuring Russian-style logwork at the mouth of the Stewart River, giving rise to speculation that the Russians might have set up a trading location there many decades before. They talked of hearing sketchy tales from local Indians substantiating the idea. *Rien de certain, naturellement!*

"Indeed, the Russians had established a trading enterprise on the lower half of the Alaskan Yukon River, extending their presence upstream as far as the Tanana River mouth where, in 1861, they built a trading post. In 1863, they paddled up the Yukon as far as the mouth of the Porcupine River and scoped out Fort Youcon. At the time of their reconnaissance why did not the Russians drive the Bay Company out? Possibly, it was because they may not have had the force on the river to do it. Or, they may not have had equipment with them to fix the location in relation to the international boundary.

"Their trading presence on the middle Yukon and their foray farther upstream to Fort Youcon notwithstanding, with few exceptions, the Russian presence had been concentrated on the coast, their North American empire being founded upon sea otter, fur seal and other marine mammal pelts. *Ils étaient de bons hommes d'affaires.* Because of their thin inland experience and their secrecy regarding what they did know, what might lie within the vast interior was mostly a mystery to their American and British competitors. *C' était l inconnu.*"

Rod Perry: *A major reason the trapper and fur trader ranged far ahead of the prospector as civilization advanced west across North America was that as soon as the earliest European settlers set foot on the eastern shore, they stepped into a land rich in valuable fur bearers from Atlantic to Pacific, while—with notable exceptions in Virginia, the Carolinas and Georgia—few substantial finds of precious metals were made until they probed the western third of the continent some 225 years later. Therefore, trapping was established as a profession from the beginning, but prospecting as an occupation did not exist, in general, until trappers had already ranged from shore to shore.*

Moses Mercier: "The great California Gold Rush of 1848 gave birth to a new breed: the full-time prospector. The 'have nots' and latecomers to Sutter's Mill had spread out, discovering other deposits and triggering a succession of rushes across the western United States and north into British Columbia. Before those purposeful searches led to discoveries, prior finds in the East had been coincidental. But in the West, each new discovery attracted more men to devote themselves to full-time prospecting. These were men of extremely adventurous, irrepressible spirit who felt confident that, sooner or later if they kept diligently searching, they themselves would strike it rich. *Ils étaient intre'pides.*

"The attraction of beaver and marten pelts had been strong enough to draw men to the farthest reaches of the continent. But to come back to my point, *mon ami,* it was as nothing compared to the attraction produced by the lure of gold. Gold has captured and held the imagination, inflamed the passions and seized the very souls of men throughout all cultures and ages. There is something about the lustrous metal itself that sets off an age-old fascination and lust that goes beyond the mere desire for instant riches won in a twinkling. It is, as I say, *comme un deable!* It sets off a craving as old as the race itself, a pull that has been able to energize and motivate to the extent of driving, even crazing men to go to unimaginable lengths. In its economic development, society has decreed it the standard of all value. Alchemists strived to make it, misers have gloated over it. Abundance gives its owner standing, influence and power. One old miner philosophized that the frenzied rush for riches could not have been more remarkable had the only way to save the immortal soul been to find and mine for gold.

"They met head on the pitiless natural forces; no wilderness was too desolate, no mountain range too formidable, no river course too fraught with dangers and no distance too daunting to discourage the indomitable gold-hunters' search for the yellow metal. Neither hunger nor loneliness nor other privations, nothing could stop them. *Rein!* Nothing! When they worked their way North in the summer heat, dense clouds of the most ravenous, blood-sucking insects on the planet could not drive them mad enough to deter them from their quest. Under the Aurora Borealis, winter temperatures down to 100 degrees below the frost point could not freeze out their hope fires of finding their own El Dorado. *Il était étonnant!* With each new discovery amid varying geological features these prospectors accumulated more knowledge about what surface indications might signal the presence of gold below."

Chapter 2

Furs and Gold Open the Yukon Basin

WERE A RAVEN TO LIFT OFF from the tidal flats at the
head of Southeastern Alaska's Lynn Canal, point his beak
due east and catch a thermal updraft to carry him high above
the intervening mountains, his flight would take him—in just
18 miles!—to a view of the headwaters of not only one of the
most famous, but one of the most remarkable rivers in the
world. One might assume that waters arising in such
proximity to the Pacific would soon find their way to that
close-by ocean.

But no. As if above anything so ordinary and predictable,
and as if disdaining to be defined as an indistinct, minor
stream, finishing its course while still insignificantly small,
it instead is seemingly determined to take charge of its own
destiny and do something unique and make a name for itself.
This unusual river immediately does an astonishing thing:
it turns its back on the nearby Pacific and chooses a
roundabout way to an entirely different, far-away sea.
The course it takes before it discharges its mighty flow into
saltwater is a path equal in distance to almost one-tenth
of the entire girth of the globe. In doing so, it becomes the
tenth-longest river in the world, the fourth-longest in North
America. *(Depending upon which headwaters is chosen as its
beginning, it may be measured to rank second, third or fourth.)*

The Yukon River does not gain its distinction as one of the
world's foremost drainages based upon its length alone but
because of its volume: It drains some 327,000 square miles,
the entire heartland of a vast subcontinent. Along its almost
2,200-mile course to the distant sea its great tide gathers

other rivers mighty in their own rights, themselves hundreds of miles long. Some, such as the Pelly, Stewart, Porcupine, Tanana and Koyukuk, flow the better part of a thousand.

As if controlling a guessing game and presenting deceptions to throw contestants off, it travels mostly northward along its 700-mile length within Yukon Territory and, after crossing the international boundary into Alaska, continues that course another 250 miles as if it were heading for the Arctic Ocean. Just as it crosses the Arctic Circle and one is convinced—as were some early explorers—that its destination must surely be the polar sea just 300 miles farther north, it throws a curve: it turns abruptly west and southwest and does not deign to join even the saltwater of its choosing until it has flowed another 1,150 miles across the Great Land. Then and only then does it finally submit its volume to the patiently waiting Bering Sea.

Eighteen miles as the raven flies, just a portage as a man walks of a mere 32 miles through the mountains from saltwater, only that short distance to reach a passageway equal in length to one-tenth the circumference of the earth. Cleaving as it does through the heart of the entire Yukon Territory-Alaska northwestern subcontinent, it presents access to the vast interior as a navigable summer waterway and a frozen winter thoroughfare.

The great river has not only made a name for itself because of the length it achieves and the volume it gathers on its way to the sea. Throughout history, few of the earth's rivers have gathered such fame as this river of glory and romance, the legendary Yukon, the fabled Highway of the North.

Moses Mercier: "In 1848, as I recall, *(comme je me rappelled)*, the year gold was discovered in California and a year after Alexander Murray had pushed Hudson's Bay Company interests to the mouth of the Porcupine in Russian Alaska, Robert Campbell established Fort Selkirk for the HBC several hundred miles upstream from Fort Youcon, near where the Pelly River joins the Yukon. The trading post stood about halfway between the present sites of Whitehorse and Dawson, Yukon Territory. Campbell picked the most strategic location for hundreds of miles, *c' était si bon!* Han and Gwitch'in Athapaskans, from far to the north, regularly made the trek south to the Pelly mouth, joining Northern and Southern Tutchone to trade with Tagish Athapaskans who served as middlemen for Tlingit Indian traders who brought goods over the mountains from the Alaska coast.

"A look at the map of the Southeast Alaska coastline shows that the Coast Range north and south of Juneau throws up an imposing 200-mile-long barrier of ragged crags. *Il est comme un mur!* To the south, this dauntingly inhospitable wall begins near Wrangell, where the Stikine River, from its origin in British Columbia, cuts through the range to saltwater. The wall extends northward without offering practical passage through the peaks, ice caps and glaciers (discounting the Taku River course as largely impractical) all the way to the head of Lynn Canal. There, occurs an ice-free gap.

"That gap, it fortuitously happens, *(si bon, si bon!)*, lies precisely at the point where the Yukon River source and Pacific are so close. It also happens that the break through the mountains offers not one, but two useful passes. Yet a third break and a third useful pass lies not far to the west.

"*Naturellement*, over the millennia, the closest native peoples, the Tlingit, had found and used the White Pass, the parallel Chilkoot Pass a few miles to the north as well as the Chilkat Pass farther west. Alaska's warlike Tlingits, aggressive and domineering, tightly controlled a highly organized trading system that reached from their coastal villages inland to trade with the comparatively mild and docile Athapaskans of the upper Yukon. The Tagish Indians of the upper river were employed—actually almost enslaved—by the Tlingits as middlemen. On pain of death, the Tagish and

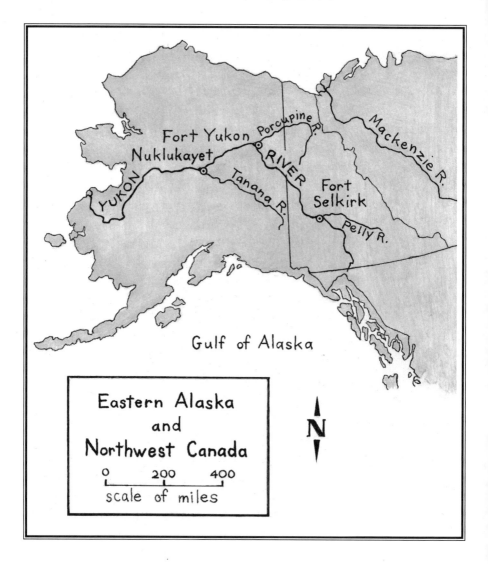

Eastern Alaska
and
Northwest Canada

0   200   400
scale of miles

other interior tribes were forbidden by the Tlingits to venture over the passes to the sea. *C'était mauvais, mon ami.* Over time, the Tlingits had so intermarried with the Tagish and were so commercially intertwined with them that the latter had left behind their Athapaskan language and spoke Tlingit.

"Each Tlingit chief had an exclusive trading partner, the chief of an Athapaskan group. The Tlingits took yearly—sometimes twice yearly—trading trips into the interior, often lasting a month or more. As many as 100 men made the trip. The coastal people were tremendous packers, *très, très, fort!* Though one early explorer estimated that the native men averaged but 140 pounds in weight, each carried 100 to 130 pounds over the steep and precarious terrain and one was known to have shouldered some 160 pounds over the pass. A white trader of the day estimated that the amount of trade goods carried into the interior yearly amounted to some eight tons. This was serious commerce.

"The jealously guarded passes were known as The Grease Trails. A primary trade item, carried inland in sealskin bladders, was oil rendered from the eulachon, or candlefish, a small, smelt-like ocean fish that enters coastal rivers to spawn. Interior Athapaskans prized the oil *un grand prix!* as a delectable dietary enhancement and food preservative.

"With the arrival of Europeans along the coast, the Tlingits became purveyors of the white man's trade goods to the Athapaskans and their power and wealth grew even more. The Athapaskans, superb hunters and trappers, traded furs, hides and copper nuggets in return.

"After establishing Fort Selkirk, Robert Campbell learned of Chilkoot Pass as soon as the first Tlingit trading party came through.

"For the Hudson's Bay Company, getting goods into Fort Selkirk and taking furs out was an incredibly expensive, laborious ordeal. Between the time post supplies and trade goods left England and were transported, post to post, toboggan to toboggan and canoe to canoe from York Factory thousands of overland and waterway miles across Canada, and the time the company's voyageurs and seamen had reversed that path taking furs back, seven long years had been consumed in the turnaround to get Fort Selkirk furs to the London market.

"If that did not already render it too economically inefficient, Campbell had to compete at a disadvantage with his own company. The Tlingits also trafficked in goods they procured from the Hudson's Bay Company trade steamer, the *Beaver*, the first motorized ship to ply the northwest coast. They could procure HBC trade items on the coast and pack them into the Upper Yukon at a fraction of the cost of moving those same goods into Fort Selkirk over the cross-Canada route that Campbell was forced to employ.

"Campbell enthusiastically reported to HBC headquarters that the pass was short and might offer excellent prospects for supplying their most western posts from the Pacific. *Quelle trouvaille!* What a find! He yearned to look over the route to evaluate possibilities.

"Hudson's Bay Company Governor George Simpson flatly rejected Campbell's request to explore it: *Mais non, non!* 'That you suggest (bringing in trade goods) from Lynn's Canal, even if practicable, I could not recommend to the Council, as if we obtained our supplies from thence, we should be opening a communication to the most valuable part of the Northern Department by which strangers might find their way thither....'

"Too much general knowledge threatened their trade. The firm's most valued possession was its internal monopoly and unchallenged control of the fur trade wherever they could maintain it. The company did not even hint that the pass existed and successfully kept outsiders from believing that such a route could be found.

"As it turned out, Campbell would not need to use the pass anyway. Angered about the interference with their trading monopoly among the northern Athapaskans, in 1852 a Chilkat war party marched in from the coast. Some say they came up the Chilkat River Valley over their trade route that intersected the Yukon at the Pelly mouth (later called the Dalton Trail). Regardless of the route they used, when they arrived they ran off the company traders, then plundered and burned Fort Selkirk.

"Campbell set off on one of the most astonishing overland treks in the annals of the North. The steel-willed explorer-

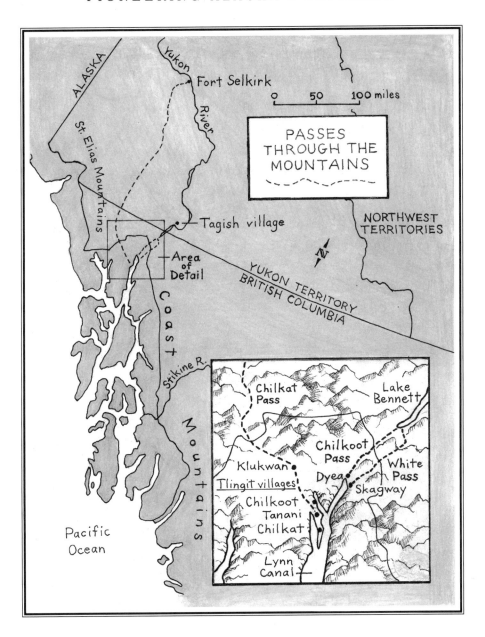

trader traveled some 3,300 miles—over 2,000 miles of that distance across the almost uninhabited Canadian subarctic by snowshoe in the dead of winter—to reach Lachine, Quebec, to petition HBC headquarters for permission to rebuild Fort Selkirk. Unswayed by his amazing loyalty and incredible feat of endurance, officials—*pouf!*—flatly denied his request. *Ainsi, si triste* . . . The location was too remote to be profitable and its operation was too complicated to be continued. As it turned out, Selkirk would not be rebuilt by the Company for some 80 years.

"The Bay Company had found traces of gold along the upper Yukon. But they guarded that information, just as they guarded topographical information to keep their country private. They considered the fur trade far more lucrative. It is believed that as early as 1804 the Russian American Company had found gold and suppressed the information for identical reasons.

"The Protestant missionary Rev. William West Kirkby arrived at Fort Youcon in 1861 and was soon joined by Rev. Robert McDonald. The latter discovered promising gold prospects on a tributary of Birch Creek. However, his focus was on souls, not gold. Word of the Reverend's discovery did not gain wide circulation, possibly because continuation of the missionaries' welcome at the Bay Company's post depended upon suppression of the information. His find was not followed up until some 30 years later when the biggest strikes along the Yukon to that date generated a major gold rush to the area and Preacher Creek was named in McDonald's honor. *Merveilleux!*

"Americans first gained widespread information about the Yukon when, in 1866, the Western Union Telegraph Expedition was organized to survey the Russian Alaskan part of a planned telegraph line that would circle the Northern Hemisphere, joining North America, Russia and Europe. Though they abandoned the venture when, after a number of failures, the rival Transatlantic Cable was finally laid, the United States benefited from the aborted try. Gaining official access into Russian Alaska because of the cooperative nature of the venture between governments, expedition scientists

Robert Kennicott and William H. Dall wrote a report detailing resources of the Yukon River. During the trip beginning from the mouth and extending to Ft. Youcon, where he stayed with the Hudson's Bay traders, Dall described scores of new plants and animals, including the Dall sheep, subsequently named for him.

"*Ainsi, mon ami . . .* in 1867, while in the Yukon River village of Nulato, Dall heard from a Russian-American Fur Company officer that the United States had just purchased Alaska from Russia. Because both Russian and British fur company secrecy had so effectively sealed off even the hint that gold had been discovered within their realms, the United States actually purchased Alaska for its furs, fisheries and timber. They simply had little idea that untold treasures lay underground.

"Immediately, the American firm of Hutchinson, Kohl & Company bought all of the Russian American Company's ships, warehouses and trading posts throughout Alaska. Though the inventory was concentrated along Alaska's long coastline, the Russian company's posts on the Yukon—such as Russian Mission, Nulato and their farthest upriver post at the mouth of the Tanana were part of the sale. *Les Yankees ambitieux* soon cast nationalistic and profit-seeking eyes at Hudson's Bay Company presence far upriver.

"In 1869, the first sternwheeler to ply the Yukon headed upstream. U.S. Army Engineer, Captain Charles Raymond steamed some 1,100 miles eastward from the sea, tied up at Fort Yukon and took readings to determine the geographic position. Having affirmed that the post was well west of the 141st meridian, he ordered the fort's evacuation.

"*Brievment*, between the departure of the Russians from their few posts on the lower and middle river and the expulsion of the trespassing Hudson's Bay Company from Fort Youcon, there existed not a single white man along the entire 2,000-mile-plus course of the great Yukon River.

"In his 'Report of a Reconnaissance of the Yukon River,

Alaska Territory,' Raymond wrote, 'The Stars and Stripes now float at Fort Yukon. Anyone who desires to is at liberty to look for mines.' Frederick Whymper, who served as official artist for the Overland Telegraph Company, was the first to publish mention of gold in the Yukon Valley. In his 1869 travel book on Alaska, Whymper reported that Hudson's Bay Company men had found "minute specks of gold" in the area of Ft. Yukon." *Petit? Combien drôle!*

———•————•———

Alma Preston: "According to Dad Leinhart, Moses Mercier knew all the original Yukoners well, the two groups led by Harper and McQuesten that came into the country by way of the old trade route down the Porcupine. Old Moses thought very well of every one of those men but his favorite was Frederick Hart, lifelong pal of Arthur Harper. Both Harper and Hart had been born in County Antrim, Ireland. They had mined in California, and had joined in British Columbia's Frazier Canyon and Caribou Rushes. Hart didn't stay in the country as long as Harper, in fact he left the North after a very few years. But he knew western and northern gold mining history and was highly interested in fur trade history so he and Mercier really hit it off. They visited every chance they got and after Hart left the country, he and Moses corresponded. And a couple of times when Moses went Outside he visited Hart. Dad said he heard that Hart came back in '97 at the time of the Klondike Rush but took sick and died in Dawson.

"Remember that Dad had that steel-trap memory? I'm not even going to try to imitate Dad trying to sound like a French Canuck mimicking an Irishman! (Alma laughs heartily.) But once Moses Mercier and Frederick Hart were sitting with a writer sent up to write stories for his magazine. The poor fellow drowned later; we heard he walked too close to a high cutbank somewhere up river and the edge caved off with him.

Maybe his notes went with him but his work never got to the magazine. Anyway here's how Moses quoted Hart explaining how prospecting opened the Upper Yukon."

———— ◆ ————

Frederick Hart: "Sir, Moses, here, and I can tell you this is the way it started, can we not, Moses? I thought so. Well, I'm thankful for a guy like you to get it down the way it happened. After California, prospectors like my pal Arthur Harper and me, had looked all over the American West and after the big placers of the Frazier, the Caribou and the Cassiar in British Columbia had dropped off, some of us gold-hunters looked north toward the subarctic and arctic. Art Harper especially could not let go of the idea that within all of the great expanses of the north that had never been prospected, there had to be the geological features we had learned were gold-bearing. I think he might have read of gold findings in the Yukon Basin in Fredrick Wymper's travel book. I know he read the writings of W.P. Blake because he showed them to me. Blake was an American geologist who went with a Russian expedition up the Stikine River in 1863. Everyone knew that the gold-bearing zone stretched through the western mountains of both Americas north into British Columbia. Reading Blake convinced us it would logically extend on north into the Canadian Yukon and Alaska.

"Then somehow Art got his hands on an Arrowsmith map. You'd have thought he'd struck the mother lode! Let me explain. Aaron Arrowsmith was the finest mapmaker of his day. He founded the Arrowsmith Map Company of London. After the Hudson's Bay Company let him into their archives of journals and surveys, he came out with his Map of North America. That was in 1775. President Jefferson used Arrowsmith planning Lewis and Clark's exploration. He gave the two a copy to carry.

"Studying the map, Art reasoned it out this way, and I fully agreed: tributaries of the Mackenzie contained areas rich in gold. They had their headwaters in the same mountainous area the Yukon does. It made sense the Yukon should also hold rich deposits.

"Of course, Arthur could only dream of what might lay on the Russian side. He was brave and driven, but not enough to dare the jaws of the Russian Bear. Besides, he was no outlaw. At the same time, far northwestern Canada was big enough for Art without Alaska and he thought about it day and night.

"Then the United States bought Alaska from Russia in 1867. Now that whole land to the north suddenly became officially open to us. Arthur didn't just itch to go, he went around like he was ready to explode. As we prospected and mined around B. C., his conversations with other gold-hunters always turned talk to the far north. Watching Art's effect on them, I could see that few of even these men used to peril and hardship were daring enough to plan seriously to head into that great unknown.

"Art Harper and the rest of the most daring vanguard were simply tremendous outdoorsmen. You could say they redefined the word, intrepid. They compared to the earlier Mountain Men of the West. They just had an unquenchable thirst to know what lay over the horizon. And they had unlimited confidence in their own strength, wits and wilderness skills. The last supply source could be left far behind and they'd not give it a second thought. No one I knew bested Art in these regards.

"Some of the other lads prospecting British Columbia spilled over into Southeastern Alaska. The first gold they found were in some small lodes around Sitka in 1871. People besides miners wouldn't think we could possibly communicate with each other but there were enough of us milling around the country we could carry letters or spoken messages. The Sitka finds drew a few score who used the old Russian capital as a base. From there, they began a search up and down the coastline.

"In 1872, while the coast was being prospected, we were poking around Peace River country inland. Art Harper just couldn't take it anymore. He was just bursting his britches to have a go at the north and had me caught up in it, too. We found three others crazy enough to take the plunge. They were tough and skillful and would make a good team. We were already traveling in dug-out canoes we bought from the Indians. After paddling the Peace, we left Munson Creek off of the Peace River in the fall and crossed the height of land into the Liard basin. While we wintered over, the five or us whipsawed lumber and built a boat. Then at ice-out we went down the Sikanni Chief and Fort Nelson Rivers to the Nelson mouth.

"There, in Northeastern British Columbia we had a most surprising meeting. We bumped into another party of prospectors as crazed for the Far North as we were. Some members of our groups would turn out lifelong friends and partners. Standing there we could have never guessed that some would even go down in history.

"Leroy 'Jack' McQuesten led the other group and Alfred Mayo with him. These were real men, tremendous men. Like my friend Art Harper, they were of strong moral character, indomitable spirit. And like Art, they had a vision that was broader and much longer in range than the rank-and-file gold-hunter."

———◆——◆——◆———

Rod Perry: *Those adventurers were destined to become famous not only in the early developmental history of Yukon Territory and Alaska but geographical place names and the contributions of their descendants will forever keep their names well known.*

The descendants of Arthur Harper and Al Mayo remain especially numerous along the Alaskan Yukon. Archdeacon Hudson Stuck chose Arthur's son, Walter Harper along with Harry Karstens (the Seventy-Mile Kid) to join him on the first successful ascent of Mount McKinley. By the very fact that it was Stuck who had conceived and organized the expedition and chosen its members, he had every legitimate reason to stand on top first. But consistent with the character of the great churchman and adventurer, at the top he stepped back, thinking it appropriate that a native Alaskan should be first to set foot on the summit.

Iditarod Race legend Susan Butcher introduced the blood of Blackie, a prepotent male sled dog owned by racer, Clyde Mayo of Rampart into her winning line.

Frederick Hart: "Jack McQuesten had been attracted to the West by the California gold rush, the same as Art Harper. And like Art, during the early 1860s, he prospected north into British Columbia. Jack hit both the Frazer and Finlay River rushes.

"After that he mainly trapped and fur traded for almost a decade, some of that time for the Hudson's Bay Company. While working in the fur trade, he was intrigued by stories about the Pelly and Yukon Rivers told by Bay Company employees who had worked there many years before. Jack kept mulling over his own conclusions, identical to those of Harper. He, too, thought that the mineralized zone of the western mountains surely must extend into the Upper Yukon and Russian America.

"It seems McQuesten's last location was so remote he did not find out until1871 that the United States had bought Alaska. When he heard the news he instantly began preparing to investigate the Yukon. By the next year he had found good partners. With Alfred Mayo, who was an ex-circus acrobat ('No better trail companion ever lived,' McQuesten claimed) and George Nicholson, he put together an outfit. They started up the Liard River intending to follow the old abandoned Bay Company route. Jack had heard the canoemen talk about it. The route ascended the swift Frances River, to Frances Lake. Then they would portage along the Finlayson to the Pelly River which would take them downstream to the upper Yukon.

"But while they wintered at the Bay post at the mouth of the Nelson, the agent drummed it into their heads to give up on that route. He knew the country. He asked Jack, Al and George, 'Why, after all the work we put into establishing our posts at Frances Lake and Pelly Banks where the portage trail from Frances hits the Pelly—and throw in Robert Campbell's burned-out Fort Selkirk at the Pelly mouth, just why do you think we abandoned them? You think it was because there was no fur there?

"I'll tell you why, and may that evil country be forever damned! Hells Gate! Devil's Gorge! Rapids of the Drowned! I warn you, in the years the company ran those posts, eight voyageurs—eight, I tell you, and every one of them superb rivermen—eight of them drowned, devoured by the cursed Liard. Two were my friends, fine men both. The Malevolent River or River of Malediction Campbell called it. And if the Liard isn't detestable enough, the Frances is swifter yet! Three other company men starved to death along your intended route, Mr. McQuesten. Don't go that way, I tell you. There's too much danger, it's too difficult, and no supply.'

"By the time we showed up, he had Jack, Al and George convinced to take the trunk line north. The famous old HBC trade route went down the Liard, down the Mckenzie almost to its very mouth on the Arctic Ocean, up the Peel, over Rat Portage and down the Porcupine to Fort Yukon. It was many hundreds of miles longer—really, just shy of a thousand farther—but it was all flat water with several Bay posts along the way.

"That spring when we pulled into the Fort Nelson post the McQuesten party was just getting ready to leave. We had gone over and over Arrowsmith. It was clear the shortest way to the Yukon was via the Liard, Frances and Pelly. Arthur and I and the boys planned to reach the Yukon by the same way McQuesten first intended. But it didn't take the post agent and McQuesten long to sell us. We headed out the longer, safer way.

"After months by river and portage, we four came into Fort Yukon July 15, 1873. I say four because Sam Wilkinson decided to stay back and prospect the Liard. Moses, remember how surprised you were when four strange white men showed up? As you know, it was because McQuesten made a side trip to finish some business at Fort Resolution on Great Slave Lake that his party didn't get to the Yukon until about a month later. Jack told us how thankful he was when you spared them that 50 pounds of flour after two years without.

"From the fur trade, McQuesten had a lot of experience with sled dogs. He had four with him when he got to the Yukon.

"By the time Jack and Al and the lads got there, our bunch had been gone a month, bucking the swift current up the Yukon, prospecting along the way. We found fine gold on the lower Fortymile. We didn't prospect up that river further because local Indians warned of an impassable canyon upstream. Turned out to be blarney. We went on up the Yukon to the White River. We turned from hunting gold to looking for copper up the White until the current stopped us. We wintered over there on almost straight moose.

"That same winter of 1873–74, the McQuesten Party wintered at the mouth of Beaver Creek. They had gone up the Yukon to that tributary after hearing talk around Fort Yukon of Reverend McDonald's gold find a dozen years before. After prospecting and finding some fine gold on the Beaver Creek bars they built winter quarters. They got by on moose and whitefish, hardly anything else.

"Jack, Al and George came back up to Ft. Yukon on April 2nd over the ice. Immediately Jack and one of the others left on a very tough trip of several hundred miles that took five weeks to go and come back. They snowshoed up the Porcupine with Jack's dogs pulling a cariole and went over Rat Portage to La Pierre House part way over to the Mckenzie. Jack had to attend to some business with the Hudson's Bay Company. They just got back to Ft. Yukon in the nick of time the very day—May 10—the ice went out. In their boat they followed

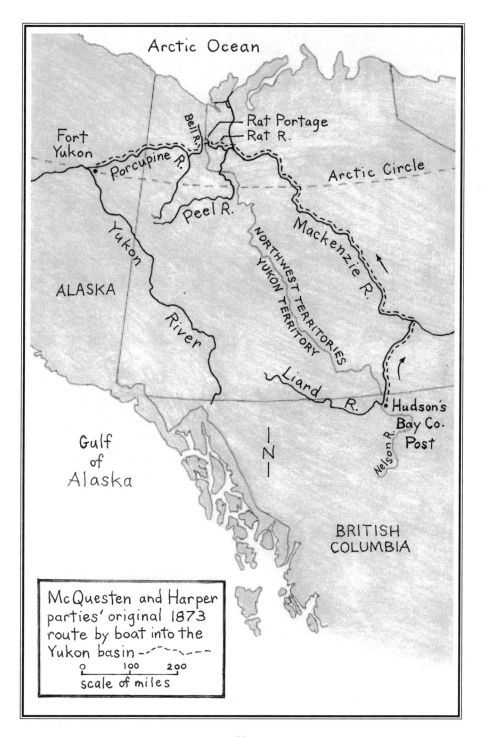

Arctic Ocean

Rat Portage
Rat R.

Fort
Yukon

Bell R.

Porcupine R.

Arctic Circle

Peel R.

Mackenzie R.

Yukon

NORTHWEST TERRITORIES
YUKON TERRITORY

ALASKA

River

Liard

R.

Hudson's
Bay Co.
Post

Nelson R.

Gulf
of
Alaska

N

BRITISH
COLUMBIA

McQuesten and Harper
parties' original 1873
route by boat into the
Yukon basin

0   100   200
scale of miles

breakup downriver to the Alaska Commercial Company station at the mouth of the Tanana, hoping to get supplies.

"Not long after their arrival, our party drifted in, down from our winter on the White. We, too, hoped to stock up on provisions and gear. However, that station was as thinly stocked as Ft. Yukon. How could they have known two groups of white prospectors were going to come crashing in? They were just stocked to trade with the local Indians and barely that.

"The Alaska Commercial Company (ACC) had bought out Hutchinson, Kohl & Company, giving it a virtual trading monopoly on the river. However, they had done nothing to expand the Russian American and Hudson's Bay properties on the Yukon they had taken over but had merely maintained the fur-trading operations as they found them. They hired Mr. Mercier here as to give them an experienced agent at Fort Youcon for a smooth transition from Bay ownership.

"Just before our Harper and McQuesten parties arrived, only a half dozen or so white men populated the whole 2,000-plus-mile-long river. The little steamer *Yukon* made just one trip yearly to take furs out and supply the ACC trading posts. In addition to trade goods the Indians wanted, what the company brought up was only enough to maintain the personnel who ran the posts. It had to last them until next year's boat. So you can see that when our two prospecting parties blew in from out of nowhere there had been almost nothing to spare to supply us.

"Our whole first year on the Yukon, all of us had lived the futility of being forced to focus a big part of our attention on scraping up enough to keep our bellies from rubbing on our backbones. It wasn't that we weren't accomplished at living off the land, it's just that it took time; Heavens sake, the Indians were even better at it, and they spent most of their existence just rounding up enough to eat to stay alive. We sure hadn't come all that way just to practice skills as hunter-gatherers. We needed to train our time on prospecting and mining. We just simply had to do something to fix things.

"Prospectors, see, are like armies, they function on their bellies. We had to find more than a dependable source for merely *enough* to eat, we needed feed that was healthier, too. Just like early sailors brought on scurvy and other ailments from poor diets, we knew a diet of straight fish and game would eventually break us down. All of us could see the futility of trying to work in a region so lacking supplies. If our groups as well as future prospectors were going to have any chance to find the minerals all of us—especially Art and Jack—were sure were present, set-up of a more assured supply system was just an absolute must. Some of us, especially Jack, determined to concentrate on setting up a dependable source of provisions and miner's supplies.

"Well, even though we found the shelves pretty bare at the Tanana post, we knew trusty ol' Mr. Mercier would be coming down from Fort Yukon. He'd be on his annual spring trip down to the ACC distribution center at St. Michael's on the Bering Sea to deliver his furs and pick up his yearly supplies and trade goods. By the time he showed up we had a plan cooking. All of us took the thousand or so mile trip with Moses to the Redoubt. His brother, Franc Mercier, was in charge. There on June 25, 1874, McQuesten, Mayo and I, Fredrick Hart entered into an agreement to act as Alaska Commercial agents. We worked out a veritable franchise for the upper river. We took on a small load of supplies—all they could spare because they hadn't expected us either—totaling about three tons. The plan was for us to found and run a new trading operation. Harper, George Finch and a new guy named John McKniff got a separate supply to keep them prospecting.

"With five boats in tow, the *Yukon* steamed upstream. It was quite a sight to behold, the little steamer straining to pull all those boats. We made only three miles an hour on the lower river. Every 10 hours or so, we'd have to pull up to some driftwood pile and take on four cords of fuel. To establish trading relations with the river people, we put in at the villages along the way.

"While at Koyukuk Station, my lifelong friend, Arthur Harper, who I thought I knew so well, completely surprises me. He's 39 years old. I thought he was a confirmed bachelor, but something must have gotten into him. He spots a Koyukon girl. Her name's Jenny Bosco, only 14. Faster than I know what's happening—Moses, he has the boiler fired up with a full head of steam and needs to get going—in quick order Art checks around to find a little about her, asks her to marry him, arranges with her parents, has the wedding on the spot, and steams away upriver with her, all so fast it makes my head swirl.

"The *Yukon* finally arrived at the Tanana mouth where the newly weds and the rest had determined to prospect. You might think that offloading the tonnage—you know, the goods for the ACC station, plus Art's party getting off with their supplies—along with relieving the drag by getting free of four of the skiffs we'd been towing, you'd think it would've so lightened us the steamer'd be able to take off like the guy who carries an anvil just so he can drop it when he sees the pack of wolves on his trail. But the little boat still struggled to make headway as the current of the upper river increased.

"At the village of Kokrines, Al Mayo added to the load when he found and hastily married his own 14-year-old bride. She was Margaret, daughter of the chief of Nuklukayet at the Tanana mouth. She and Jenny (Bosco) Harper were cousins.

"Not to be outdone while there at Kokrines, Jack McQuesten met *his* 14-year-old bride-to-be, Katherine. She was home for the summer from the Russian Orthodox school at Russian Mission. Katherine was some piece of work. Not only was she fluent in her native Athapaskan, she knew perfect Russian and could do OK in English. Of the three young girls, she was the only one with a whit of book-learning or exposure to Western culture. It was easy to see that Jack and Kate were instantly smitten with each other, but as it turned out they would not marry until she was 18. About this time I was getting pretty jumpy, thinking I'd better just hide somewhere under the deck.

"Now look, I want to make something clear. And Moses, you can vouch for this too. While at first glance those three unions might look like three lustful older men preying upon vulnerable young girls—maybe the kids were only going to get used and thrown away—if that's the thinking, I want to snuff it right now. That was anything but the case. Each of the three was a man of absolutely sterling character, too high to consider such a thing. And the young ladies? Their people often had a short, short lifespan. So they married in their early to mid-teens. There just weren't any left of the quality of those three young ladies after they were older than 14 or 15.

"I want to tell you something else, and Moses will back this up, too. Much credit for the successes of the trading businesses eventually founded by Arthur Harper, Jack McQuesten and Al Mayo would be readily given to the talent, hard work and dedication of their wives. They made faithful partners who would mix the traders into the culture of the river. They did that not only through their blood ties but through their skills as translators and ambassadors.

"It was not until August 7th that our good captain Moses, here, nosed his great ship up to the bank at Fort Yukon. A few days after offloading Fort Yukon cargo, Jack, Al Mayo and I and another fellow pointed the prow of the *Yukon* upstream. That was historic, the first time a motorized vessel had plied the river above the Porcupine. (I guess, looking back, everything we did was historic.) On the 20th of August, 1874 McQuesten picked out a site six miles downstream from the mouth of the Tron-duick River—later to be named the Klondike. We discharged our supplies and there, built the first of Jack's trading post/supply depots on the Yukon River. We didn't get to any prospecting that summer but we sure got a lot done to start a set-up for future prospectors to get out there and hunt gold instead of food.

"Through Jack's considerable time spent working for the Hudson's Bay Company he knew the company history of the founding and destruction of Ft. Selkirk and the fact that the coastal Tlingits had trade trails into the upper river. He even suspected the trails came in from the head of Lynn Canal. Jack kept contact with quite a few prospectors looking along the coast north from Sitka. It was known that the Tlingit villages up there were powerful through trading. Maybe Jack just put two and two together. Another thing, having a whole summer on the river in the company of Mr. Mercier, here, and even having had some touch with the local Indians around Fort Yukon, McQuesten learned all the people of the interior could tell him about the Tlingit's trade and their trail between the coast and Yukon headwaters.

"The rest of us would write a letter once in awhile, but Harper and McQuesten were just tireless letter writers. They knew a lot of letters had very little chance of ever catching up with their wandering prospector friends working remote country, leaving no word where they were going because sometimes they didn't know themselves or would change plans on the way. But Arthur and Jack never tired of casting their bread upon the waters. Enough letters cast out there and chances are some would connect. In the years to come, both would deluge friends they had prospected and mined with in British Columbia with letters promoting the Yukon. Then the recipients would spread the information. Many of the earliest vanguard of prospectors who would shortly push into the country would say their decision to prospect the Yukon Basin started with word that spread throughout the gold fields from the letters of Harper or McQuesten.

"It is very likely that as the Alaska Commercial Company's supply ship left St. Michael for the States following our visit it carried many letters the two wrote steaming down river. You can bet those letters were packed with valuable information. They probably got the blood stirring in many of their adventurous, gold-seeking friends far down south. As it turned out, the letters of Arthur and Jack would play a big part in fostering not one, but many gold rushes. Their letters would help open up and found the North Country.

"McQuesten named the station, Fort Reliance. Because there were yet no other prospectors in the region and gold had not yet been discovered, and because of his past experience in the fur trade, we focused our business on the surest quick income, we traded with the Indians for furs.

"One advancement that Jack brought into the country was a much heavier emphasis on the use of dogs for freighting and travel than before on the upper river. Among the natives who adopted the traders' practice, it brought on big changes. The early practice we saw was the native people using double-ended sleds pulled by their women. They were so poor they couldn't keep many dogs, so few they just supplemented the women. When they increased the use of dogs to haul freight and run traplines, they expanded their range and caught more furs. More furs meant more wealth to keep bigger teams. That meant yet greater range and even more furs. The Indians of the region began to rely more heavily upon trapping and trading as a means of gaining their necessities.

"The season after Jack started Reliance, the ACC reorganized and things really shuffled around. The company put their fur traders on commission. Mercier saw an opportunity too good to turn down so he left to build his Belle Isle trading post near Eagle. I worked here and there. Jack McQuesten went down to be agent at Fort Yukon. Arthur Harper came aboard as a partner in the business. With Al Mayo he manned Fort Reliance for the next three years, but just as a summer enterprise. Each of those winters they would drop down to the more well-appointed Fort Yukon to winter, the first two with McQuesten. It was a treat for the young wives as well as for the three fast friends. The third year, Jack ran the company's Tanana post. After a season there he returned to Fort Reliance and began operating it year round. Art and Al spread out to other posts.

"Well, sir, I hope that gives you enough for your magazine piece. If your readers are as interested in history of the North as Moses and I are, and if they wonder how the country got opened up for the first prospectors, I pretty well covered it. By the way, you say you're going to be around for a few more days. If Mr. Mercier or I think of anything I should have included, I'll look you up."

———◆———◆———

Alfred Hulse Brooks: "During the next few years, with ACC support, Arthur Harper, Jack McQuesten and Al Mayo would found a number of Yukon River trading posts. Their enterprises stretched out over 800-odd river miles between the mouth of the Tanana and the mouth of the Pelly, responding to the supply needs of various gold strikes on one side of the international border or the other. It may be truly stated that without the foundational supply base these pioneer pioneers set in place to attract prospectors and support them in their efforts, none of the gold strikes of the Yukon Basin or Seward Peninsula would have happened as they did and it is probable that the continent's far northwest would have lain dormant for decades into the 20th century."

Chapter 3

The Trickle Begins

ACROSS THE COAST RANGE from the transmontaigne area of the upper Yukon, in 1875 a daring prospector named George Holt furtively slipped into the dense forest at the end of saltwater on Lynn Canal, searched out the Tlingit's trail over the Chilkoot Pass and penetrated the fastness of the upper Yukon. How he had acquired knowledge of the tribe's secret is lost to history, but the contents of the letters of Harper and McQuesten were known to some of the prospectors based out of Sitka who were searching along the Southeast Alaska Coast. Whatever his source of information—some reports say he was guided by two Indians, (if true, they must not have placed a very high value on their lives), he gained the distinction of becoming the first white man known to cross the pass.

Instead of following the watercourse far down the upper Yukon, Holt turned eastward at Marsh Lake, crossed the height of land and prospected the Teslin River, a move that probably saved him from detection by natives traveling their summer Yukon trade route. Though his pack contained a small quantity of gold when Holt cautiously retraced his steps in the fall, his main triumph was going in, then making it back out without the knowledge of the Tlingits. Had he been caught in the act, the consequences would have no doubt been dire.

Holt came into Sitka, freely talked about his findings and encouraged others to duplicate his feat. Holt knew that since he had broadcast his accomplishment, the Chilkats would double their watch and never allow him back over their trail without military support. During the winter of 1875–76 he and the post commander formulated a plan to send an officer

67

with him the next spring. However, the government withdrew U.S. troops from Sitka before the plan could be carried out. As far as is known, Holt never went back.

Rod Perry: *George Holt did not emerge from all of his experiences with natives so successfully. In 1886, Indians killed him at the Alaska Commercial Company post at Knik, Alaska, later to be an important jumping off point on the Iditarod Trail.*

Word that circulated among west coast prospectors about Holt's findings on the upper Yukon and his access via the Chilkoot Pass added to Harper and McQuesten's beckoning, informative letters increased the lure and led numerous prospectors to lay definite plans to enter the country.

Soon, George Finch (who had originally accompanied Arthur Harper to the Yukon) somehow made it over the Chilkoot Pass and back. Here and there, a few others arrived in upper Lynn Canal, intending to make the trek. However, the watchful Tlingits, enforcing exclusive right of passage over the trade route they had considered their proprietary domain for hundreds of years, harshly thwarted all other attempts through the 1870s.

Alfred Hulse Brooks: "Meanwhile, Harper, McQuesten and Mayo, but especially the former two, continued in their unique partnership, each in his own way laying down a critical foundation for those who would follow."

Frederick Hart: "Sir, I'm glad we could get back to you. Mr. Mercier and I were talking after the other day, and he reminded me of something we just can't let you go home to your magazine without. A man never had a truer, kinder friend than my lifelong pal, Arthur Harper and I almost left out something he should be credited with.

"Art had joined Jack McQuesten in the fur trade but it was gold that occupied his thinking. Furs were to him merely a way to finance his next prospecting trip. Art was just the quintessential prospector. He just knew that if he combed enough country he would eventually make a big find. That confidence filled him and never died. On that first upriver trip we made after we came in in '73 we prospected some up the Stewart River. Now, he did not formally record his journeys, but through the following years I know Art made as many short forays and lengthy expeditions as his trading business would allow. On one of his long trips, in1876 he looked for color all the way to the head of the Fortymile River. From there he portaged over to the Sixtymile and prospected that drainage. He found color on his way back downstream to the Yukon. Several times he made lengthy trips into the Tanana country. On one trip into the Tanana he entered the headwaters by going over the divide from the Fortymile. Sir, you might not be familiar with the map but the Fortymile is well over a hundred miles long as the river flows. On a trip in 1878, he journeyed up the Tanana some 250 miles from its mouth in the company of Al Mayo. You probably don't know but they had to build a new boat from spruce boards they whipsawed every drainage they traveled.

"Arthur Harper was the first to find gold on the Stewart, the Fortymile, the Sixtymile, and the Tanana, including black sand and fine gold dust brought back from the vicinity of the lower Chena River. But Harper never found gold in paying quantities.

"Although he, himself failed to ever find any deposits worth mining, Sir, it may be truly said, and my friend, Moses Mercier, here, will vouchsafe this as fact: Arthur Harper and no other should gain tribute as the chief pioneer discoverer of gold in the Yukon Basin."

Alfred Hulse Brooks: "Most importantly for those who would follow, Harper's arduous trips, though often fraught with peril and deprivation and always laborious in the extreme, gave him an overall feel for the distribution of gold deposits and a general familiarity with the unmapped uplands and drainages of the central Yukon Basin, knowledge which he freely shared. Harper's discoveries and information led to the main strikes at Fortymile, the Klondike and Fairbanks, which in turn led to finds at other Alaska locations, in a sense, even Nome."

——————

While Arthur Harper, the prospector was the key discoverer, his faithful friend and long business associate, Jack McQuesten, was to play such an important role in the industrial development of the country that he would become known to history variously as the "Father of the Yukon," "Father of the Country" and "Guardian Angel of the Miners." In the years following his initial prospecting upon his arrival on the Yukon, McQuesten seldom, if ever took part in the search for gold. Instead, as per the arrangement he made with Harper, he concentrated on providing a support base for his partner so that Harper could prospect for the group. He concentrated on the fur trade with the Athapaskans, the only viable source of income in the early days, making many trips to St. Michael with furs and bringing back supplies either from St. Michael, Seattle or San Francisco.

With families to raise and educate and with growing business interests as the partners spread out to more effectively capture the fur trade, it grew impractical even for Harper and Mayo to be gone on numerous long prospecting trips and they, like McQuesten settled increasingly into management of their various trading and supply stations.

While the partners anchored their business in the fur trade, they never lost the vision that first attracted them to the North

Country and viewed their fur business as a necessary means to an end, the end being gold.

Out on the Southeast Alaska coast in 1880, a party of 19 prospectors appealed to Commander Beardslee of the *U.S.S. Jamestown* stationed at Sitka to force open the Chilkoot Pass route. Seeing that the group was comprised of serious, experienced men headed up by Edmund Bean, an old California Gold Rush prospector, the commander wrote a letter to the Chilkat chiefs and dispatched Lt. E.P. McClellan with a steam launch carrying 18 armed officers and crew and two Indian interpreters to accompany the prospectors' boats to the Chilkat Village for a confrontation.

Commander Beardslee's persuasive letter-writing and the skills of his interpreters changed the Tlingit's attitude about maintaining monopolistic dominion over the pass. Or perhaps it was the Gattling gun mounted on the bow. Whatever swayed the Tlingits, the meeting ended their several-hundred-year-long stranglehold on use of the pass. Ever commercially minded though, the tribe instantly adapted: they became packers for hire.

The expedition left the head of Lynn Canal May 20. On June 17th, Bean wrote to Beardslee and hired one of the packers to deliver it. The letter told of being camped on a lake shore over the pass and building boats.

By November 15 the party returned to Sitka. They reported the finding of some gold, nothing outstanding, but they at least substantiated Holt's claims of gold to be found on the Hootalinqua, as the miners misnamed the Teslin.

———◆——◆———

Alfred Hulse Brooks: "I have said that Alaska owes credit for its modern history to the opening of the Canadian Yukon and the great rush to the Klondike. I must turn about and say that a much smaller, yet important part that credit must be handed back to Alaska. First, the approach to the Chilkoot Pass begins in Alaska and it was due to Alaskan efforts that the Tlingit's deadly grip on its use was relaxed. Second, the same year the Bean Party went over the pass and back, two men based out of Sitka, Richard T. Harris and Joseph Juneau (nephew of the founder of Milwaukee, Wisconsin) made a rich strike at the present site of Juneau, Alaska, on August 17th. (You know, folks, coincidentally, that is same day of the year, 16 years later, that gold would be found on the Klondike.) The pair's findings led to the establishment of the incredibly rich Alaska-Juneau Mine. The discovery of a gold-bearing quartz ledge across the channel from the present site of Juneau by French Pete in about 1881 and its sale for a pittance to John Tredwell, led to the development of the wonderful Glory Hole of the Tredwell Mine.

"Placer, or free gold, is what most prospectors seek because it can usually be mined with no more than a pick, shovel and a strong back. Hardrock mining is altogether different. The gold lies within the solid rock. Miners must tunnel into a mountain or dig deep open pits to get at gold-bearing ore. The ore is then pulverized with big machinery to separate rock from gold. Often tons must be crushed for each ounce of gold.

"The nature of the lode mining effort around Juneau necessitated enormous capital investment in machinery, the employment of large numbers of miners and the establishment of well-built, permanent company mining camps to house and feed the men so work could go on regardless of season. These great camps were destined to play an important part in the opening of the Canadian and Alaskan Yukon Basin. They not only drew miners from throughout the West, they formed a strategic staging base from which a few of the more intrepid could set forth on their long expeditions over the Chilkoot Pass.

"After working the winter in the Juneau or Tredwell mine, some of the hardiest, most adventurous prospectors boated north 100 miles to the head of Lynn Canal, crossed the pass, built boats or rafts from native timber, sailed and rowed down the Yukon several hundred miles, prospected all summer, then traveled through fall to beat the onset of winter back to the haven of the Juneau or Tredwell. [Let it be inserted here that few have the experience to even imagine the grueling details of the journey of hundreds of miles back *against* the swift flow of the Yukon.] At the mines they could count on rehiring to labor another winter, staying warm and well-fed and earning enough for another stake to outfit for a further go at the Yukon. Had they not been able to rely upon this nearby support base for security and replenishment, the initial trickle of gold-seekers heading over the pass each summer would have remained just that for many more years, a mere trickle."

———————

In 1881, four men crossed the Chilkoot Pass and became the first to find gold in actual paying quantities in the interior. They noted at least some color on every bar they tried for 200 miles up a Yukon tributary, the Big Salmon River. Enthusiastically, they reported that some bars not only paid, but paid well.

At first, it was but an almost unnoticed trickle of gold-seekers who crested the pass. But the silence of the little-known Yukon began to break. Year by year, a few more arrived. About 50 came over each year from 1881 to 1883, and 75 the following year, most descending the Yukon to the mouths of the Pelly and Teslin Rivers then prospecting up those tributaries. In 1886, on the Cassiar bars along the Yukon just below the mouth of the Teslin River and the on bars along the Stewart River, the finds of encouraging colors made them major points of activity.

———————

Alfred Hulse Brooks: "It was in 1882 when the first of those prospectors venturing in from Juneau over the Chilkoot pushed their way far enough north to take advantage of the beginnings of the infrastructure, meager though it was, that Harper and McQuesten, through a decade of hard labors, had been establishing for them. They would find the beginnings of a Yukon riverboat service. Fort Reliance, though thinly provisioned, served as a supply hub and winter quarters. Just as important was the vast body of information about the country related to topography, travel and prospecting conditions and subsistence tips the two men had to offer. By sheer dint of their own vision and almost unaided effort, these pioneer pioneers had opened up the Yukon drainage to the prospector. Therefore, much of the later development of Alaska and the Yukon must be considered to stand upon their shoulders."

About a dozen of these adventurers forged north to Fort Reliance that September of 1882. It must almost be a foregone conclusion that it was correspondence from Harper and McQuesten that gave them knowledge of the fort's existence and the confidence to push farther down the Yukon to winter there. As stated, the pattern of other, earlier prospectors had been to use late summer and early fall to beat a retreat from the farthest extent of their midsummer explorations in order to winter back on saltwater. Because most of them had penetrated into the country fully 400 to 700 hundred miles from Juneau, and the way back involved at least a month of arduous poling and lining their boats upstream then sailing and rowing up the lake system, the prevailing practice had dictated a timely start in order to get back over the Coast Range before the fall storm season set in and barred the pass. By choosing to winter over in the interior this small vanguard who floated into Fort Reliance not only demonstrated confidence that the Yukon Basin held rich gold deposits worth the commitment of more than a short summer foray, these forerunners demonstrated that serious gold seekers could gamble enough on supplies being available through Harper and McQuesten to stay in the country and double their prospecting time instead of wasting much of the limited season, their energy and supplies making the arduous, yearly, 1,000-plus-mile round trip.

Rod Perry: *That winter of 1882 was a watershed for the partners' operations, as well as for the opening and future development of the Yukon Basin. The traders had been on the Upper Yukon the better part of a decade "going before, preparing the way in the wilderness." From 1882 on, the rate at which there would be an increase in men who would dedicate themselves to the country would pick up momentum.*

Our close family friend, Nome miner Al Preston, knew many of the old-time dog punchers from the upper country because many of them migrated among all the big strikes. Although as with most miners, Al was too occupied with mining to keep a team, he loved dogs and life on the trail. He spent a lot of time in the company of the drivers when errands and business took him into town from his claim.

Ben Atwater was a well-known sourdough of the Upper Yukon who later went to Nome, Fairbanks and Iditarod. His grandson, Ted Atwater of Willow, was a close friend of my friends, Mike Lee and his former wife Carolyn, who introduced me to mushing dogs. Ted was a wonderful sled-builder, crafting one from native birch for Mike. He made another for Tom Mercer to take on the first Iditarod Race. The hat which the old sourdough on the cover of this book wears was given to him by Ted Atwater.

The deep, but flinty sound of Al's voice drifts back to me.

Al Preston: "I knew Old Ben Atwater, one of the first prospectors into the Upper Country. Later he became a famous mail carrier. His big, black, retriever-malemute

Ben Atwater, Mail Carrier, with His Dogsled Team, ca. 1898
University of Washington Libraries, Special Collections, Hegg052

crosses were the fastest mail team anyone had ever seen. You'd know him as far as you could see him by his great, black beard. Many years after he made his way into the Upper Yukon he looked back on the difficulty and told me about how it was."

***

Old Ben Atwater: "Al, 'arduous' hardly describes our prospecting trips into the Yukon and back out. Sometimes we went maybe 1,400 miles before we got back to Juneau. We only had about five months to do it. Looks to me like those writers and historians back in America tend to live in the city library. Probably die up here pretty quick. Might be at ease handling a typewriter, but, far's I can see, couldn't tell one end of an axe or paddle from the other and wouldn't know a tumpline or gee pole from Adam's off ox. Ever since the gold rushes made big news and people want to read about us, they sit back there trying to write like authorities on the North. Maybe I shouldn't be so critical, and I s'pose they do the best they can. Al, you and I know you can't look at even the best map and have so much as an inkling. They'd never guess unless they've been here and even then they couldn't imagine unless they did it just like we did for as far and long as we did. It's pretty plain those librarians never traveled on foot or river themselves, at least not like we did. They just don't have any personal experience to even guess what we had to do. So they can't know how tough it was for us to get around in the old days.

"Most readers don't know enough about it to know the writers don't know anything so they don't know the writers are leaving anything out. It don't even enter the minds of most historians to try to fill in their readers about the backbreaking labor and miseries. They got no idea how much harder foot travel in the Yukon and Alaska is than where they live. Black spruce muskegs are so spongy they eat up your energy when you're packing a heavy load and the packs we humped over the pass were staggering. We had food staples to last months, clothing, simple shelter, hunting and fishing gear, and boatbuilding, camp and prospecting tools. Weighed way over 120 pounds a lot of times. Tundra tussock country was a killer, just maddening. Then there were always tangles of alder brush and downed timber you could hardly fight your way through. Took the spirit right out of you. Beaver swamps, side channels and ox bows along the rivers, they made every mile just a real battle ground.

"Even if the soft, librarian types have tried enough foot travel to amount to anything, even bushwhacking with no trail at all through wilderness farther south, it's almost sure to be a stroll in the park held up to the same number of Yukon or Alaska wilderness miles. Al, you know what I'm talking about.

"Those historians that write about our prospecting expeditions up or down a river never mention that first we had to build a boat. If the library guy does mention it, he doesn't put in what it takes to do it. He couldn't set up a sawpit, and he wouldn't know the first thing about whipsawing boards from rough logs. Fact, most wouldn't know a whipsaw from a two-man misery whip. Huh! And the logs aren't always very good. Sometimes they are small, or knotty. But you've got to have a boat so you take whatever the country gives. Man on the scaffold pulls up, man in the pit pulls down. Stroke by stroke, terribly hard and pure misery. Every minute your motions and body heat draw mosquitoes, no-see-ums and black flies by the thousands, maybe millions. The man on the scaffold works like a dog hauling the saw up, but I'd rather man the upstroke any day. The pitchy sawdust that showers down is torture. The itchy stuff sticks to the sweating body and it blinds the eyes of the man in the pit as he looks up to keep the cut running true to the line. I'll tell you, whipsawing lumber's the greatest test of a friendship I can think of. Put two angels straight from Heaven on opposite ends of a whipsaw and they'd be fighting before the first board's finished. Takes about a week for a couple of experienced men to build a boat, longer if the logs are small and knotty.

"Yes, those writers never lined or polled a heavy, 20- to 28-foot-long boat made of green lumber upstream against a swift current day after day. So the historian just writes that the expedition went up such and such a river. Then when he just mentions in passing that we left one river and crossed a divide to follow another, did you ever see him include that the first boat we had built and all the blood, sweat and tears that went into it had to be left behind? Or see him say that when we got to the next drainage, another sawpit had to be set up, a new pile of lumber had to be whipsawed and we had to go through the torture all over again to build the next boat? Al, you and I know travel in the north country was just hellacious hard work."

———— ••◆•• ————

Al Preston: "One time I was traveling with a guy, can't remember his name, but he was keeping a journal that he thought he might turn into a book if he ever made it back out of the North. He read me something about the terrible insects that I wrote down and saved because he described it perfectly, way better than I could. Ben, it fits in with what you were saying about how tough the traveling was in the territories:

'These black swarms are veritable thorns in the flesh and ravagers of the soul. Men must go to every length to prevent them from devouring the body and eroding the nerves. We miners suffer untold tortures from their attacks, no matter how we protect against them. A strong wind is a welcomed relief and a hard freeze seems like the gentle caress of Nature, even if we understand that it signals the beginning of months of Arctic temperatures and may be the harbinger of a winter of starvation.' "

———— ••◆•• ————

In the Yukon and Alaska, fiendish hordes of blood-sucking insects billowed out of the vegetation at every footstep to follow along in clouds so dense that any encounter suffered in the "South 48" may be dismissed with a wave of the hand as comparatively insignificant. Many ranked mosquitoes as the worst obstacle of all. At their thickest, with no modern repellants yet available, they were almost impossible to cope with. Pack horses were covered with canvas sheets and their nostrils had to be periodically cleaned to keep them breathing clearly. After several horses on one expedition drowned in a river trying to escape the hordes, the men kept smudge fires burning when they camped for the night so the horses could gain relief. Then the animals grew so thin and weak refusing to leave the smoke to graze that some had to be shot. Some of the early prospectors reported their head nets becoming so covered with insects seeking entry they could hardly breathe. Not a few who had previously conquered all other hardships gave up the country, driven raving mad by the onslaught of the pests that pressed them with no respite day and night.

The dozen-odd of the vanguard who chose to hole up at McQuesten's haven, almost 700 miles from Juneau, included in their number Captain William Moore, who would go on to found Skagway, Alaska; Joe Ladue, who would found Dawson, Yukon Territory; and Howard Franklin, who would discover gold on the Fortymile so he could be credited as starting the town of Fortymile, Yukon Territory. Frank Densmore and Thomas Boswell, also counted among their number, were destined as well to play important roles in the development of the North Country. The men built small cabins and must have laid in a good supply of fish, caribou and moose (the local Athapaskans favored the nearby Klondike Valley as a moose hunting ground) because McQuesten apparently had not known they were coming, so would not have stocked much more food than he had planned to trade for furs and consume himself.

Jack McQuesten thoroughly enjoyed the winter. It was the first time since he came back to Fort Reliance that he had men whose chosen tongue was English with whom to converse. The men spent most of their evenings gathered at his main building visiting and playing cards. During that winter they laid the ground for what would grow into the fraternal brotherhood, Yukon Order of Pioneers.

Their wintering over broke ground, setting an example soon duplicated by many others.

Al Preston: "There was a world of difference in the skills at living and traveling in the wild between the old sourdoughs and most of those who came in later during the gold rushes. Those earliest gold-hunters who came into the country over the Chilkoot before '97, tended to be experienced, professional prospectors. They were hardened outdoorsmen out of the mold of Old Ben Atwater, himself. They knew what to take and what to leave out. They never left out essentials. But at the same time you'd never see them packing one thing they didn't really need. They had to be good at finding fish and game to make up most of their diet because they could have never carried enough staples over the pass to keep them all season. The ones who decided to overwinter were sure of their ability to travel the distances and live off the country until they could reach one of the remote trading posts of Harper or McQuesten or at least get to a native village or mining center before their supplies ran out.

"I once cut out a passage from *National Geographic Magazine*, quoting a guy sent up to write about the early times. I met the writer, Israel Russell his name was, and he seemed like a decent enough sort. He described those forerunners who broke trail and moiled for gold across the North: 'My companions were rough and uncouth as men could well be. Their hair and beards had grown long, and their faces were tanned and weather-beaten by constant exposure. Their garments, then in the last stages of serviceability, had been made by those who wore them, from any material that chanced to be available, from buckskin and fur to flour-sacks, and had been repaired without regard to color or texture . . . One not accustomed to the vicissitudes of exploration, coming suddenly on such a scene, would certainly believe he had stumbled on a band of the most desperate outlaws.

'They were a rough, hardy race, made up, it would seem, of representatives of nearly every nation on earth. Some are typical frontiersmen, dressed in buckskin, who are never at home except on the outskirts of civilization. Others were of doubtful character, and it is said are seldom known by their rightful names. The remote gulches of the Yukon country seem to offer safe asylums for men who are 'wanted' in other districts. Despite the varied character of its inhabitants, this remote community is orderly and but few disturbances have been known.' "

<hr />

The earliest men into the country had to improvise in many ways and some of the improvisations exhibited a lot of creative thought. Jack McQuesten invented an ingenious thermometer that was widely used throughout the region. It consisted of a row of vials mounted on a rack, the first containing quicksilver, the next Jamaica Ginger Extract, the third coal oil and the fourth Perry Davis Pain Killer. The four congealed in that order every 10 degrees Fahrenheit from minus-40 to minus-70. When Pain Killer went past merely congealing and crystallized the men knew it had to be minus-75 degrees or lower. It was said that a man considering a journey went without a worry at frozen quicksilver, proceeded with caution at Extract, took pause at kerosene and dived back into his cabin and stoked a big fire at Pain Killer.

With the nearest medical and dental help one or two month's travel away (that is, if traveling conditions were good and the man seeking help was in condition to make good time) men doctored themselves, even to setting their own broken bones. Should some sourdough need something on the order of an amputation, say the removal of a gangrenous leg, if he were fortunate enough he might find some old coot up the creek to perform it. If the patient (victim) was really lucky, the enlisted doctor might even bring a fairly clean crosscut saw and a jug of strong whiskey.

One of the most well-known written records of life in the early days on the upper Yukon tells of an old prospector who suffered such severe tooth aches he was driven to pull all of his own teeth. Upon healing, he became tired of gumming his food so turned his miner's ingenuity to doing something about it. Selecting a bear of just the right size, he shot it, and from the bruin's pearly gnashers fabricated what must have been one of the most remarkable sets of dentures ever created, featuring incisors, canines, molars, the works.

Anxious to try out his new choppers, the old sourdough set about testing his workmanship on the donor, the first recorded instance of a bear eaten with its own teeth!

——————•—•—————

Old Ben Atwater: "Another example of how we got by was our making "bone butter." All the old sourdoughs made it 'cause one of the things we missed most was butter. Here's how you do it: You cut several sets of caribou antlers into 10-inch pieces. Then you boil them in a large cauldron for two nights and a day. You remove the 'bones' and cool the liquid. Wait for it to set up on the surface and you can lift a couple of inches of 'butter' off the top. Then add salt to your taste; the saltier it is, the longer it will stay fresh in warm weather. The butter will be white instead of yellow and don't expect it to taste quite the same, but after you've been in the upper country long enough you'll think it's just as good as sweet cream butter. The only trouble, it takes a lot of valuable time."

——————•—•—————

As the number of prospectors increased and the need to spend more time mining and less time subsisting grew, Harper and McQuesten tried not just to respond to that demand, but stay one jump ahead of it. In the Yukon Basin every major gold discovery lay relatively close to the big river or one of its tributaries, enabling them to freight in the miners' needs efficiently by ship from San Francisco or Seattle to St. Michael, then up the Yukon by river boat.

That is, if nothing went wrong along the supply chain. The fall after the 12 miners wintered over with Jack McQuesten, all but Joe Ladue and George Powers were forced to buck the current of the Yukon several hundred miles and go back out over the Chilkoot to winter. McQuesten's steamer had broken down, rendering Fort Reliance provisionless. Four other miners who had come in from Juneau and successfully prospected the Stewart River dropped down to Fort Reliance, expecting to winter there. Instead they found it abandoned. Everyone had gone down to the mouth of the Tanana where there was food. Circumstantial evidence suggests that Al Harper may have been manning the company post there and that McQuesten possibly limped in to winter at Tanana with his decrepit steamer carrying what few supplies he had left over from what he had brought into Fort Reliance the previous year.

Also wintering that year near the Tanana mouth was a party headed by Ed Sheiffelin, the wealthy discoverer of the rich mines of Tombstone, Arizona. As deck cargo on a ship he had chartered, his 12- by 40-foot steamer, *New Racket* had been brought to the Yukon earlier in 1882 and the party had used it in their summer-fall prospecting venture in the vicinities of the Tanana mouth and Ramparts on the Yukon. When he and his men folded their venture, at least one representative of the newly reorganized partnership of Harper, Mayo and McQuesten was there to buy the boat.

Alfred Hulse Brooks: "The traders differed from many who would eventually come in to compete for the Yukoner's dollar. While most of the prospectors were so focused on their own searching and digging they could not see much else, Harper, McQuesten and Mayo had a much broader view. They had been up and down the river for years. They knew the entire country. Being experienced prospectors themselves gave them the advantage of being able to step back, study the big picture, and make sagacious predictions regarding where the best chances lay for someone to make the next strike. They often backed prospectors, grubstaking them to investigate country they thought held promise. However, beyond any thought of their own financial benefit, the two, especially Jack McQuesten, gained the well-loved reputation of never turning away a prospector who had come up short in his search for gold. He was the veritable guardian angel of the prospector. Often, McQuesten sacrificed personally to help miners down on their luck. Other companies that would soon arrive typically resisted such investing in futures. They firmly demanded cash on the barrel head for all purchases.

"McQuesten had another practice that endeared him to the miners. During the early years, a severe shortage of provisions seemed to be the order of things each winter. He instituted a personal policy of apportioning his limited supplies equally among everyone. Financial standing had no bearing. One fall when supplies were thin the joke went up and down the river that each man's share came to two bags of flour and instructions detailing a new way to catch rabbits! When things got that tight, many men would leave the country by way of the Chilkoot or St. Michael in the fall, returning the following summer.

———•———•———

Out in the Pacific Northwest, General Nelson A. Miles, commander of the U.S. Army's Department of the Columbia which watched over the northwest coast, coveted northern extension of his jurisdiction. In 1883, despite opposition from Washington D.C. and the refusal of the War Department to sanction it, Miles dispatched First Lieutenant Fredrick Schwatka into the Upper Yukon on an overall geographical, ethnological, economic and military fact-finding mission. Not only did Schwatka's superiors send him off without bothering to secure higher approval up the Army chain of command, they sent the military expedition into a foreign country without that government's permission or even notification. The lieutenant and his party of six men slipped away on his quickly convened, clandestine reconnaissance, in his words, "like a thief in the night."

At the head of Lynn Canal, Schwatka was fortunate to encounter the superintendent of a nearby salmon cannery who briefed the lieutenant on the packing abilities of the Chilkats and what to pay them. The ever commercially minded Chilkats not only freighted the gear for the expedition over the steep pass, the sure-footed, bull-strong Natives even piggy-backed the explorers themselves during their fording of the Taiya River.

Frederick Hart: "Arthur Harper met Lt. Schwatka as he rafted into his trading station and later got hold of one of his reports. Here's what Art told me the lieutenant said at the time and told him when they met later about what he had published in his journals. I can almost hear Schwatka . . ."

Lt. Fredrick Schwatka: "That portage over the pass was indeed a steep climb. But Mr. Harper, compared to battling 2,000 miles upstream against swift current to accomplish such a survey as we made, well, that mere 32 miles was mere trivia.

When I reached the Yukon so close to it's source and found that it lay so close to the Pacific, I was just dumbfounded that U.S. government mapmakers had been so inaccurate in their placement of the river's headwaters. To show our disgust my men used the maps for target practice.

"It truly amazed me that early explorers had not taken my top-to-bottom route to explore the Yukon instead of starting from the mouth and fighting the current over 2,000 miles which would consume a whole season of the hardest labor to get to where our packers took us in two days. In fact it might have taken even two seasons in the days before your resupply posts; they would have had to hunt and fish along the way. And once they reached the upper waters they would have had to float the entire distance back to the mouth. All because they did not know of this short pass.

"As I wrote in my journal, 'Why this route had not been picked out long ago by some explorer, who could thereby traverse the whole river in a single summer instead of combating its swift current from its mouth, seems singular, and can only be explained by supposing that those who would place sufficient reliance on the Indian reports to put in their maps the gross inaccuracies that fill even our Government charts of the Yukon's source, would be very likely to place reliance on the same Indians; and these from time immemorial, have united in pronouncing this part of the river unavailable even by canoes, filled as it is with rapids, whirlpools and cascades.' "

"As I made my way downriver, I took note of the mining and prospecting activity on the upper Yukon. Jack McQuesten, piloting the recently purchased *New Racket*, passed me on his way upstream. He said he had 30 tons of tools, gear and supplies on board, destined for the miners on the Cassiar bars."

Rod Perry: *The passage upriver of the* New Racket *happened to be McQuesten's first haul dedicated largely to the outfitting and supplying of the growing number of prospectors working the upper river. Closing in on their first decade in the Yukon, the partner's enterprise had concentrated almost solely on the native fur trade.*

———◆———◆———

Lt. Fredrick Schwatka: "Our expedition accomplished the first complete survey of the third largest river of our country. We did it with 'far less money in our hands to conduct it through its long journey than was afterward appropriated by Congress to publish its report.' Both the official and popular reports of our expedition were published in 1885. It became the first widespread mention of the Yukon and its resources to reach the American press. Mine was, as far as I know, the first published description of the crossing of the Chilkoot Pass."

———◆———◆———

One prospector who was lured north in the early 1880s was George Washington Carmack. Carmack befriended Tagish Athapaskans, Skookum Jim and his cousin, Tagish (later, Dawson) Charlie, and began to live with their people. He married one of Skookum Jim's sisters, and, when she died, following the Tagish custom, married another sister, whom George called Kate.

Carmack's first notable find, probably aided by his relatives' intimate knowledge of the country, was a major coal deposit. He attempted to develop a coal mine, building a cabin that became a trading post and, years later, grew into the Yukon River village that now bears his name.

In 1885, the year of Schwatka's expedition report, prospectors mined the first truly paying quantity of gold in the region along the Stewart River bars. The Schwatka publicity and reports of gold brought over 200 prospectors across the Chilkoot Pass the next year, 1886. About $100,000 in gold was taken by miners scattered along the Stewart and upper Yukon Rivers that season. In response, Alfred Harper and Jack McQuesten set up a trading post at the mouth of the Stewart. Then McQuesten took a late boat out to San Francisco to procure their goods for the following year.

After McQuesten's departure, in the waning days of fall Howard Franklin struck gold 25 miles up the Fortymile River in Alaska and soon thereafter on a tributary, Franklin Creek. Before Franklin's discovery, prospecting along the Yukon had been limited to the search for gold-bearing bars where the force of the current and the yearly cataclysm of spring ice breakup tended to stir light gold up from deeper deposits. Therefore, previous gold production had only been in dust form. Franklin's find of a continuous bedrock paystreak was a first for the region and the coarse gold it yielded suddenly revolutionized the way prospectors sought and mined gold in the Yukon basin. The miners found that Fortymile gold lay close to the surface on most of the claims, giving them quick returns for their labors.

Most of the Stewart River miners rushed to the exciting new site, leaving Al Harper's new post virtually devoid of customers. The myriad forks and tributary creeks of the Fortymile River are located in Alaska, but the river flows into the Yukon just east of the international boundary. The town of Fortymile, Yukon Territory (40 miles downstream from Fort Reliance), was quickly established at the confluence to service the new location. Harper would have to wait until spring ice-out to move operations down to the new townsite. In the meantime, dog teams kept the trail hard-beaten, hauling his supplies down from the Stewart to the miners.

Arthur Harper read Franklin's discovery of coarse gold as a clue that a lode must be nearby. If his hunch proved true it would draw far more miners to the area than he and Jack McQuesten had planned for prior to the latter's departure on his buying trip, not only causing the partners to miss profits but, more importantly, setting up the potential for a life-threatening food shortage the following year.

Harper decided that he must try to get word Outside to his partner. Additionally, he felt duty-bound to follow the Code of the Miners and get word to some 200 Yukon regulars who had been diligently exploring the country but were wintering over around Juneau. He hired Tom Williams to carry a letter containing news of the strike some 600 miles to Lynn Canal and once there, devise some way to forward it to McQuesten. They knew the trip would be extremely hazardous, there being no record of anyone daring to cross the Chilkoot Pass in mid winter. Adding to the peril was that Williams' primary experience was as a riverman; he was neither an experienced dog driver nor winter traveler. But even the savvy sourdoughs who watched him leave could not have predicted the extent of the terrible trail conditions, blizzards and minus-40- to minus-70-degree temperatures that Williams and an 18-year-old Indian boy named Bob who accompanied him would encounter.

By the time Williams and Bob reached the pass they had eaten all of their sled dogs and were barely staving off death by eating dry flour. While waiting out a blizzard just below the pass, holed up for several days in a snow cave, Williams' endurance gave out. He badly froze his fingers and toes. Upon emerging, he barely staggered along with Bob's help. Soon he could not even do that. For five days the weakened Bob carried him a few steps at a time over the pass and down the other side. Finally they encountered a group who loaded Williams on a sled and took him to the Healy and Wilson trading post at Dyea on Lynn Canal.

Questioned about why he had taken such a seemingly foolhardy risk as coming out during winter, Williams could only mumble faintly that he was on an important mission. He lasted but two days then died. The boy, however, who spoke little English, conveyed the message that in their dire circumstances, they had left Harper's packet in the snow near the pass and in the packet laid the important reason for which Wilson had given his life. A party ventured back and retrieved the communiqué. It eventually reached McQuesten in time.

The following summer, McQuesten and Harper moved their Stewart River post down to Fortymile and provisioned it with supplies he had just brought in from San Francisco.

***

Alfred Hulse Brooks: "William Ogilvie was a Canadian government surveyor who would later be appointed commissioner of Yukon Territory. In 1887, he performed much of the official surveying and mapping of the 141st parallel, the boundary between Alaska and Yukon Territory. He and I later became close friends. George Carmack, Skookum Jim and Tagish Charlie packed Ogilvie's supplies over the Chilkoot, [and] traveled with his survey party to Fortymile that summer. I mention the three packers because they would eventually play such an important part in the most defining moment in the history of the region.

"That same year, as part of the Ogilvie survey, Skookum Jim showed Captain William Moore, founder of Skagway, Alaska, the pass that paralleled the Chilkoot, which Ogilvie named the White Pass. The natives had managed to keep the existence of the White Pass secret for 40 years after Robert Campbell of the Hudson's Bay Company had found out about the Chilkoot Pass."

***

While the men were occupied in the survey, a prospector worked his way 40 miles up Yukon Territory's Tron-duick (Klondike) River, but reportedly found little.

A major competitor to the Alaska Commercial Company arrived on the Yukon in 1892 when the Chicago-based North American Trade and Transportation Company (NAT&T) began to establish stores along the river.

The year 1893 saw the United States fall into a major depression. Financial panic hit the American economy. Many within the population were at a loss to know where to find their next dollar and were forced into a search mode. More men turned their eyes north.

About 180 river miles downstream from the Alaska-Canada border, small findings in 1891 and 1892 were followed by the most sizeable discovery of gold along the Yukon up to that time, the 1893 Birch Creek strike. The two Russian-Creole discoverers, Sergei Cherosky and Pitka Pavaloff worked for Jack McQuesten and he had grubstaked them. On Preacher Creek, and along several other creeks near Birch Creek, prospectors made several other large 1893 discoveries. The richest diggings lay many miles back from the main river. Along the stretch of the Yukon closest to the finds, in the most well-situated location offering high ground for a town site with water deep enough for riverboats to pull up closely, the Alaska town of Circle City quickly grew as a service center for the district.

Jack McQuesten again moved in response to the miners' needs. In 1894 he established an Alaska Commercial Company store at Circle City. The following year the NAT&T built a rival store there. Circle City became known as the largest log town in the world. At its peak it boasted a library, a post office, two theaters, an opera house, eight dance halls and more than 25 saloons. The nature of the mining in the Circle district made it unproductive to accomplish anything but freighting after freeze-up so almost the whole population who used Circle City as a base came in from their outlaying claims to winter in town. Those were idyllic days at Circle City about which old-timers later happily referred. The acknowledged leader of the community, by virtue of his sharp intelligence, open generosity, impeccable integrity and trust in the eyes of his fellow pioneers was Jack McQuesten.

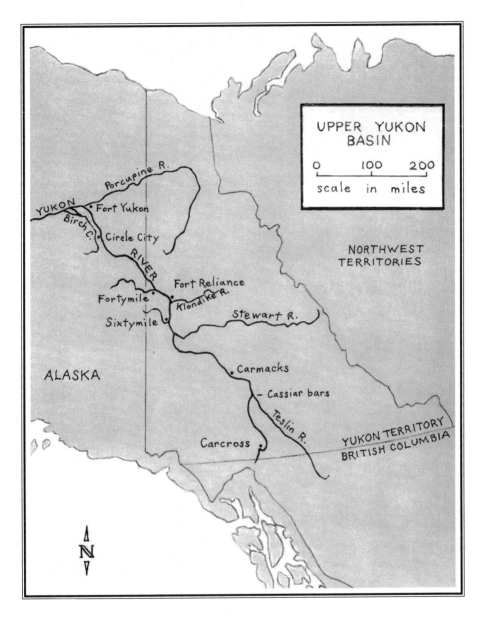

Alma Preston: "Rod, maybe you've heard of The Goin' Kid. Talk about live energy! He could hardly sit still and was always happiest while on the move. Back in the old days he and his team were known from Skagway to Kotzebue and from Seward to Coldfoot, one of the greatest names on the northern trails. He had an interesting way of talking, it was very 'country' but fast and full of action. He told me about how it was just before the big strike."

———•———•———

The Goin' Kid: "Most miners workin' so-so Fortymile claims abandon their diggin's 'n' stampede down to the richer strike. Almost all the miners work in partnerships. Nothin' better'n a true, loyal, hardworkin' partner. On better Fortymile locations, many partnerships diversify. One stays workin' it to keep their proven Fortymile diggin's bringin' income. Smart, bird-in-the-hand. The other partner drops way down to Circle City. He's goin' to see if he can find a bird in the bush to expand joint holdin's. The ones who stay keep producin'. In 1895, they take $400,000 worth of gold out of there. Several hundred people keep usin' the town of Fortymile as headquarters. In 1896 on just two creeks in the Fortymile District, Miller Creek and Glacier Creek, miners take out about $300,000 in gold.

"As it's about to play out, the luckiest thing some of the ones who stay around Fortymile country ever do is to stay put. They don't know it but they're keepin' themselves closest to a giant strike about to happen. At least the ones around Fortymile that're close to town 'n' not way on back up the river. The close ones're ready to be among the first to reach one of the greatest gold deposits the world's ever seen. They'll get first pick of the claims. Before a year's passed, many Fortymilers're goin' to be rich. 'Course, they'll make their partners down in the Circle City district just filthy rich, too."

———•———•———

As the United States and Canada were primed by the economic depression word of the gold finds along the Yukon circulated among opportunistic types who kept their ear to the ground. From mid-March through April of 1896, a notable increase in the number of gold-seekers left Seattle bound for Circle City and Fortymile.

The majority of the early gold discoveries lay relatively close to the great waterway. Thus, most of the needs were boated in during the ice-free summers under steam power. But the situation cried out for winter transport after freeze-up because seven to eight months a year was a long time to go without contact or supply from the outside world. The problem initially was that the early strikes were too small and there were yet too few people in the North to warrant the expense and effort of constructing year-round, overland transportation lines. But all of that was about to change. One of the greatest watershed occurrences in the history of the North was in the offing, destined to blow the lid off transportation and supply systems serving the Yukon Basin.

TRAILBREAKERS

Chapter 4

The Klondike Strike

AFTER PACKING AS FAR AS FORTYMILE for William Ogilvie
as Ogilvie surveyed the Alaska-Yukon boundary in 1887,
George Carmack brought his wife, Kate to Fortymile and
began to headquarter there, half a thousand river miles
downstream from the present location of Carcross, where
they had been living with Skookum Jim and the rest of
their Tagish relatives.

In the late summer of 1896, word reached Skookum Jim
that George and Kate were fishing on the Klondike River. He
and his relative, Tagish Charlie, and Charlie's nephew, Patsy
Henderson, ventured downriver to join George and Kate. The
three found the pair fishing for salmon at a long-established
native fish camp at the mouth of the Klondike, a river from
the northeast flowing into the Yukon about 120 miles above
the U.S.-Canada boundary and just six miles above the old
site of Jack McQuesten's Fort Reliance.

Shortly, the group met Robert Henderson, a miner from
Nova Scotia. They could not dream that the encounter would
not only dramatically impact, beyond their wildest imagination,
the lives of not only everyone there but that the happenstance
was destined to explode upon and change the history of the
entire northwest part of the continent.

Henderson had turned to gold prospecting as a profession
some years before, first in Colorado then in the Yukon. He
had come over the Chilkoot Pass in 1894, headed for either
Fortymile or Birch Creek, when he chanced to meet Joe
Ladue. Ladue, with Al Harper, had recently established a
trading post at the mouth of the Sixtymile River. Like Harper,

McQuesten and Mayo, Ladue possessed an unbridled enthusiasm for the future of the Yukon Basin and, being a seasoned prospector himself, had particular faith in the potential of the area draining into the Yukon near his new post. Joe Ladue and Robert Henderson hit it off immediately. The trading post owner convinced the newcomer to remain in the area, which, like the rest of the Canadian Yukon had been nearly deserted by miners following the rushes to Fortymile and Birch Creek.

The Nova Scotian, after securing a grubstake from his new friend, had launched a dedicated search for gold up the Indian River which drains into the Yukon just south of the Klondike. With a companion he had ascended a northern tributary, Quartz Creek, to the divide where they could look over into Klondike drainage. Impressed enough to try the creek, the men went back to get more supplies from Ladue, then devoted the next year to mining Quartz Creek and prospecting Indian River.

From the Quartz Creek bars, Henderson had mined about $600 in the spring of 1896, almost a year's wages for a laborer back in the States. Buoyed by that success and optimistic that the region held something even better, with four others he had again ascended Quartz Creek and crossed over the divide into the Klondike drainage into which he had previously gazed. Dropping down into a tributary creek he named Gold Bottom, the men had found good prospects and begun mining. Taking the first gold from the basin, Robert Henderson became the true discoverer of the Klondike. By the time the men had $700 to show for their efforts they had run out of food. Henderson decided to follow Gold Bottom down to the Klondike, thence to the Yukon and up to Ladue's Sixtymile post.

Returning with a boatload of supplies, Henderson's appearance poling upstream surprised George Carmack at his fish camp. Honor-bound to follow the traditional Code of the Miners, Henderson openly informed Carmack of his discoveries and his general belief that the nearby country held great promise. Henderson encouraged him to prospect in the vicinity and even invited him to stake a claim near his own. He requested that he be quickly informed if Carmack found anything profitable. However, Henderson, holding Carmack's Tagish relatives in obvious disdain, emphatically stated that he did not want any "d—d Siwashes" (meaning Indians) mining near him! When the offended Carmack shot back that he would be loyal to his wife and companions in any venture, the two men parted somewhat disagreeably.

Carmack had been a casual prospector, at most. At the time he was thinking more about prospects for cutting a raft of building logs for which he had an offer and floating them down to Fortymile. The group looked for suitable timber up the Klondike, hunting moose and casually prospecting as they went. Finally, being out of food and tobacco, and deciding to look over Henderson's prospects, Carmack and the men took a route up a tributary known to the natives as Rabbit Creek, finding a few colors as they went, then crossed over a divide, bushwhacking 25 miles from their camp to Henderson's.

George Carmack: "Twenty-five miles cross-country when you're hungry takes a lot out of you. When we got there, Henderson sure gave us the cold shoulder. He did sell us a little food, enough for a meal or two just to get us back over to our camp. But he flatly refused my relatives tobacco. Henderson strongly stated again, 'I told you once and I'll tell you again, I do not want them mining anywhere close to me! As I was later quoted, 'His childish unreasoning prejudice would not even allow him to stake on the same creek with the despised Siwashes so his obstinacy cost him a fortune.' "

Carmack and his company were hungry. On their way back from Henderson's, while diligently hunting moose, they looked for stands of suitable house logs and evaluated Rabbit Creek to see if it were possible to float them down its course. Additionally, they poked a little here and there for gold. By all accounts, no one had ever prospected the stream. The few gold-seekers who had previously searched up the Klondike had missed the Rabbit Creek mouth entirely because it spread out into a low area of shallow slackwater behind an island at the confluence.

During their hunt for meat, logs, water and gold, Skookum Jim killed a moose. They camped for a couple of days to butcher and eat. Influenced by Henderson's original enthusiastic advice and their previous finding of color on the way to the miner's camp, they conducted some light prospecting around the kill site. Nearby, at a point where bedrock rose to the surface, Skookum Jim (some said it was his sister, Kate) made a startling discovery, rich almost beyond belief. Carmack later said that as they lifted slabs of rock the gold appeared "like cheese on a sandwich!" With the moose to sustain them, the men prospected hard for two days, searching for what they thought would be the richest ground. On August 17, George Carmack four-sided a small spruce in the middle of the valley and wrote on it with pencil words that would turn the history of the Canadian Yukon and Alaska: "To Whom It May Concern: I do, this day, locate and claim, by right of discovery, five hundred feet, running up stream from this notice. Located this 17th day of August, 1896. G.W. Carmack."

For Jim they staked One Above, Carmack took One Below for himself (the person who is recorded as the discoverer of a new strike is due a second claim) and Two Below went to Charlie.

The group renamed the stream, Bonanza Creek. The area held such rich deposits that over $30 million—about $4.5 billion adjusting for more than 100 years of inflation and the vast increase in the price per ounce of gold—eventually would be taken from the gravel of El Dorado Creek, just one, mere five-mile-long tributary to Bonanza Creek!

It was decided that Carmack should record the claims. They reasoned that, given the prevalent racist attitudes, other miners would not recognize the claim of a native. Therefore, George Carmack is widely credited with making the discovery.

On their way to Fortymile to record, at the mouth of Rabbit Creek they met four men directed to the Klondike River by Joe Ladue. Carmack redirected them up Rabbit Creek. He did the same with two Frenchmen they ran into at the Klondike mouth, where Carmack sent Jim back to look after their interests and begin work on the claims. Carmack tipped off other miners they passed on their way down to Fortymile.

To his everlasting discredit, Carmack, in his offended pride, refused to honor the Code of the Miners. He could have taken the moral high road and risen above Henderson's racial insults. He could have sent one of his party to Gold Bottom to inform the man who was greatly responsible for Carmack even looking for gold on Rabbit Creek, prejudiced though he was. Instead, sinking to the character level of the Nova Scotian, George Carmack headed to Fortymile to record the claim, leaving Robert Henderson to unknowingly mine comparatively inferior ground just a day's walk over the divide.

George Carmack: "What's it to him who's working a claim that's not his? Especially if we had staked claims well separated from his. He was so narrow-minded and hateful. When he insulted my relatives he was denigrating me for marrying into their people. I suppose I could have sent Charlie over to his camp again to give Henderson the heads up. But I'll tell you, with no trail, a 50-mile tramp isn't something to be taken lightly; you don't just do it with a wave of the hand. And after his hateful rejection just a few days before? If it was still grating on me, just imagine how Charlie must have felt to be so despised. Think how it would have been between the two of us if I had insisted he go.

"I don't know, maybe I should have seen to it that he get the earliest tip. Maybe returning good for evil and letting him feel small and cheap all of his days would have made for even better payback. But there were other prospectors in the area and I was in a hurry to get down to Fortymile so we'd be first to record and get that extra discovery claim. Join that with the combination of our excitement and our feelings about Henderson and you can see why I did what I did. Finally, if he didn't even want my relatives on the same drainage with him over on his Gold Bottom show, how would he have been satisfied working Rabbit Creek—we renamed it Bonanza— with Kate, Jim and Charlie anywhere on the same drainage?"

Chapter 5

---◆---

Miners Positioned in the Yukon
Lead the Stampede

The Goin' Kid: "In Fortymile, most of the hands in town're new to the country, just cheechakos. The old-timers're back on the creeks workin' their claims. Many of the greenhorns're just millin' around idle. They aren't necessarily lazy, most of 'em have given the country all they had. They'd tuckered themselves clean out gettin' into the Yukon and prospectin' hard all summer. All with no luck. Now summer's endin'. Most of 'em're hangin' around with faces long as a horse, just down 'n' dejected 'n' plannin' to quit the country. Quite a few of 'em have tied on a long drunk. The more sober of the drunks can only stand if they're holdin' onto somethin'.

"Then Carmack arrives.

"Before recordin' the claim, Carmack stands before a group in a Fortymile saloon and announces his find. All the old-timers think of George as a poor prospector. He's always braggin' to make himself look good. They've never thought he was a man whose word could be altogether trusted. So the few sourdoughs in town influence the newcomers who look up to them. At first, nobody believes him. But you know, seein's believin'. The greatest gold stampede the world's ever known erupts when the small poke George Carmack throws down hits the table. They just pour out of town like the gold out of that poke.

"Remember I told you how lucky 'twas goin' to turn out for men to stay around instead of rushin' down to Circle City? Fortymile's only 53 miles downriver from the mouth of the

Klondike. They're goin' to be the first big group to reach Bonanza and Eldorado Creeks. The news spreads fast as men can run, pole and paddle."

AFTER ALERTING THE CROWD, Carmack went to the North West Mounted Police post to record the four claims. Imagine the irony and his dismay when he was told that the gold he had brought was insufficient to pay the filing fees! However, consistent with the character admired by all along the upper river, Inspector Charles Constantine settled Carmack's fears by gracing him with time to go back and pan out enough gold to pay.

Old Ben Atwater: "Even a few of the Fortymilers who'd been in a drunken stupor for weeks weren't left behind. Friends dumped them into the bottom of their boats and shipped them upriver like so much ballast. They scarcely realized they were passengers. One souse I knew of didn't sober up enough to know he'd even left Fortymile until his partners had him within 15 miles of the Klondike. Hanged if that drunk didn't end up staking a one of the richest claims in the country!"

Word of the blockbuster strike traveled up the Yukon as well as down. Sent for by Bonanza and El Dorado claim-holders who employed Indians as messengers to alert their friends, many of the miners from the Sixtymile River, just 45 miles above the Klondike, as well as from the Stewart River and other upriver diggings threw down what they were doing at the tidings and, hardly stopping to grab anything but the essential pick, shovel, pan and hip boots, stampeded to the Klondike.

Rod Perry: *As it is written, "the rain falls on both the just and unjust." It must have been maddening and discouraging to the worthy old-timers that a disproportionate amount of the gold rained down on others. Circumstances dealt such a cruel blow to many of the most knowledgeable, dedicated miners, those whom had been in the country the longest and were the most industrious. The persistence and diligent labor that had previously rewarded many of them with paying mines worked against them. When news of Carmack's strike reached Fortymile and the other trading posts that served as supply hubs for the various mining districts, most of the real sourdoughs were hard at work on their distant claims far back on the creeks (where an average of 25 cents a pan was considered top paydirt) so they were the last to get the report. Shopkeepers, newcomers, drunks, gamblers and others who happened to be around the supply centers were therefore the most available to stampede to the Klondike (where some pans of $800 would eventually be reported.) They staked their choice of the most promising-looking ground long before news reached most of the old-time miners.*

———————

Old Ben Atwater: "I knew a guy named Bill Liggett, a real first-class prospector and smart as anything. When Bill first heard the rumors he just shrugged his shoulders. Seasoned sourdoughs like he was, we all remembered many a stampede that had led excited men, usually tenderfoot cheechakos to rush off to worthless ground. That just wasted what little time, energy and money they had. Like I said, Bill was an excellent prospector. And he was a careful businessman. He had already developed some successful finds during his years in the region and took his money Outside and invested it. At the time Lyin' George and his party made the Klondike strike, Liggett was working a very profitable claim, which he was didn't want to leave.

"At first he pooh-poohed the fabulous rumors. The tales that rode the winds up and down the creeks from claim to claim seemed pretty far-fetched. Just way too tall to be true. But Bill told me finally [that] reports just stacked up too fast one on top of the other for him to keep discounting them. The moment he believed, he made a lightening-quick decision.

"Bill Liggett told me he just dropped his pick right where he stood. He hot-footed to his cabin, snatched up only a very few essentials and dashed down the gulch to the Yukon. He left behind his lucrative claim and his snug little cabin and cache. Most valuable left behind was a year's stock of provisions. Bill did what not many would do, but it turned out he knew what he was doing; keeping things light and fast was most important. He even left his tools, camp gear and rifle. He never saw any of those things again. Liggett leaped into his skiff and poled like the devil himself was sitting right on the stern threatening Bill with his pitchfork if he let up one bit. He pushed to his limits day and night 'til he reached the Klondike. But when he got up there, all he found was a sea of fresh-skinned spruce stakes gleaming white as porcupine quills—every piece of decent ground along the two main creeks was already staked.

"A number of other sourdoughs like me had finally come to see if it was just another wild goose chase or a real find. Most of us thought the surface indications were all wrong—'willows lean the wrong way, valley too broad, soil wrong, water doesn't taste right—and we turned our back on it. That left the discovery mostly to the know-nothings who went out and staked the whole blame country.

"Liggett was smarter. He could see that the landscape didn't look right, yet he looked into it more carefully and saw the early test pans had showed it held gold, maybe lots of gold. He walked around until he picked out what he thought looked like the most promising part of the new strike. He just goes right up to one of the claimholders. The guy was a newcomer who didn't really know what the ground held yet.

Ol' Bill offers the guy more money than he'd seen in all his born days, just too much to turn down. A three-eights share in Claim No. 13 on El Dorado Creek is what he bought. Out of that little part of one claim—a 'fraction' is what we call it—Liggett turned out one of the richest of the 'Klondike Kings.' "

Rod Perry: *And what became of Robert Henderson, who deserved credit as being the true discoverer of the Klondike's riches? In a case of poetic justice, Henderson indeed got to maintain his prejudiced parameters: He did not have to mine near any "d—d Siwashes." Though he was working just over the hill, he did not learn about the great strike until three weeks after Carmack and his Indian relatives struck it rich. By then it was too late. Within just two weeks, by the end of August 1896, the whole length of Bonanza and El Dorado Creeks had been staked. When he belatedly heard the news, he just sat down and buried his face in his hands, in his utter disappointment unable to so much as speak. Later, the Canadian government would recognize him for his part in the discovery and reward him with a small pension.*

The Goin' Kid: "Back at Fortymile, the main center of minin' activity lies 85 miles up that river. On the most distant forks some're workin' ground over a hundred miles upstream. News quickly spreads upstream, claim to claim, to miners nearer Fortymile. But it's not 'til the river freezes that the first dog-team freighters begin to get way up to the most distant camps with the supply orders. It's not 'til we pull in that word of the Klondike penetrates to the farthest miners.

"You know what? When they do hear, most of the old sourdoughs with the longest experience choose to stay put. The tend to be the least likely to leave profitable diggin's to go flyin' off chasin' after wild tales of some fabulous, new strike that seems too outlandishly rich to be possible. To make it worse, the delay stretches out for 'em. While some rumors tell of unbelievable indications, others're discouragin'.

"It's hard enough to get a good idea of what their claims have to offer for the new Klondikers who're right there. They can only tell what's on the surface. To keep their test holes from floodin' they have to wait 'til the ground freezes before they dig down to bedrock. The heaviest deposits'll eventually be found 12 to 20 feet down. So if the Klondike miners themselves right on their claims find it hard to get a handle on it, it's really hazy for the old Fortymilers because they're so far from what's goin' on up there."

Old Ben Atwater: "It was bad enough that most of the best ground on the Bonanza and El Dorado bottoms were staked by the time many of the old Fortymilers got there, but they faced the additional problem: They had to somehow get by on starvation rations. We dog punchers had already freighted half of their yearly supplies up to their former diggings far up the Fortymile. When the men abandoned their claims and rushed off for the Klondike, just like Bill Liggett they turned their back on all their supplies and left 'em behind.

"Right after freeze-up's a busy time for freighters anyway but now in addition to the usual hauling we had to turn around, go up and haul everything from the claims back down to Fortymile. The round trip from a lot of the heaviest upstream mining action averaged about 170 miles. Next the supplies had to be taken up the Yukon to the Klondike and out to the miner's new claims. Depending on the location, that could be another 80 miles.

"Every dog puncher in the Upper Country was employed full-time. The Malemute Kid, The Goin' Kid, The Seventymile Kid, my buddy Art Walden, me and a few others just drove ourselves and our teams until they got so sour that even when you went out to feed them they'd try to hide, and that's no exaggeration. We tried to pace them, but we knew men might starve if we didn't keep ahead of it. Our rehauls added tremendously to their cost of the already-expensive food and equipment which made it tough on them. I don't doubt a starving man would pay a fancy price for our service, much more than the going rate. But none of us wanted to hold anyone up and take advantage of their straits and gouge them. But as the Good Word says, 'A workman is worthy of his hire' and we were well-worth our pay. We worked so constantly, all of us dog punchers came out of that fall with a nice tidy income."

———— • ———— • ————

Joe Ladue, sensing the importance of the new strike, sagaciously staked the only logical ground suited for a town site at the mouth of the Klondike. Knowing the several hundred early entrants into the district had left their food behind to travel light, enabling them to get there quickly, he lost no time in moving the Sixtymile trading post and his sawmill downriver to his new town location he named Dawson. However, Ladue and Harper had only originally provisioned the little post at Sixtymile for the much smaller number of miners that had been working that river, so when its supply reached Dawson it was not nearly sufficient to sustain through the winter what amounted to a gathering of almost the entire white population of the upper Yukon Basin.

———— • ———— • ————

Moses Mercier: "As an experienced former Alaska Commercial Company post agent, I know that for McQuesten, Harper and their partners, supplying their trading posts had always been speculative. *Ils étaient des joueurs.* If they overestimated business, they ended up sitting on stock that did not move quickly and experienced cash-flow problems. On the other hand, if they underestimated and ran out before those depending upon them filled their needs, severe privation could discourage prospecting and mining activity and either cause their customers to leave the area or open the way for competitors to move in. Only if they supplied their stores with close to the exact amount needed, they experienced a fast turnaround on their investment and kept their market thriving and their business profitable.

"The great, continuing problem remained the lack of winter transport. Being limited to the four-month river shipping season forced suppliers into sending out orders at the end of summer for an inventory that wouldn't arrive until the beginning of the following summer. It was an inventory that would have to last until the summer after that. For instance, the last boats to make it out of the river before ice-up in September of 1896 not only carried last-minute notes to friends and relatives about the new strike on the Klondike, but they also carried orders for supplies that would not begin arriving until early June of 1897 and keep coming in through the '97 summer. My friend, *pouvez-vous imaginer cela?* Miners would desperately depend upon those supplies to keep them fed and equipped until June of 1898 when the '98 shipping season would begin. September 1896 to June 1898 was closing in on two years. Obviously having to prognosticate the number of prospectors that would be in the country and trying to forecast where, along hundreds of miles of the Yukon their shifting activity might place them made it a great guessing game and held back development of the country.

"For McQuesten, Harper, Mayo and the other trading and supply ventures, by the 1890s, almost all of the supplies were shipped out of San Francisco and Seattle. Because Seattle was also the port of embarkation and return for most of the gold-seekers, the traders were able to keep fairly close tabs. As their yearly tallies had always showed but a gradual climb in numbers, the suppliers had generally been able to come somewhat close to keeping up with the increasing demand for the almost two decades leading up to the Klondike strike. But there was no way in the fall of 1895—when they had been ordering their June 1896 through June 1897 supplies, they could have guessed what was coming and thereby adequately provisioned the Klondike! *C était impossible!* And in the fall of 1896, if they could not have foreseen how big the new strike would be, nor that the population would double in the coming year, how, in their wildest dreams—*rêves fantastiques!*—could they have guessed that in two years the population of Dawson alone—not counting the numbers mining out on the claims and scattered around the remainder of the Yukon Basin—would be some 20 times what it had been before the Klondike strike!"

Old Ben Atwater: "I told you about going up the Fortymile to bring back the supplies for a lot of the miners who had stampeded off to Klondike and left their outfit behind. Well, there were a lot of men that couldn't afford to relocate their food from their old claims to the Klondike like that. And it was frustrating for the suppliers, too. In that fall of 1896, Jack McQuesten, Arthur Harper, their new partner, Joe Ladue, and all of the other traders were just flat stuck there frozen in with no way to respond and nothing to respond with.

"You know, the strike had come so late in the season that most of the miners had already bought their winter supplies from the companies. Of course, they hauled it all out to their various mining locations. That distributed almost all the traders' stock out into the far-flung cabins and caches, some of them more than a hundred miles away. It was just like someone dipping into a bag of seed and broadcasting it out over the land until the bag is almost empty. Anyway, the trading companies were left with their usual low, freeze-up inventory.

"Jack McQuesten and the others might have guessed the tonnage needed under normal circumstances fairly close. But all of their careful preplanning, their expensive expediting down in Seattle and 'Frisco, and their shipping, and mainly the thousands of tons of their valuable stores themselves, they could never have guessed that most all of it would end up as good as *wasted*. Wasted, because once the miners bought their supplies, freighted them out to their cabins, then went and left those purchases far behind when they go and stampede off to the Klondike, well, just think about it: The effect turned out the same as if the traders had sold most of their inventory only to have the miners take the goods down off the shelves, load it all in wheelbarrows, then turn right around, roll it out and dump it all in the Yukon River!"

———————

The Northwest Mounted Police report for 1896 noted that an unusually early cold snap hit the upper Yukon that fall. Ice began to run heavily September 2, almost stopping navigation. After opening up for a few days it froze tight, bringing navigation to an untimely halt.

Chapter 6

———◆———

Early Stampeders from "Outside"
Beat the Big Rush

Rod Perry: *In the fall of 1896, William Ogilvie, stationed in Fortymile, had sent word of the strike out to his superiors in Ottawa by one of the last outbound steamboats of the season. His report received but minimal attention.*

However, a few other early reports besides Ogilvie's—those letters that had just made it out on the last boats that fall—did have an effect. Probably mainly limited to Yukoner's private communiqués to relatives and personal friends, the news did not attract widespread media notice. Even if it had, the unknowing would not have thought it sounded different enough from other announcements of periodic discoveries that had come down from the North County over the preceding two decades to create more than casual interest.

However, to people who had been personal recipients of the inside information, those early tidings of the Klondike strike were convincing enough to cause great excitement. From those insiders, word must have radiated out to numerous others, inside tips that the strike gave indications that it could well surpass all others in the annals of the North. Amid visions of instant wealth simply waiting to be claimed, many began assembling prospecting outfits and preparing to head to the Yukon early in the spring of 1897.

Even as glowing as the reports sounded to those north-bound possessors of early information, they could not have guessed the full extent of the discovery, for even most of the miners themselves who were mucking away that winter in the Klondike would not know for sure until May of 1897.

Old Ben Atwater: "Because such a large number on the Klondike were former Fortymile miners, many had partners in Circle City and wanted to get news of the great strike to them. However, the Klondikers simply could not tear themselves away from developing their claims that indeed appeared fabulous. News did not travel the 300 miles down the Yukon from Dawson by steamer because, before the extent of the strike was known, the early freeze-up had driven riverboats into winter moorage.

"Dog teams had not been immediately available to run the news down because all of the upriver drivers were busy under contract to relocate supplies from the Fortymile up to the new diggings. However, in December a freight team driven by Walden—that's my old pal, Art Walden—finally broke away and headed to Circle City with a packet of letters from the new strike. On his way he was caught up by the first official U.S. Mail team to make a regular run from Lynn Canal hauling Circle City mail. The two teams pulled into the village within a couple of hours of each other in January.

"As word went out that the first dog teams of the season had come in with mail, every man in Circle City gathered at Harry Ash's tavern. Art, the dog driver from the Klondike, threw his packet down on the bar and ordered a mug of beef tea. Just leaving Walden to make his own, Harry grabbed the bundle and thumbed through fast as he could 'til he found a letter from his partner. As he read his pulse must have been going crazy. Suddenly, in his excitement he vaulted right over the bar, Walden told me, shouting out to the crowd to help themselves to his entire stock of whiskey; he was heading to the Klondike! As letter after letter told men they were partners in claims that might make them rich beyond their wildest dreams, they didn't even wait to uncork the bottles. They simply knocked the necks off to get at the whiskey and started dancing and whooping like wild men.

"But, same as with Fortymile, many of the foremost miners who headquartered at Circle were working profitable diggings as far as three to four days travel out on the creeks. Again, they were the some of the last to find out and take action.

"You know, that packet of mail killed Circle City as a boom town. Just rang the death knell. It would live on as an inhabited village, alright. But it would never again have the population and it wouldn't be the center of commerce and society it used to be. Up to then, the going price for a town lot and cabin was $500. Sled dogs had been selling for $25 to $50 each. As Walden, who had delivered the mail, was immediately offered three of the best cabins for any one dog in his team he told me that must mean that the price of a dog just shot up to $1,500! Either that or it meant that the price of a cabin had cratered out at $8 to $17. Actually, Art had a good sense of humor and I figure the real values for both settled somewhere in between. The animals were so valuable, in such demand, that during the rare times when they went up for sale they began to be sold by their weight. At first they were going for $1.50 and finally it worked up to $2.50 a pound.

"The town virtually emptied. Every Man Jack loaded hand sleds and hit the river. It was going to be a real ordeal. Almost a 300-mile trudge up to Dawson. You know all about hand sleds, Al. Up there just like here around Nome, no one worth his salt would be caught without one. Most places they call them Yukon sleds. Well, a long line started to stretch out up the river. Everyone necking their sled, pulling by passing a loop of rope from the front corners of the sled under their arm pits and around the back of their neck. Men steered with a gee pole. Why am I telling you Al, as you know all this?

"Anyway, every man understood perfectly he couldn't hope to buy so much as a morsel of food or any supplies in such a new camp when they got to Dawson. They knew the first steamboat wouldn't make it in 'til the middle of the next July. Half a year. Clear to then they'd have to scrape by on what they could drag upriver from Circle City themselves.

"The miners considered a sled load of 200 pounds to be the absolute limit one man could tow and still make 15 miles a day. That was their common expectation when the going was so exhausting. Men traveled in pairs. Each one necked a sled but they only took one camp outfit to save weight. Any way you figure it, it seems impossible for a man to tow on a hand sled enough food to get him by for six months. Especially when part of the load's taken up with trail gear and mining equipment. And even more especially when the terrific labor of pulling a steel-shod sled almost 300 miles in temperatures far below zero and over trails that continually blew in demanded eating much of the load during the march itself. But somehow those rawhide-tough miners would all make it through to Dawson. Further, they would somehow winter over on what they brought. Though by spring ice-out, many would be down to diets of almost nothing but flour, every one would scrape by until the first supply boat.

"At the going rate of $1.20 a pound, I joined Walden and the Malemute Kid and a couple other freighters hauling up from Circle City all winter long. Some of us made three round trips, 1,800 miles. And that was after our earlier work between the Fortymile and the Klondike."

———————

OUT ON THE KLONDIKE CREEKS, beyond the sinking of test holes few could progress into extensive mining development of their claims through the winter of 1896–1897 because the labor it required was hard to hire. Most of the people in the country were too busy sinking test holes on their own claims to work for someone else. Everyone worked on pure speculation, driven on by reports coming from other claims, first, reports of wonderful test pans before bedrock was even reached, then tales of staggering wealth at the bottom. The miners bent to the task, driving themselves to their limit, hardly stopping to eat, sleep, bathe or change clothes in a feverish effort to sink shafts through the frozen overburden to bedrock. The few with access to more labor began to thaw underground drifts to follow pay streaks.

The typical prospect hole was two-and-one-half feet wide by six feet long. The men built a fire of six-foot dry logs then completely covered the fire with green logs. To seal off the cracks between the green logs the men banked the fire with dirt. With the limited flow of oxygen the fire would burn all night and the covering of barely burnable green wood and dirt kept much of the heat available to thaw downward. The next morning they would the remove unburned logs, banking dirt, what they had thawed and what they could manage to pick and shovel from the frozen ground below. Ten inches by thawing and six inches by pick and shovel was considered good progress. They repeated the process each day. After digging down 11 feet, it grew impossible to efficiently throw dirt out of the hole with a shovel, so the men would construct over the hole a log frame and a crude windlass with a seven-inch log for a drum. One man ran the windlass, another worked at the bottom. As soon as they hit gravel they checked their prospect by running a test pan every foot until they hit bedrock. If they found gold in paying quantity (paydirt), they melted (drifted) their way sideways, tunneling to follow the paystreak. The frozen ground generally needed no shoring to prevent cave-ins.

Paydirt along Bonanza and El Dorado Creeks generally lay 12 to 20 feet below the surface on the ancient streambed. It was difficult to see what the frozen ground held. Periodically, however, they washed out a test pan with melted snow. Pans commonly tested out at between $5 and $100 to the pan. Miners used to previously finding eight or ten cents to the pan on the best claims almost refused to believe what they were seeing, even as they held the riches right in their hands. Excitement over the results drove the men on.

On March 25, 1897—spring in the south but still winter in the Yukon—the *City of Mexico* left Seattle with over 600 stampeders, little doubt mostly responders to the last letters that made it out of the Yukon before fall freeze-up. For the rest of the spring, eager gold-seekers jammed every northbound ship, the forerunners of the great rush that would follow.

Up north, back in the Klondike, many miners began to look emaciated by springtime. There they were, starving—some showing obvious symptoms of scurvy—while sitting atop piles of muck and gravel worth fortunes. Every waking moment the men dreamed of extravagant meals their hoped-for money could buy in far-off cities. However, though many would soon be unimaginably wealthy, there in the Klondike they could not buy so much as a loaf of bread.

After such a long, hard winter, the Klondikers could hardly wait to find out what had been the fruits of their labors. As soon as the first available water began to run in the creeks, the miners built sluice boxes and proceeded to "clean up." What those who had staked the most productive claims found settled behind the riffles made their eyes bulge out like doorknobs. Pans were found that spring as rich as $500. By comparison, the best pans in California had run 35 to 40 cents and had been thought of as unbelievably rich.

When spring cleanup revealed that their winter labors had made many Klondike miners fabulously rich, the strike became news of truly stupendous proportions. However, the news would have to wait until someone could reach the outside world to break it. The first to take the word out were some of the miners themselves.

Immediately on the heels of breakup, as soon as sternwheelers could ply the river, many Klondike miners headed Outside. Some had sold their claims, thinking their pay streak would play out. Others just needed a break from the privation. They had only begun to tap the wealth of their claims but the claims would be there when they got back.

On July 14, 1897, the Alaska Commercial steamship *Excelsior* tied up at the San Francisco dock. A number of Klondike miners disembarked with one-half million dollars in gold. (Converted to Year 2000 dollars, their gold would have been worth about $12 million.) Wondrous stories hit the news wires and swept the nation like wildfire.

———————

Al Preston: "The story was told of one of those miners. He'd lived a solitary existence for several years on his remote mine on the Fortymile. Then he'd rushed to the Klondike and overwintered on his claim. Upon reaching San Francisco and registering at his hotel, the first thing he does is start running a bath. As the tub fills and he begins peeling off clothes, he comes to a pair of woolen long johns and discovers two pairs of socks he'd totally forgotten he owned.

Once bathed and dressed, he sits down in the restaurant and orders a lavish dinner fit for a king—or three kings. Before the waiter leaves with the order, the old sourdough gives instructions to bring him a plateful of beans so he can occupy himself while he waits for his feast.

As the waiter approaches with the first course, he notices the bush rat muttering intently into his plate. The old-timer's apparently engaged in an earnest and animated discourse with the beans.

At the waiter's arrival, the man from the Klondike looks up briefly, then resumes his conversation. Shaking a finger at the beans as he pushes the plate aside, he sternly orders, "OK, boys, now you just stand back and watch a man eat a real meal!"

———————

Three days after the *Excelsior* reached San Francisco, the rusted hulk of the Pacific Whaling Company steamship *Portland* eased into Seattle harbor before an awaiting crowd of over 5,000 at the dock. They watched as 68 gaunt, weatherbeaten men in patched and mended garments brought over $1 million in gold (about $24 million in 2000 dollars) down the gangplank in old satchels, wooden boxes, cans and canvas bags tied up with rope.

The Seattle Post-Intelligencer headlines cried out, "GOLD! GOLD! GOLD! GOLD! Sixty-eight rich men on the steamer *Portland*. STACKS OF YELLOW METAL."

The continent was primed to catch gold fever. Citizens had been mired in the despair of the severe depression from which they could see no end. In the United States, the luster was off the promise of a developing nation that had previously offered unlimited opportunity. From colonial times, anyone who wished to create a new beginning had been able to heed the call, "Go West, Young Man!" But by the 1890s the country had been all but settled coast to coast. The economic aspect of the siren call that had attracted the world's downtrodden, huddled masses had ceased to deliver to immigrants in the same measure that it had for over 200 years. Millions lived in poverty, having no outlook offering hope that their situation would brighten. As well, the great strike came at a time when the national treasury had been almost emptied of gold.

The press played on the sensational discovery. Exaggerated reports blew an already giant strike into mythical proportions. They painted the picture of a land where anyone could dig almost anywhere and bring back riches. Once they had created hysteria, newspapers fanned the flames. Thousands swallowed the bait.

The excitement swung the mood of the nation. One informal investigation into the passenger make-up of railways heading west found some 210,000 who stated that their goal was the Klondike. That was far more than had responded to the other great gold rushes outside the continental United States, those to South Africa or Australia. Adding to those railway travelers were the many who stampeded to the Klondike from the far reaches of the earth. The great rush seemed to be on everyone's lips. Money that had been hoarded came out and begun to circulate. The country's atmosphere became one of festive self-confidence.

Ten thousand scrambled to head north immediately. The last days of summer and the autumn of 1897 saw the first ships full of the media-driven masses head north to beat the onset of winter across the Chilkoot Pass and White Pass.

Craft of every description and state of seaworthiness— anything available from Tierra del Fuego to Barrow, retired or active, joined the fleet. Even derelicts that had lain in "bone yards" for years were resurrected and pressed into service.

One collier, having been emptied of its usual cargo, had its filthy black hold hastily furbished with what passed for "berths" for 600 passengers. Another ship, terribly overloaded, weighed anchor for the North Country with a deck load piled so high that the helmsman could not see directly ahead. A small launch embarked stuffed with men so consumed with visions of gold they seemed not to care that the closest qualification its captain had for piloting an ocean-going vessel had been driving a horse-drawn milk wagon on the streets of San Francisco!

The voyage of the ship *Eliza Anderson* seemed doomed to failure at the beginning, but by its finish, its passengers must have hoped the blind luck that accompanied their voyage would transfer unchecked once they reached the goldfields. First, the ship cast off from Seattle headed north—at least the captain hoped they were headed north—without a compass. They soon rammed another ship. Next, crossing the dangerous Gulf of Alaska, they barely survived a driving storm. Then, only half way to the mouth of the Yukon, their destination, they ran out of fuel.

Incredibly, their luck swung around. Somehow, they managed to safely make their way into a sheltered cove on Kodiak Island. Then, while walking the nearby shoreline, someone discovered a rich vein of coal. Farther along on the voyage, just when it seemed that all would be lost as the ship was close to being dashed on the rocks, a remarkably gifted stowaway emerged from hiding and saved the ship!

Though the season saw an increase in the incidence of shipwrecks, many made it through. As soon as the gold-crazed hordes disembarked at the head of Lynn Canal, Skagway and Dyea sprang up as instant towns to service them.

The earliest arrivals of the onrushing horde began to pull into Dawson and rush out to the Klondike creeks to stake their fortune.

Rod Perry: *The misconceptions of various new arrivals to the Klondike may be grouped under several headings: two are cynical, the third harbors false hopes. In the first group, many experienced miners among the earliest arrivals turn negative without so much as brushing the surface. "It just doesn't look right," they say. In the second group are a number like Robert Henderson. He arrives three weeks after the strike but turns away in disgust when he finds all of Bonanza and El Dorado creeks staked. This second group assumes there is no worthwhile ground left. The third group, a naïve wave of newcomers, comes roaring in thinking they will find the whole discovery open to their staking and they're as good as rich just because they are many months ahead of the hordes who follow. Of course, the reality is that the main creeks had been staked end to end months before word of the strike even reached them. Many immediately leave, shocked when their false hopes are dashed.*

All of the groups were wrong. Rich deposits still lay hidden nearby.

Old Ben Atwater: "Remember that a bunch of us old sourdoughs looked at the surface indications, the way the willows leaned wrong, the water didn't taste right and so forth and talked ourselves right out of staking? Well, the gold seemed to play another cruel trick on many of us most experienced miners. It caused our very experience that we gained through seasons of back-breaking labor and privation to play against us. Wherever we'd prospected through the American West, British Columbia and elsewhere along the Yukon we had always found gold settled at the lowest point. It's the heaviest material in the formation. The lowest point is in the creek bottoms. For sure it's never on the hillsides above. So when us old hands arrived just a few days or weeks late or even months, and saw all the rich Bonanza and El Dorado Creek bottoms staked, our so-called "knowledge" led us to turn away to look elsewhere without another thought. We just left it to raw, inexperienced Johnny-come-latelys who would come in the next summer and didn't know any better, to prospect above on the hillsides. It was the greenest cheechakos you ever saw that located the fabulous bench claims in places like the famous White Channel. Those turned out to be ancient stream courses. Bonanza and El Dorado flowed up there in past ages and left deposits worth millions of dollars."

———— ⋅•◆•⋅ ————

At the end of the first winter of the strike, by which time most of the miners from all of the other mining districts in the Yukon Basin had relocated in the Klondike, the April 1897 population of Dawson had been 1,500. But by fall, with the coming of the first seekers from the outside world, those who had heeded the initial word of the strike and headed north before the first Klondike gold had arrived at San Francisco and Seattle, the town had swelled to 3,500.

———— ⋅•◆•⋅ ————

Old Ben Atwater: "A lot of these new gold-seekers were of a different cut than the experienced prospectors who came in before the Klondike Strike. No doubt the new ones included a fair number of hardened outdoorsmen. But a big share had little, if any experience that would prepare them for such a trip and life. Their ranks were made up of shopkeepers, bankers, tradesmen, doctors, attorneys, menial laborers and the like. Many were town and city dwellers. Not many knew anything first hand of scaling mountains, building boats and running wild rivers, traveling the wilderness, enduring mosquitoes and black flies or, especially, living and working year-round in the subarctic. Few but the farmers among them knew a thing about working draft animals. That would result in thousands of horses dying on the trail. They didn't know how to dress, how to outfit for the trip to the Klondike or what they would need once they got here. Many traveled light to get here quickly. The fools thought they would be able to buy whatever supplies and gear they needed when they got to Dawson. They would be in for a very rude awakening."

Rod Perry: *Regarding supplying the region, there were no more knowledgeable people in the North than the established trading companies. It can hardly be imagined how frustrated and frantic they must have felt, for with all of their experience in the feeding and equipping of Yukon miners over the past seasons, they fell far short in their estimates regarding the numbers and lack of preparedness of the crowds that would descend upon them by the fall of 1897. With no precedent to refer to, how could they or anyone else accurately guess the country's supply needs? And without the ability to place a quick order and get a timely shipment back, there was no way to adjust the status quo.*

Chapter 7

The 1897–1898 Food Shortage

WHILE THE FIRST WHO STAKED the Klondike had mucked and moiled and starved on their claims through the winter of 1896–97, those last letters of the season they had managed to send out of the Yukon to friends and relatives via the final downriver boats before freeze-up were effecting foundations of a repeat food shortage the following winter of 1897–98. The earliest respondents to the previous fall's letters had shipped north beginning in March and on through the summer in time to enter the upper Yukon during the short northern access window. They trickled in through the summer. By fall new entrees from over the passes were arriving at the rate of about 75 a day. Not one in 10 brought provisions enough to feed himself until the opening of shipping the following summer. Word of $15-a-day wages and gold being carelessly cast about had begun to seep out. Incoming pilgrims deduced that the Yukon must be a land of abundance. Most had traveled light to beat the rush and naively depended upon being able to gain equipment and supplies once they got to Dawson. Once they arrived it took awhile for the reality to set in that while steamers from downriver had supplied Dawson with plenty of whiskey to last the winter, they had not brought nearly enough food. While that might have satisfied some, those who did not relish the idea of starvation began to sweat.

By the time reality set in, it was too late for many to escape. In the fall of 1897 the big river dropped to an unusually low level, preventing the last few steamers that had been expected from getting up over the shallow Yukon Flats ahead of the initial freeze-up. An evident disaster loomed.

Then the river, though running ice, reopened barely enough to allow navigation. The Alaska Commercial Company, having a steamboat docked in Dawson, hurriedly sent a picked crew under Captain Hanson down to Fort Yukon, some 375 miles away, hoping they could beat the final freeze-up and bring up a load of food the company had stored there. On the way down it was noticed that the water level was dropping at an alarming rate.

They churned into Fort Yukon, loaded 300 to 400 tons of food in record time and pulled out on the high boil. But only 20 miles upriver the steamer grounded on a sandbar. Dropping down a few miles, they offloaded half of the goods on an island, then turned back upstream to try to make it over the shallows with the lightened load. But the river had fallen still farther and again prevented their passage. They dropped down to the island again and offloaded the rest of the cargo.

They had failed to relieve Dawson's impending food crisis. Now it was doubly vital that the gold town be alerted that hoped-for provisions would not be coming. As many as possible needed to flee the country before the final freeze-up stopped navigation. Captain Hanson and the men returned to try to get over the shallows, this time with an empty boat. But the river had continued to fall. Once more they could not get across.

The steamer dropped back down to Fort Yukon whereupon Captain Hanson began one of the noblest missions in the annals of the north. He hired some Fort Yukon Indians and their birch-bark canoe to take him to warn the citizens of Dawson, warn them to boat down to Fort Yukon—where there was food—while they still had the chance, that no more steamers could be expected. Immediately they pointed their bow toward the Klondike, 375 miles away against the swift current.

Most of the crew steamed downriver, the Captain having promised free transportation to San Francisco if they could beat ice-up and get the boat to St. Michael. Three others, desperate to get back to their Klondike gold claims, food or no, flew at the task of building a poling boat and heading upriver to beat the ice.

Two of the crew, dog drivers, decided to spend the winter freelancing, buying dogs at Fort Yukon and hauling goods from the island cache up to Dawson.

———————

Alma Preston: "Rod, our friend, The Goin' Kid was right in the middle of that whole debacle and here's the way he told the incredible story to me . . ."

———————

The Goin' Kid: "Art Walden 'n' I take one of the steamer's lifeboats. A few days later we start pollin' up to the food cache on the island to secure it for the winter. Now that round-bottom 'n' fore and aft rocker no doubt let the thing pivot 'n' ride stormy sea waves like a gull. But the shape makes it almost impossible to pole upstream. The consarned beast will just not keel, it wants to spin like a dang bowl. But it's all we have so we bend to the task. Exasperating! says Walden, along with a lot of stronger language I won't repeat.

"When we come up on the island a few days later, what do we behold but a crazy runnin' up and down the bank wildly wavin' us in to land. Who should it turn out to be but Captain Hanson. The birch-bark canoe he'd hired had leaked so bad the Indians dropped 'im off at the food cache. They promised to get another canoe at Fort Yukon. They said they'd come back for 'im to keep their mission goin'. So he'd built 'im a shelter of packin' boxes. Just sittin' there most of a week, he read labels for somethin' to do. And worried himself sick about the people up in Dawson. And fretted about losin' time because freeze-up's not goin' to wait. The new canoe and Fort Yukon men haven't showed up.

"Art and I change plans instantly. Now we're in with Hanson in his rescue mission. An extra man to help line the boat helps. But then, the first snow, a half a foot, makes the footin' hellacious. Takes us four days of the most terrible labor to line the 60 miles along the bank from the island to Circle City. Captain Hanson hires another birch-bark and a new crew of natives. He tells Walden and me to follow any way we can 'n' off he goes on his desperate dash. Dawson's now about 295 miles away against the current.

"All that Walden and I can find's a leaky birch-bark. We take two days to cover it with canvas. No one's ever seen the likes, but in those two days the Yukon begins to rise. Now all the old Circle City sourdoughs predict another steamboat'll make it up over the flats."

———————◆—◆———————

Rod Perry: *Not only Dawson, but Circle City itself is in dire straits. After the town exodus to the Klondike the winter before, only 80 miners remained working the district. Not a crumb of food had been dropped at Circle since the year before. Though each passing steamer promised that the one coming behind would offload provisions, riverboat after riverboat bypassed Circle City, running their cargos on up to Dawson where the desperate demand had driven up prices.*

The Circle City men were in no danger of actual starvation because they could make their way 80 miles down to Fort Yukon where warehouses held plenty. However, because their mines were located so many miles back in the country behind Circle City, most had to be supplied by sled over winter trails, a task that required a whole winter of repetitious trips. If, instead of spending the season freighting from Circle City to their claims, the miners were forced to take up the whole winter sledding their supplies from Fort Yukon, they faced losing the entire following year of mining, just consuming what they had brought up from Fort Yukon, and many would go broke.

The Goin' Kid: "At a miners meetin' the men decide to stage a holdup of the next Dawson-bound boat. If indeed one even makes it up over the flats. The boys'll make it polite, but it'll be forceful. They mean business, they're desperate. If the boat goes on by Circle City, a group of the boys camped out above'll get a signal. They'll stop the boat at a swift narrows above the town with a shot 'r two through the pilot house. The meetin' agrees they'll help unload Circle City's own cargo 'n pay for it at Dawson prices.

"We don't have long to wait. The N.A.T.&T. flagship *Portius B. Weire* rounds the bend. Not suspectin' a thing, they nose in, tie up 'n' drop the gangplank. The company superintendant comes ashore. The miners, just as calm 'n' polite as can be, confront the supe' with their case. But the man has his own company orders. He turns 'n' barks out for a deckhand to the cast off the hawser from its tie-up to a stump. Next thing the deckhand sees is a dozen leveled Winchesters. He freezes. A pilot then steps to the bow all brave. He's about to take an axe to the line. Then he looks again. Now the same dozen muzzles are swung around on him. He sees the grim glares down their barrels 'n' thinks better of it.

"The supe' refuses the miner's demands. The miners refuse to allow the boat to leave. For three whole days while the supe' folds his arms 'n' the Winchesters threaten, it's a standoff . Time wastes. Signs of oncomin' winter are everywhere. A little ice starts runnin'. The captain knows once it begins to run heavy, he's stuck right where he is for the winter. For all he knows, the boat might well be destroyed by the ice.

"The Circle City boys all have friends 'n' partners up on the Klondike 'n' don't want to see 'em starve. A few leaders reason if they force things they can relieve the captain of responsibility to his company because he didn't give permission. They think he might even be hopin' that's what they'll do so he can get goin'. Losin' some supplies isn't anywhere close to as bad as losing the NAT&T's fanciest boat. So they end the stalemate by forcefully offloadin' 80 outfits from the hold themselves. Mannerly as you please, they carry the goods into the company store. They pay full Dawson prices to the NAT&T agent. And then they empty the shelves 'n' take the goods to their own cabins.

"Walden 'n' I're refused passage upriver. Not only's the captain in a hostile mood toward Circle City in general, everybody knows Walden 'n' I contract a lot for the rival Alaska Commercial Company. But we, along with four others march aboard. We just dare the man to throw us off. Not wanting more trouble and wasted time, he gives in, casts off and steams up river.

"Everything goes well enough for a few days. Then we come up on those Dawson miners pollin' their new-built boat up from Fort Yukon. When the captain finds they're A.C.C. employees 'n', especially, friends of us six who'd forced passage, he refuses to pick 'em up. But the pilot probably figures he'd rather lose his job than face the wrath of the whole river. He defies orders, swings over 'n' takes 'em aboard. While they're tyin' their boat in tow, I wink at Walden 'n' nod my head toward the captain: later, he's still goin' to look good to company bosses when they find out he ordered the pilot not to pick up rivals.

"Meanwhile, Captain Hanson's been drivin' himself 'n' his hired canoemen night 'n' day. He's bucked the swift current 375 miles since Fort Yukon 'n' flowin' ice the last part. 'Just valiant! An epic feat of heroism' is what Walden calls it. Hanson's birch-bark had only just pulled into the big eddy in front of Dawson an hour before. He's in the middle of pleading to the big crowd. Get out of the town, he's begging them, while they still have the chance. That, or risk starvation. No paddlewheeler can possibly make it up over the flats, he's just explainin' to the crowd, when he practically stops in mid-word 'n' signals for silence. Everyone listens.

A long, drawn-out whistle echoes up the river. It's the approachin' *Portius B. Wiere.*"

———◆———◆———

Rod Perry: However, the good Captain's convincing warning does bear fruit. It primes many to leave when they discover that the *Wiere*, the same as the trusty old *Bella* which comes in close behind, are only carrying light loads. A good part of the cargo is whiskey. Many Dawsonites ship out immediately, some on the steamboats, others in small boats of their own. A number drop down to winter in Fort Yukon. The rest of the evacuees grab the chance to get completely out of the starving country by way of St. Michael and the last ships of the season outbound to Seattle, Portland 'n San Francisco. Captain Hanson's effective reduction of Dawson's population ends up saving the town, relieving demands on the thin food supply just enough for everyone to narrowly scrape by on starvation rations.

Chapter 8

The Great Klondike Rush of 1898

SEATTLE, PORTLAND AND SAN FRANCISCO vied to establish themselves as the main supply point for Alaska and the Yukon. In October 1897, a Seattle newspaper had printed an eight-page Klondike edition and sent it to every postmaster and public library in the country as well as to thousands of businessmen and politicians.

Rod Perry: *As we have seen, many, if not most among the first wave who had rushed from the outside into the Klondike had gone in without adequate supplies. The two companies that dominated trade and transportation on the river had pulled out all the stops in a race against falling temperatures and water levels to bolster supplies 1,500 miles upriver. Leslie's Weekly, a publication with strong interest in the North, had reported that if even one of the steamers that left Saint Michael were to fail to make it to Dawson before freeze-up, one-third of the Klondike population could starve.*

As we know, barely enough supplies did reach Dawson before ice-up the fall of 1897 to just fend off starvation of the number already there. And the rush had barely started.

With a teeming horde on the way, the North West Mounted Police could see a looming disaster. In February of 1898 they announced a policy that no one else would be allowed into Yukon Territory unless they brought in one ton of supplies and gear, considered enough to make them self sufficient for one year. The Mounties set up scales near the summit of the Chilkoot and White Passes to weigh the miner's outfits.

About seven of the first 12 miles of the Chilkoot Trail lay either over level ground or climbed slowly enough to make it possible to pull sleds and transport heavy loads. Once the incline became steeper, however, it became necessary to divide each man's "ton" into lighter increments. Carried in 100-pound parcels, the ton took 20 trips. Many men broke their loads down to 50 pounds for the hardest going. It was said that for every mile of the steep parts of the trail, the average stampeder walked ahead 40 miles packed, then returned 40 empty. The final pitch to the summit of 1,500 steps carved in the ice up which men trudged in a crowded, slow-moving line, took an average of five hours each trip.

Horses were used by many until the way grew too steep. When their final load was packed that far, they were abandoned for others to use or were shot.

Canyon City was set up as a permanent settlement seven miles from the top. Entrepreneurs built a steam-powered tram that included the longest cable span in the world, 2,200 feet. When running at capacity, it could haul nine tons per hour for those who could pay. Professional packers offered their services to carry loads the final pitch to the summit for $1 per pound.

Tent cities sprang up along the trail featuring supply dumps, saloons, bunkhouses, brothels, casinos and, as one stampeder put it, "humanity pressed so close you can hardly breathe."

Unusually heavy snows fell on the Chilkoot during February and March of 1898 then were followed by several warm days and fresh snow. Experienced mountaineers warned of impending danger and cautioned the throngs to wait. The lure of gold was too strong, however, and thousands pressed on.

The Goin' Kid: "At 2 a.m. on April 2, 1898, Palm Sunday, a small avalanche buries about 20 men. Another slide at

9:30 a.m. covers three. All are rescued. About 200 decide
to heed warnings 'n' evacuate. Just before noon, a massive
avalanche bears down on some of the evacuees 'n' a number
of men diggin' supplies out from the prior slides. About 60
men 're buried under 30 feet of snow. Only Shorty Fisher's
freight dog, Jack survives. By the time they get to 'im he's
been buried eight days. Someone claims him, they give him
a couple of days to catch up 'n' Jack's put right back to work."

Promoters billed the White Pass as an easy wagon road
the entire way. After a relatively broad, but terribly muddy
first few miles, however, the way narrowed. Then it traversed
steep sections where one misstep could mean a drop of
hundreds of feet. Some places were too narrow for two laden
horses to pass. All of the repetitious ferrying of loads tempted
stampeders (many who had no experience in the use of beasts
of burden) to greatly overload their pack animals. Horses
broke legs negotiating boulder fields, strained themselves in
the deep quagmires and tumbled down precipices, perishing
by the thousands.

By September 1897, conditions deteriorated to the point
that the White Pass trail was virtually impassable. Strong
men, it was reported, were seen returning, tears streaming
down their cheeks, completely physically and emotionally
broken, while the stream of gold-crazed humanity passed
on, indifferent to their sufferings.

Through the mountains, stampeders following both trails
risked disease, malnutrition, hypothermia and even, it was
reported, death from suicide and murder. Of the estimated
5,000 who missed getting to Skagway earlier and did not set
out until the fall of 1897, some estimated that no more than
500 made it through that winter.

Al Preston: "Rod, here is what I clipped from an article quoting Canada's Minister of the Interior. Remember, he's commenting on that winter between the winter of Carmack's discovery in 1896–97 and the main rush to come later, in the summer of 1898. The minister is writing at the end of the 1897–98 winter."

———————

Interior Minister Clifford Sifton: "The inhumanity this trail had been witness to, the heartbreak and suffering which so many have undergone, cannot be imagined."

———————

Compiled records of various railway companies indicated that some quarter million citizens started west intending to join the rush. Of the approximately 100,000 men and women who actually started in 1897 and 1898, no more than 40,000—probably far fewer—eventually reached the Yukon. Everywhere along the trail were piles of left-behind supplies, many marked with signs welcoming others to "help yourself."

After the Mounties' "ton-or-turn-back" requirement went into effect, the average time it took to cover the 32-mile-long Chilkoot Pass or the 40-mile-long White Pass totaled three months. Those who made it over the passes gathered where the trails converged at Lake Bennett. There, they stopped to fell trees, whipsaw lumber and build boats, quickly denuding the slopes of timber. On May 29, 1898, the ice went out and an armada of several thousand craft began their float of over 500 danger-fraught miles to Dawson.

Several dangerous rapids between the headwaters and Dawson took their toll in lives and lost outfits. Most of the gold-seekers were inexperienced boat builders and lacked river-running skills. The crafts were almost universally too heavily laden. Most careful travelers unloaded and portaged all or most of their cargo around Whitehorse Rapids and Five

Finger Rapids but the portages were so long and the work took so many days that the lure of arriving at the foot of the torrent in a brief, few minutes influenced many to cast their fate to the tumult and "shoot the chutes." Some chose to just shove their unmanned, empty craft into the current above, hope for the best and catch them below from another boat. Reportedly, the first man to successfully brave the rapids with a full cargo shot through with his boat laden to the gunwales with whiskey.

Old Ben Atwater: "The prize for the most bizarre load had to go to the enterprising opportunist who brought in a scow load of cats. Just how on earth did the man cage, feed, care for and relay that many panthers from saltwater over the mountains to Yukon headwaters? Nobody knows. But think about it; his logistics must have been something to behold!

Now, when he got to the summit of the pass and checked in to clear customs, he really set those Canadian officials to scratching their heads. They'd never seen such an import. They had no written guidelines on what to assess the man. What they finally charged was their usual duty to trappers: $1 each on the fur.

"When the load reached Dawson the cargo sold as fast as the townspeople could slap down an ounce of gold per kitty. Al, you shoulda seen those new arrivals tear into the town's booming mouse population. Man, they were going through the vermin like a dose of salts through the hired hand! Their pace of mouse extermination was only exceeded by the speed the cats themselves were cleaned out by Dawson's loose huskies!"

Following the disappointment of finding that they were almost two years too late, and that gold did not, indeed lay under every rock, most of the late hopefuls did not even go prospecting. Only some 4,000 who reached the Klondike found so much as a trace of gold, although it was a few of the most driven of the 98'ers who, finding everything staked closer to Dawson, indeed made some of most remote discoveries far back on the fringes of the district. Thousands of the newcomers left the country at first opportunity. Many others, however, either went to work laboring in the various support service industries or toiling at the standard $15 a day wage for the few hundred whose claims held substantial deposits.

Chapter 9

---◆---

Travel Options to the Klondike in '98

Rod Perry: *Some who traveled to the gold fields took the "poor man's route" and trekked by way of the Chilkoot Pass or its close neighbor, the White Pass, into the upper Yukon. Others, who had the resources to pay and could find space on the overcrowded boats, took the "rich man's route," travelling by water all the way to the diggings. There were several other ways to reach the northern gold fields but only a small minority took them.*

THE DALTON TRAIL, which began at the present location of Haines, Alaska, was perceived by many, at least those with pack animals, to be the best route of all. It was the third of the three "grease trails" of the Chilkat Tlingits. It went overland about 245 long, but relatively easy, miles, following the route of today's Haines Cutoff. It hit the Yukon at Fort Selkirk.

One reason it was not more popular during the Klondike rush was that since Jack Dalton had learned the way by following Chilkat packers in 1890, he had established a lucrative trading business along the trail and regarded the route, save for Native use, as his private cattle drive trail for supplying inland miners as well as his tightly held, for-profit toll road. Therefore, until about 1896, he did not advertise it as a way to reach the gold fields. By that time, the Chilkoot and White Passes were so widely known that few gold-seekers took other pathways to reach the Klondike.

Rod Perry: *Jack Dalton led a long, fabulously adventurous, sometimes violent, life, serving a pivotal role in many business*

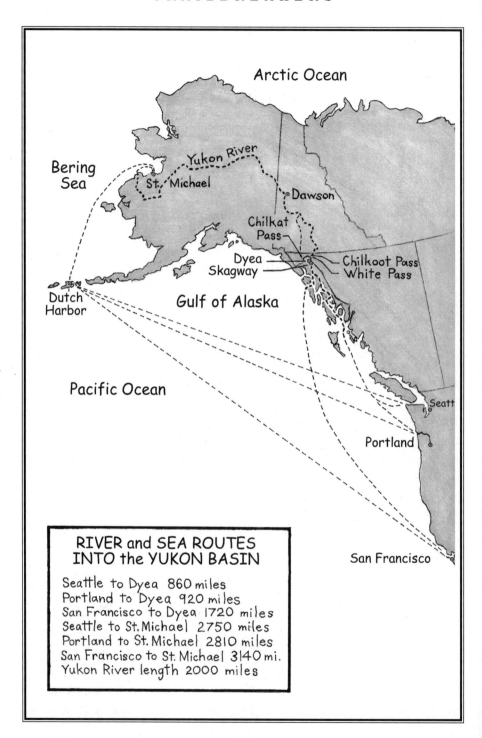

Arctic Ocean

Bering
Sea

Yukon River

St. Michael

Dawson

Chilkat
Pass

Dyea
Skagway

Chilkoot Pass
White Pass

Dutch
Harbor

Gulf of Alaska

Pacific Ocean

Seatt

Portland

San Francisco

**RIVER and SEA ROUTES
INTO the YUKON BASIN**

Seattle to Dyea 860 miles
Portland to Dyea 920 miles
San Francisco to Dyea 1720 miles
Seattle to St. Michael 2750 miles
Portland to St. Michael 2810 miles
San Francisco to St. Michael 3140 mi.
Yukon River length 2000 miles

explorations and commercial ventures central to a significant part of early-day Alaskan development. Jack Dalton's second son, James W. Dalton, an engineer, served in Dutch Harbor alongside Al Preston in the Naval Construction Battalion, the "Sea Bees. (Like many of Alaska's miners, Al patriotically put down his pick and shovel to serve his nation at war. Al was working at Dutch Harbor when the Japanese bombed the base on Alaska's Aleutian Islands on June 3, 1942.)

Later, James Dalton served as a supervisor of the Distant Early Warning System (DEW Line) Cold War defense system in Alaska. Early on, oil companies exploring Alaska's North Slope consulted with him for his expertise in Arctic engineering. The 414-mile-long supply road to Alaska's oil fields on the Arctic Ocean was named the James W. Dalton Highway in his honor.

James Dalton's wife, Kathleen "Mike" Dalton, widowed when he died of a sudden heart attack in 1957, continued to be prominent in the civic life of Fairbanks. In the early winter of 1983–84, I was privileged to work shoulder-to-shoulder with Mike Dalton as she dived into helping Yukon Quest International Sled Dog Race founder Leroy Shank and our core group get the thousand-mile event that leads from Fairbanks, Alaska, to Whitehorse, Yukon Territory, off and running.

For transportation of passengers, both the poor man's and rich man's routes had their advantages and disadvantages. The Chilkoot and White Pass routes were shorter, only 1,600 miles or so north from Seattle to the Klondike River. They began with a relatively short, easy ocean voyage. From Seattle, for most of the almost 1,000 miles up the coast of British Columbia and Southeastern Alaska, shipping cruised within the protected waters of the Inside Passage. From the head of Lynn Canal, it was "only 32 miles" over the Chilkoot Trail and "slightly more than 40 miles" (but, oh, what miles they were) over the White Pass to the headwaters of the Yukon. From there they could float downstream with the current, albeit, a current that included two sets of perilous rapids.

Gold-seekers taking either of the poor man's routes could also start earlier in the season. By crossing the passes well before ice-out and building boats or rafts, they could be poised to float to the diggings the moment the Yukon broke up.

The offsetting disadvantages were several. The final pitch to the summit of the Chilkoot Pass was so steep that the trekker could reach out and touch the ground ahead. In winter, avalanches thundered down from the slopes above. The White Pass was not much better, evidenced by the fact that several thousand horses died as stampeders attempted to use pack animals in the crossing.

Once they packed across either pass and descended to the chain of lakes connected to the upper river, it was necessary for travelers to stop and construct rafts or painstakingly whipsaw lumber and build boats from native materials. Beyond the lakes, they floated anywhere from 300 to 800 miles of river, depending upon where they stopped to prospect. Once they reached their destination, they had but a bare minimum of supplies and gear to support their prospecting efforts.

The advantage for gold-seekers taking the all-water passage from Seattle to the upper Yukon was that they could outfit themselves with as much in the way of equipment and supplies as they wished, and get it there with little or no physical effort of their own. As sail and steam did the work, passengers could sit back and view the scenery all the way.

Passage on sternwheelers plying the Yukon was hard to come by. There were only a few such specialized craft working the river, just enough to take care of the pre-rush needs. It would take shipbuilders awhile to catch up with the exploding demand. Therefore, boat owners charged premium prices.

Rod Perry: *The all-water route held several other disadvantages. First, to go by ship all the way up the coast, across the Gulf of Alaska, around the Alaska Peninsula and across the Bering Sea to the Yukon mouth was a trip of over 2,500 miles in length, more or less, and the voyage was often* *ravaged by tremendous storms. It was far greater undertaking than the short, easy sail up the inside passage to Skagway or Dyea. Naturally, it was much more expensive. Second, the Yukon remained ice locked about eight months of the year. If, in an attempt to beat the rush, arrivals reached the Yukon mouth before ice-out, they had to await breakup then steam about 1,500 miles upstream. Hazardous navigational conditions ended on the upper river before they did far downstream. In a race to a new strike those waiting at the Yukon mouth would lose to those who went over either the Chilkoot Pass or White Pass in early spring and had their boats built in time to float the few hundred miles down the Yukon as soon as the ice went out.*

Not only was the Chilkoot Trail many times too steep to negotiate readily by draft or pack animals, the climb was so grueling that a traveler's outfit had to be broken down into small loads and back-packed over the summit in repetitious trips. The White Pass offered different challenges but was just as difficult. Therefore, while the Chilkoot and White Pass Trails served adequately for the mere passage of miners hauling just enough to get them into the country to start prospecting, the effort required was far too labor-intensive to be practical for trading posts and stores to use in the large-scale transport of the heavy supply upon which the miners who stayed in the North depended.

To move large amounts of equipment and supplies into the gold country, shipment by water was the only practical way. Not only was it economically efficient, but beyond loading and offloading, delivering the tonnage required minimal physical effort. Very little that equipped and supplied any of the diggings along the Yukon River and its tributaries prior to 1900 came into the country any other way.

At first, people like famed sourdough "Klondike Mike" Mahoney filled part of the winter demand. In 1897 he carried mail at $1 a letter between Dawson and Skagway. His 1,200-mile round trips took one month. As he started from either end, his sled carried 250 pounds of mail and 500 pounds of food and gear for himself and his dogs. He also brought newspapers which were read to gathered miners for a fee as he distributed the mail in the far-flung camps.

By 1898 the population in the Klondike overwhelmed Mahoney's efforts to fill the need. The North West Mounted Police took over. Relays of men and teams going day and night could complete the trip one way in a week.

Rod Perry: *It was one thing for the Mounties to haul 250 pounds of mail at a time on those Pony Express-like relays. But if it had been 250 pounds of freight it would have filled only the bare needs of a tiny percentage of the populace, a mere drop in the bucket of the supply needs of 30,000 desperate inhabitants. Clearly, the Klondike cried out for something with greater carrying capacity than piecemeal dog team supply.*

Albert Hulse Brooks: "Before the Klondike rush, the major holdup to the region's development had been that the gold country was isolated from the industrialized world for two-thirds of the year. Cut off from freeze-up in late September to breakup in late May, the lack of travel, communication and supply simply strangled the region.

"I say eight months because, in addition to deep winter, hazardous river ice conditions during spring and fall shut down not only steamboat traffic, but over-the-ice hauling by dog team and horse-drawn sledge. Most transportation from Lynn Canal through the mountains into the Yukon Basin was at least slowed, if not stopped during spring and fall as well.

"Before 1898–99, there were so few prospectors and miners working the country, with just a limited amount of gold being produced that there were relatively small requirements for supply of food and equipment. So this had never come close to making a road project of the size and scope needed to breach the mountain barrier worthy of the slightest consideration. That changed with the great rush to the Klondike."

Chapter 10

---◆---

The White Pass Railroad and Overland Wagon Road

IT TOOK SOMETHING CATACLYSMIC, an explosion the size of the booming Klondike strike to blow things wide open for development of winter transportation into the northern interior. Until 1896, the population of Yukon Territory stood at about 5,000 people, mostly First Nations people plus the very hardiest, most intrepid explorers, fur traders, prospectors, missionaries and a handful of merchant companies and river transportation interests. The Yukon River on the Alaska side was likewise sparsely populated with the same mix. But by 1899, the great rush of humanity into the Klondike caused a previously almost unpeopled area in an almost unmapped region of the North to explode into an instant wilderness metropolis of 30,000 inhabitants, the largest Canadian population center west of Winnipeg, Manitoba.

Before, in both Canada and the United States, the few stories coming out of the Yukon River had been colorful, but of minor importance on the overall scale of national news. The great rush, however, commonly created sensational, front-page, national coverage and became an everyday conversational topic across the continent. Among the people of Canada and the United States, the Yukon Territory and Alaska grew greatly within the public perception as valued possessions.

---◆---

Old Ben Atwater: "Interestingly, at Dawson's peak, I figured U.S. citizens outnumbered Canadians maybe 15 to one.

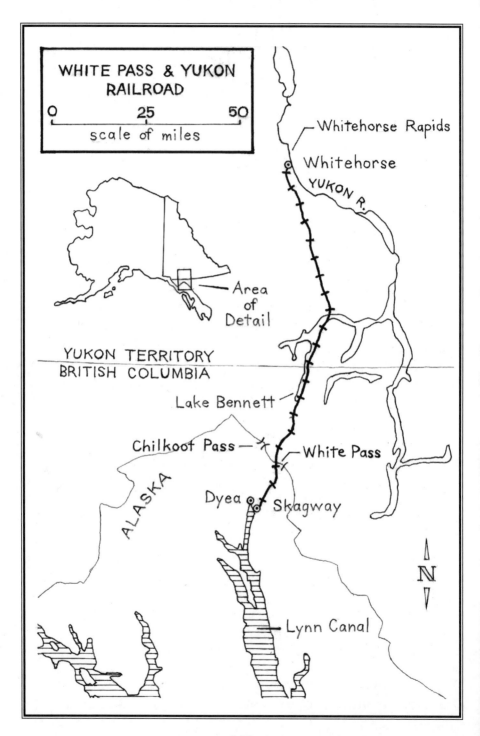

WHITE PASS & YUKON
RAILROAD

0   25   50
scale of miles

Whitehorse Rapids

Whitehorse

YUKON R.

Area
of
Detail

YUKON TERRITORY
BRITISH COLUMBIA

Lake Bennett

Chilkoot Pass

White Pass

ALASKA

Dyea   Skagway

Lynn Canal

N

Americans held most of the claims. No wonder United States citizens felt such a strong connection to the Klondike. We felt like our stake east of Ogilvie's survey line was as important as that of Canadians."

———•——•——•———

Alfred Hulse Brooks: "With the exploding population and economic importance, the far North was desperate for a better transportation system. Not only could such a booming area not *thrive* with a mere four-month transportation system, such a large population and that much industry could hardly *survive*, having to cope as they did with virtually all movement of travelers, mail and freight to and from the outside world shut down eight months a year and having to guess the needs and supply the region up to 20 months in advance."

———•——•——•———

Rod Perry: *The Yukon and Alaska, according to the prevailing opinion, probably held untold hidden mineral wealth, with the Klondike discovery only the tip of the iceberg. With the boom and its excitement driving thousands of prospectors to search out every nook and cranny, other rich locations, it was felt, were sure to be found. Even the most casual observation showed that lack of adequate year-round transportation constricted development of the Dawson area. How much more, analysts were saying, would it choke a country featuring a number of such finds?*

Capturing, as it had, the attention and romantic emotions of the continent, the roaring Klondike strike brought tremendous pressure upon the Canadian government and opened up lucrative opportunity for industry to throw their might into building an efficient, high-capacity transportation system over which people, mail and supplies could readily flow regardless of season.

147

Men of action sped to build a railroad from saltwater into the gold country. At the last of the 19th century, developers did not become bogged down in today's endless permit processes, congressional hearings, partisan politics, environmental concerns and the like. North America was in an empire-building mode and developers were encouraged to open up the country.

At the very peak of the Klondike Gold Rush, on May 28, 1898, the day before the ice went out on the Yukon allowing the great armada of the Chilkoot and White Pass stampeders to begin their float toward Dawson—construction of the White Pass and Yukon Railway began at Skagway.

In just one year, in a remarkable feat enabled by British financing, American engineering and Canadian contracting and powered with almost superhuman effort, the narrow-gauge roadbed was cut, filled and blasted, tunneled and trestled through the rugged Coast Range barrier into the interior. Rails reached Lake Bennett in the summer of 1899. A year later, on July 29, 1900, only 25 months after starting construction, the 110 miles of track connected Whitehorse to saltwater.

———◆—◆———

Al Preston: "I remember an old-timer of the country describing advantages he found in the new railroad: 'A journey that used to be an odyssey that took us old prospectors weeks (actually, *months* during the Klondike Rush after the Mounties started their ton-of-supplies rule) of incredible, severe exertion is now a relaxing ride, where, while carrying as much luggage or freight as he wishes to ship in, the traveler can sit nestled in comfort while he takes in glorious vistas and comes to his trip's end in a few hours, relaxed and uplifted.' "

———◆—◆———

Completion of the railroad eliminated the terribly difficult and time-consuming crossing of the Coast Range through either the White Pass or Chilkoot Pass and lopped off the miles teams had formerly had to travel between Lake Bennett and Whitehorse. But, from Whitehorse, Dawson still lay some 400 miles downriver.

Immediately, regular summer sternwheeler service commenced between Whitehorse and Dawson, extending the reach of the railroad in summer, carrying what had been brought in by locomotive power from Lynn Canal on down to the Klondike supply hub. But open summer river conditions only lasted four months. Winter travel and transport downriver from Whitehorse remained as primitive and piecemeal as before, however, and still partially stifled the region.

Canadians hurried to reduce the winter difficulty. In 1902 the territorial government contracted with the White Pass and Yukon Route to build a winter sled and wagon road from the end of steel at Whitehorse on downriver to Dawson. Called the Dawson or Overland Trail, it cut across two major bends of the Yukon, lopping over 70 miles from the primitive and dangerous 400-mile river trail it replaced. The 330-mile-long wagon and sledge road further greased the movement of mail, freight and passengers, extending the winter reach of the railroad.

Before the road, each fall between the time that flowing ice stopped river traffic and the time that newly forming ice grew strong enough, movement up and down the river had been halted for several weeks. Likewise in spring, transportation suffered a lengthy wait between the time the ice became too rotten to support winter traffic and when it went out, and another few weeks were lost. Not only was it shorter, the improved route, because it was located off the river, eliminated the need to deal with vagaries and dangers of Yukon River ice. The Overland Road thereby substantially enhanced conditions for freighting by horse-drawn wagon and sledge and gained more than two months annually for shipping and travel.

Even with the coming of the road, during the four months of open water, heavy use of the waterway between Whitehorse and Dawson by steamboats still provided by far the most efficient and economical shipping, being able to carry scores of tons at a time. However, with the advent of the Overland Road, during the eight months that the river was nonnavigable, at least teamsters were able to regularly move mail and materials by the ton into the brawling Canadian supply hub, carrying much more and doing it faster than dog teams ever had over the old, longer river route.

The Arctic Limited stage line, which regularly changed to fresh teams at waypoints along the way, covered the 330-mile distance between Whitehorse and Dawson once each week carrying passengers, baggage and light freight. At slower speeds than the Limited's fliers, private contractors moved heavy freight.

———————

Alfred Hulse Brooks: "The White Pass and Yukon Route—the combined railroad and Overland Road—was the most valuable addition to the developing infrastructure of the Yukon Territory and Alaska since the advent of the steamboat and trading post system on the Yukon River. Before the WP&YR, there had been no viable way to swiftly travel, communicate or transport anything or in and out of the North once freeze-up shut down the great waterway. Prior to the railroad, supplying the Yukon Basin depended totally upon accurately guessing the numbers and whereabouts of the population and its needs more than a year—sometimes approaching two years—in advance, something that was not always possible, as evidenced during the great shortages of the Klondike Rush.

"Finally, though, with the coming of the railroad, summer or winter, supplies and equipment could be brought into the Interior not just by the ton, but by the hundreds of tons. Mail service became regular and travelers could move readily in and out of the North. If freight were needed badly enough, even in winter an order could be sent from Dawson to Seattle and it was possible to receive it within the month, sometimes faster.

"Whereas before, no matter how badly mail, freight or people had needed to be moved between the States and the North during winter, it had been a virtual impossibility. However, once the railroad had broken through the former barrier of the Coast Range, it relaxed winter's grip for not only the Klondike region, but for the entire northwestern subcontinent. By establishing year-round transport from the North Pacific through to the Yukon drainage, though the way might include a thousand miles—or even double that—of laborious dog team freighting beyond Dawson, almost anyone, almost anywhere in the Interior of Yukon Territory and Alaska could access anything that could be carried on a sled if he was willing to pay for the effort."

Once mountains of supplies began to reach the Klondike year around, other strikes that had not been big enough to demand construction of such a winter supply system began to greatly benefit. Immediately, intrepid Alaskan dog drivers, among them The Malamute Kid, The Goin' Kid and Harry Karstens, famed as The Seventy Mile Kid beat in winter trails along several hundred miles of the upper Yukon River to access the supply wealth of Dawson for the older gold discovery sites of the late 1880s and early 1890s such as Fortymile and Circle City.

Rod Perry: *Karstens' fame was already widespread in the North when Charles Sheldon, avid hunter, naturalist and wealthy friend of Theodore Roosevelt ventured into the Alaska Range north and east of Mount McKinley to explore, study the flora and fauna, observe the change of seasons and collect museum specimens and hired Karstens to assist him. When Sheldon's work resulted in the creation of Mount McKinley— now Denali—National Park, Sheldon made sure that Karstens was installed as its first superintendent.*

When Hudson Stuck, archdeacon of the Episcopal Church in Alaska, organized the first successful climb of Mount McKinley, he chose Karstens to lead the climb. The route he chose, later named Karstens Ridge proved the most practical way to the summit until the Alaska Earthquake of Good Friday, 1964 destroyed it as an easy route. (Author's note: Read The Wilderness of Denali *by Charles Sheldon,* Ten Thousand Miles on a Dog Sled and The Ascent of Denali *by Hudson Stuck, and* My Life of High Adventure *by Grant Pearson.)*

Chapter 11

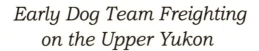

Early Dog Team Freighting on the Upper Yukon

ALL OF THE GOLD STRIKES were located well back from the Yukon along the Klondike, Sixtymile and Fortymile Rivers, Birch Creek, Preacher Creek and other tributaries. Distances as far as 100 trail miles separated some of the diggings from the main river. Therefore, freighting by dog team was crucial to moving supplies and equipment back to the mines.

Rod Perry: *Hardly any of the miners during the gold rush era owned dogs; they were too busy prospecting and mining to afford the money, time and trouble to keep a team. About the only dog teams in the country outside of small teams kept by the natives were owned by hard-working professional freighters and mail carriers. These great dog men upon whom everyone else so depended were known and looked up to throughout the whole North.*

When reporters converged upon the North to feed a nation hungry for romantic tales of gold-rush adventure, writers glorified feats of some the foremost dog punchers, grew them larger than life and they became luminaries known 'round the globe. Some of their names: Frank Tondreau, aka The Malamute Kid; Harry Karstens, The Seventy-Mile Kid; Captain Ulysses Grant Norton, the Tireless Trojan of the Trails; The Wandering Japanese, Jujira Wada; and the great Eskimo driver, Split-the-Wind. Lesser known to readers Outside but just as highly esteemed by men throughout the North were others such as The Goin' Kid and Ben Atwater, among others. These men

*Ben Atwater and His Dogsled Team Arriving at
Bennett Lake from Circle City, Alaska with U.S. Mail*
University of Washington Libraries, Special Collections, Hegg064

*contracted with either the Alaska Commercial Company, the
North American Trade and Transportation Company, a few
lesser commercial suppliers or with the miners themselves.
Some, such as Ben Atwater, contracted to carry U.S. Mail.*

The price of goods sitting in company warehouses was
already expensive, and understandably so. Trading companies
had to cover the expense of the procurement and expediting
in the States, the 2,500-mile sea voyage to St. Michael, the
1,100 to 1,700-mile sternwheeler trip against the current from
the mouth up to the various supply centers and all of the
attendant costs such as labor, fuel, storage, capital

construction and maintenance, coverage of risk from loss at sea and fires, and, of course, profit to investors. Freighting supplies and equipment from company warehouses out to the miners added greatly to the cost. At the height of the Klondike rush the going rate rose to $1.25 a pound from Dawson to the most distant claims. But there were no other options. Without the dog teams, mining would have ground to a halt.

———◆———◆———

Alma Preston: "Rod, as you can well imagine, those dog drivers worked, literally, hundreds of thousands of cumulative winter trail miles. As they did, they concocted and perfected methods and means. None I know of describes these better than our old friend, The Goin' Kid. . . ."

———◆———◆———

The Goin' Kid: "Most professional freighters in those early years along the upper Yukon used a system we perfected to the conditions 'n' kind work we were doin'. It later disappeared 'n' I never see dog freightin' done like that anymore. Here's the way it works: Yukon sleds, not basket sleds 're used. They have flat beds 7 feet long, 20 inches wide. Their supportin' cross bents clear the trail 4 inches. Runners're just 16 inches, outside to outside, to follow narrow trails. We hitch three sleds to track close one behind another by cross chainin' 'em into a train. Right crossin' to left 'n' left crossin' to right, short lengths of chain fixed to the front corners of the trailin' sled attach to the opposite rear corners of the sled ahead. This crossed-chain arrangement forces the trailers to follow just about perfectly in the tracks of the sled in front.

"Freightin' back then was very heavy. The trails were rough as a cob. That triple Yukon sled method works better'n any other. It makes it possible for one lone man to work heavier loads than other ways used anywhere else in the north. Those three 7-foot sleds spread out the load over a much longer bearin' surface than if you use just one standard 12-foot basket sled. Keeps the center of gravity lower. The jointed sled train flexes over obstacles. Think of a chain draggin' over a log. It serpentines through forest trails so twistin' you could never get a longer sled through. When one 'r more sleds tip over, one lone driver can right one at a time without havin' to unload. And when you come to places too steep, you just take 'em apart and go with one at a time up 'r down.

"The load everyone thinks of as a standard contract load, at least over flat 'r gently rollin' country, is twelve hundred pounds. We're careful to figure "draft" 'n arrange the loads to get the weight as close to the power as we can. The cargo's loaded 600 pounds on the lead sled, 400 on the mid sled 'n' 200 on the trailer. On each sled, we want the center of gravity one-third back from the front.

"Drivers figure six or seven big dogs make a full team. And these're big dogs. We dog punchers used a lot of Malamutes. They're coastal Eskimo dogs about 100 pounds weight. In fall they're brought up from the coast on the steamboats. But for heavy freightin' you can't beat McKenzie River Huskies. This breed was put together decades before by the Hudson's Bay Company. They're larger, stronger 'n' better draft animals than the coastal dogs. The finest team I've seen has a couple that weigh 160 pounds, all go not too far shy of that. And that's dogs in late winter, workin' weight.

"The team's harnessed single file. Dogs pull from leather collars akin to horse collars. The tubular leather structures're stuffed tight, usually with hair. Traces from the lead dog run from his collar to about four inches in back of the hips of dog behind. There, they snap into a ring on that second dog's traces. This hook-up's repeated all the way back 'til it reaches the last two dogs. Both of 'em're attached to a spreader bar called a whiffle-tree. The whiffle-tree's far enough behind the rear dog—called the sled dog on the upper Yukon back then—that he can readily jump out from between the traces to help the driver maneuver the sled around tight corners. The whiffle-tree's attached to the sled bridle with a five-foot-long tow line. The driver straddle's the tow line, walkin' between the sled dog 'n' the sled.

"He steers with a gee pole attached to one side of the front of the lead sled so's it angles up steeply to the driver's shoulder height. Graspin' it in his right hand, he uses the pole as a powerful steerin' lever. Over easier trails, the gee pole's angled to waist height. But over the tussock-ridden trails roughed in from the Yukon to the mines, the higher angled gee pole is a vertical lever to keep the sleds from tippin' over at the same time it's a side-to-side lever for steerin'.

"Yukon sleds have no break like on a basket sled. Goin' down steep hills, the driver unsnaps the towline from the sled bridle. Just turns the dogs loose as a harnessed team. Then he takes the sleds down by himself by leanin' back on the gee pole 'n' digging his heels in to break. Several freighters have been killed in crashes. One's gee pole broke 'n' the stub ran him through. Down the steepest slopes the safe way, sleds are turned on their sides 'n' dragged down.

"Goin' out loaded, the dogs make only about three miles an hour. Bent to their work, they don't need much room between 'em. They're harnessed up separated, nose to tail, by less'n a dog length between them. That keeps the total team length short. Then the power stays close to the load. But empty, you come back at a smart trot. Sometimes they even break into a lope. Then the team does better havin' the traces lengthened. Gives more freedom of motion. Instead of snappin' the traces of the dog in front into rings four inches behind the next dog back, they're snapped into another set of rings midway along the followin' dog. This way each dog gets a couple extra feet. Comin' back empty at five, six miles an hour, the driver still trots most of the time. There's no place to stand on a Yukon sled. If the goin's flat 'n' smooth 'n' the driver wants to ride, he has to sit or kneel perched on the load. The load goin' home carries the freighter's camp 'n' trail gear with the mid and trailer sleds lashed on top. He positioned dog food caches for the return trip on the way out.

"Shelter cabins (not tended roadhouses) are built an average day's travel—about 20 miles—apart along the main trails to the mines. They're simple, log walls, sod roofs 'n' dirt floors, a window 'r two, a door, a wood stove 'n' pole bunks piled with wild hay. Freighters haul 'n' cook their own food 'n' cut their own stove wood.

"The drivers work their teams 'bout eight hours a day durin' the short winter daylight. That leaves 'em a lot of time. On faint trails to more off-the-beaten-track diggin's, there's no shelter cabins. Dog punchers camp in the open like this: A camp location's picked where two trees stand 'bout four to six feet apart. Against 'em we pile a half cord of six-foot-long green logs to make a high wall to reflect heat. In front of the pile a big fire's kindled of dead, dry wood. Then it's fed with green logs from the pile. On the side of the fire opposite the pile, the puncher puts down a thick bed of spruce feathers. Next a canvas, then a caribou hide mattress, hair side up, then his fur sleepin' robe, last the canvas wraps over the top for warmth 'n' to guard the robe from sparks. To keep the side of the bed away from the fire from losin' heat you pile up a high wall of snow 'r hang a canvas for a reflector. Such a camp setup's comfortable at 40 below 'n' keeps it bearable way lower.

"People who don't know a lick 'bout life in cold country think you'd better not ever go to sleep, you'll never wake up. That's plain corral dust. Think 'bout it. When you're home in bed 'n' get a bit chilly it makes you uncomfortable 'n' wakes you up. You add a quilt 'n' go back to sleep. Same thing on the trail. You get uncomfortable 'n' wake up long before you get cold enough to matter. Just stay right 'n bed 'n' reach out with a long pole with a stub of a branch for a hook. Pull a few logs down, roll 'em from the top of the stack into the fire. This old camp method's largely replaced now by using light wall tents 'n' Yukon stoves.

"Sled dogs in the days before the big rush were extremely valued. But they used t' have a hard life, usually short. Before the multitudes came in, a working husky can usually be had for $3 to $5 dollars. But the great Klondike Rush skyrockets the demand way beyond the number of local native dogs. As demand rises, steamboats begin t' ship Malamutes in from the coast. Men from the States comin' up t' the gold fields bring with them every large dog they can lay their hands on that looks able t' tighten his traces. Even with the added supply few're around for purchase. During the boom years of the rush, the goin' price for a proven sled dog rises t' $300.

"Miss Alma, I'm attached to my dogs 'n' glad they have it a lot better these days. But back then, as sought-after as the animals are while they're workin' through the long winters, they drop in value t' next t' nothin' at the end of the freightin' season. Before the White Pass and Yukon Route and Overland Wagon Road created regular supply lines, facin' near starvation used to be expected every winter for the miners and us dog men ourselves. Summers were spent workin' and scraping up enough to make it through the next winter. With humans so threatened, even in summer the old-timers didn't have anything t' feed non-working dogs. The common practice was t' save only the very best. They'd shoot the rest each spring t' spare the poor animals the misery of a summer of starvation. Nobody liked it, but that was the reality of a harsh life. Dog punchers depended on findin' replacements somehow before the next freeze-up."

Rod Perry: *Surviving dogs were turned loose to fend for themselves over the summer. Most on-the-spot chronicles of the gold rush devote some space to the tremendous cunning and skill the voracious animals developed as thieves. All who would succeed along the Yukon had to learn to "think like a dog" in this aspect of dog behavior. The animals would rarely let an opportunity escape them, whether it was biting through* *tin cans, making cat-like climbs newcomers would swear no canine could accomplish, or curling up innocently near a tent, feigning sleep, patiently waiting for hours for the inhabitants to leave so that they might move in and ransack it.*

Old Ben Atwater: "Two prospectors boated down to Circle City on business. They anchored their loaded boat a ways offshore to keep it safe, then walked into town. When they got back, they were amazed and roaring angry over what they found: a pack of loose dogs had obviously sized things up, swum out, bitten through the rope holding the boat and dragged the craft ashore. The starving critters had not left one single bag of provisions unripped. They were gorged on the contents. They even ate the dry flour and the dishrag.

"Another time in Circle City a desperate, starving sled dog saw his chance when a native woman turned her back for a moment. He dashed into a cabin and made off with the body of a baby his grieving mother had been preparing for burial. As the dog dashed through town with his prize, miners gave chase. A passel of them ran him 'til the animal dropped the little corpse. Then all the men helped the poor woman bury her baby."

Rod Perry: *The tenacity and depredations of the dogs provided the chief motivation behind innovation of one of the most useful structures and picturesque symbols of the north, the elevated food cache.*

Old Ben Atwater: "In winter the dogs were too precious to destroy, but they could cause so much damage they sometimes had to tether them. In the days before steel chain became readily available, when drivers needed to tie their dogs out they borrowed an age-old native technique. They drilled a hole one inch in from each end of a two-inch-diameter, four-or five-foot-long pole. Through each end-hole a rawhide thong was passed. One end of the pole was tied to a tree or other solid object with a loop that allowed the pole to swing or circle. The other end was snubbed so close to a loop snugly circling the dog's neck that any try to turn to gnaw the pole only pushed it out of reach or tightened the loop on his neck so tight that he gave up trying.

"On the trail, I never do, but after the evening feeding, some drivers practiced turning their huskies loose to choose their own place to bed down. They didn't wander far; they didn't want to leave the source of food. When the driver was ready to move out, well-trained dogs would come mill around in position near their own collar, ready to be harnessed."

———————

The Goin' Kid: "Me, I never turn workin' dogs loose for the night. It's a sure-fire way t' loose your lash-up. The hunger of a huskie for leather has no limit. You leave their moose-hair-stuffed, leather work collars where a loose dog can get at 'em during the night, they'll be eaten up in the mornin'. Most of us teamsters built our traces of webbing rather than leather to make 'em unappealing. But if you're not careful 'n' ever get a little splash of grease or feed soaked into 'em, the dogs'll eat those, too. Even when workin', the puncher'll have to watch his harnesses 'n' lines like a hawk. While stopped you'd better keep the animals strung out. If they bunch together they eat each other's collars. Sooner or later, even if you try t' stay watchful, you can't spend every second on the alert, 'n' they'll eat up their own gear. Out in the cold, a man works up a powerful hunger, but it's left far behind by the appetite of a dog.

"While campin' on the trail, a dog of one dog puncher friend of mine slips his tether. In the mornin' the animal's fast asleep. He shows no sign—other than being untied—

that he's been up to any shenanigans durin' the night.
But then my friend gets busy loadin' his sled and harnessin'
the team. Item by item he discovers the husky's night's work.
The dog's completely eaten up the driver's valued pair of large
gauntlet gloves, every inch of babiche from the laborious
lacin' of a snowshoe, a whole, long, braided whip includin'
part of the wooden handle, a long leather gun case strap,
the leather bindin' on a canvas container 'n' part of his
own harness."

Rod Perry: *Better supply lines from saltwater into the
Yukon Basin vastly improved the lot of not only the human,
but the canine population. A growing number of enterprising
individuals began catching, drying and selling salmon to the
dog drivers which allowed the animals to be summered over.
Equipment improved. Gold strikes on the west coast exposed
upriver drivers to Russian and Eskimo sled designs and their
ways of harnessing, arranging and driving a dog team.
Dog driving on the upper Yukon evolved and many of the
freighting methods of the early days faded out.*

Chapter 12

Winter Mail in the Early Days

BEFORE BETTER TRANSPORTATION opened up the country at the turn of the century, winter travel in and out between saltwater and the Yukon Basin was uncommon. Winter mail was even less common. One winter when Circle City was at its peak, only one dog team ventured to make the perilous trip of almost 900 miles out to Lynn Canal and just two made it in.

There were no official mail carriers. Mail stacked up down in Juneau and in the offices of the various trading posts along the Yukon River. Anyone traveling in or out who was willing to add to his sled load carried the mail at $1 a letter. Those sending letters accepted that there was a good chance that the mail would never reach its destination. The trip was so long and almost impossibly grueling that everyone regarded it as a gamble whether or not the traveler could even make it through himself, even with a skeleton load. With neither a broken trail, a source of resupply nor any chance of assistance in that desolate, uninhabited country, the journey often broke down into a driver's desperate battle for his very survival. When things became that grim, the first thing to go was the mail. Letters were usually burned to protect their private nature.

In the normal course of things, a miner might write a letter and, if he received a reply within a year or 18 months, he felt fortunate that the mail had made it both ways. Of course, answers to questions he had asked a year and a half before often puzzled him. Chances were good that not only could he not remember just what it was that he had asked, by that time he probably could not remember that he had asked anything at all.

Old, outdated newspapers that were brought in along with the mail were read for a fee to groups of assembled miners at each of the mail carrier's stops. By late winter, after having been cut off from the civilized world since the close of navigation the prior fall, the miners were so starved for news they devoured each sentence with all the voracity with which a ravenous man would eat.

Chapter 13

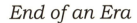

End of an Era

AND WHAT BECAME OF Arthur Harper, Leroy "Jack" McQuesten, and Al Mayo, the three "pioneer-pioneers?" When the first gold down from the Klondike aboard the steamships *Excelsior* and *Portland* broke the news of the fabulous strike to the nation, the eyes of those who gathered on the San Francisco waterfront to see the *Excelsior* in were no doubt riveted on the motley, disheveled men who staggered onto the dock under the weight of fortunes. Amid the excitement it is unlikely that anyone took notice of a lone, emaciated, gray-bearded passenger who weakly tottered down the gangplank. It was poor Arthur Harper. Sadly, the well-loved pioneer to whom so much was owed, not only by the rich men receiving the attention on the dock and the rest of those back north on the Yukon, but also the citizens of both Canada and the United States, had come Outside to die. He was broken physically from the many deprivations he had suffered and was racked with tuberculosis. Having willed his assets to his beloved family, he was headed for Yuma, Arizona, where he was advised the climate would be therapeutic. Four months later he would die there at age 62, not living to witness the gold rush he was so key in starting fully reach its zenith and not knowing his vision and faith and tireless groundwork would help spawn all of the major gold finds of the North that would follow: Nome, Fairbanks and Iditarod, as well as many lesser discoveries.

Also down the *Excelsior* plank strode burly, mustachioed Jack McQuesten with his faithful wife, Katherine, and their children. Correctly predicting that the first surge of poorly provisioned miners into the Klondike would precipitate a famine, he was moving his family out of the North Country.

It can only be imagined what the final, parting words were between Arthur Harper and Jack McQuesten, the two great "pioneer-pioneers" who had endured so much together.

That Jack McQuesten would be remembered by history variously as the "Father of the Country" the "Father of the Yukon" or "The Guardian Angel of the Miners" indicates the honor and esteem in which he was held. There was no more universally beloved soul in the entire North. One observer, William Haskell, stated, "He had come in contact with nearly all of the men who had risked their lives in search of gold in its frozen soil, and had ever been their friend. It has been said that he has outfitted, supported, and grubstaked more men, and kept them through the long winters when they were down on their luck, than any other person on the Yukon. Hundreds of men now on the river owe all of the success they have to his help, and they know it and appreciate it."

Some accounts claim that Jack McQuesten died in poverty. But other reports are more hopeful. They say McQuesten not only survived to see the trio's faith vindicated that the country held vast wealth, he invested in two of the richest Klondike claims. As well, his open-handed generosity finally benefitted him tangibly as he ended up owning shares in many claims whose holders he'd grubstaked. A multimillionaire, he moved his family to the San Francisco Bay area where he had come so often over the years to buy supplies for the partner's river posts. There they lived in their Berkeley mansion until Leroy "Jack" McQuesten went to his eternal reward in his 72nd year.

And Al Mayo? Of the three, he alone lived out his days in the North. He settled in the mining town of Rampart on the Yukon River where he lived as de facto mayor surrounded by his family until, in 1924, he died at age 77.

The "pioneer-pioneers" had opened the North. Almost all subsequent development of the interior and west coast of the entire northwestern subcontinent can be traced at least in part to their founding efforts.

From the Sled:
Progress Assessment and Perspective

Rod Perry: *Back at the beginning, you accepted my invitation to climb aboard my sled and travel with me on an adventure through history. You have proved yourself an able traveler and faithful companion. We are progressing. Our huskies have covered the miles and we are well along toward our destination: Iditarod. On long uphill pulls and through blizzards the pace has been slowed, then at times it has quickened when the way is level and hard-packed. Sometimes on the long and winding trail we have looked high into the night sky ahead and noted the Dipper. We have looked again and it was high on our right, then again and we saw it high on our left. Upon occasion we even had to turn on the sled to see it shining over our shoulder. But though the way turned briefly east, west, north or even south to best get us through the country, we trusted the trail and the trail has been taking us northwest. Yes, we are well on our way toward Iditarod.*

We pause by trailside to take stock of our progress. Looking back, the lock has been forced on the great, silent, unknown North. Indeed, it still largely remains a land of almost limitless wild expanses and great solitudes, only beginning to be explored. But the biggest obstacles have been surmounted and a base has been established. For 1,800 miles through the center of its vast heartland, the mighty river that drains it pulses with summer steamboat traffic. Winter activity along the broad thoroughfare far exceeds that of the past as settlement grows along its banks. A modern city of 30,000 booms with vigor and industry some 1,500 miles up from its mouth and serves as a transportation, communication and supply hub. A modern railroad regularly and rapidly hauls hundreds of tons at a time through ragged crags that not long before posed such an effective barrier to all but a man with a backpack. The key has been the creation of effective transportation corridors. Because of their development the eastern side of the country is no longer limited to piecemeal travel, communication and freight flow from the industrialized world in summer nor choked off completely in winter.

However, away to the west, far over a thousand trail miles distant lies a peninsula jutting into the Bering Sea that is yet largely unknown and unsettled, without any of the developed amenities we have just come from. And that is where our trail is heading. . . . on its way to Iditarod.

Chapter 14

The Nome Strike

THE SEWARD PENINSULA forms the westernmost promontory of the Alaska mainland. From the mountain above the Eskimo village of Wales, located at the tip of the peninsula, Siberia may be seen on a clear day only 60 miles distant across the Bering Straits. Though the Seward Peninsula coastline had been known since early Russian exploration, the interior lay dormant until 1866 when the Western Union Telegraph project established a route for its line across it and workers began stringing cable there. Crews had completed but 15 miles when the grand plan was abruptly aborted. Once the construction gangs pulled out, the inland area of the peninsula remained almost deserted for the following 30 years. As the caribou population was at a low ebb during that time, not even Eskimo hunters commonly ventured there. The few Americans who knew it considered it a worthless waste.

Although some prospecting took place resulting in small finds of galena and even gold, the region did not receive concerted attention until the worldwide excitement over the Klondike strike sent gold seekers searching every nook and cranny of the North. When news of Yukon gold swept San Francisco, Daniel B. Libby gathered a group that included Henry L. Blake, A.P. Mordaunt and L.F. Melsing and shipped north. They headed not for the Klondike, but for Niukluk River country on the Seward Peninsula where Libby had found gold as a young man more than 30 years before while supervising work on the Western Union cable project.

The Libby party found gold on a tributary of the Niukluk in the spring of 1898. Somewhat later that year, they made a fairly rich strike at nearby Ophir Creek which yielded $75,000 in gold. Another group that prospected nearby, included missionary Nels O. Hulteberg, mission teacher P.H. Anderson, mission doctor A.N. Kittilsen and Lapp reindeer herder Johan S. Thornesis. They staked claims nearby. The two groups established the Discovery and El Dorado Mining Districts. The town of Council came into being as the ensuing small rush brought miners to the area. However, the strike was relatively minor in the light of the blockbuster discovery that lay right around the corner, not far west.

Rod Perry: *As early as the New Years Day edition of the Nome Nugget for 1900, which would feature an article, "Who Discovered Nome's Gold?" there would be vastly varying versions regarding the who's and how's of the great Seward Peninsula discovery. Too bad the paper did not have on staff a highly skilled investigative reporter to cross-examine the principals while all of them remained close by and the happenings were still fresh. Alas, apparently no newsman of such skill and inclination was present. Besides, as usually happens during the tumult of many of the world's great events, people are too immersed in the happening itself to place much value on establishing of a correct history for the benefit of future generations. They are too physically busy to set aside time to write it. At the peak of Nome's gold frenzy, the sorting out of facts probably occupied a rock bottom rank on everyone's list of priorities.*

Henry Blake of the Libby party and the missionary, Nels Hulteberg, then looked farther west. Blake had been shown ore from the Cape Nome area by Toorig Luck, an Eskimo who, in midwinter, took them to his source. The two decided to return after the land thawed the following summer to more adequately prospect the area. Apparently, on another reconnaissance tramp across the mountains and tundra from Council to the coast west of Cape Nome, Blake gained information regarding gold in the area from Charlie Garden and his Eskimo wife, Sinuk Mary; These two formed a pair who lived a simple, subsistence lifestyle, hunting, fishing, gathering, and panning enough gold from the Sinuk River to buy staples when they took their yearly boat trip down the coast to trade.

Rod Perry: *Among a few others, the so-called Three Lucky Swedes enter into the story: Erik Lindblom [different reports spell his first name also as Eric and his last name also as Lindbloom] and John Brynteson, emigrants from Sweden, and Jafet Lindeberg, a half Lapp, half Norwegian. From there, the chronology and details of the movements of the principal discoverers of Nome's gold, as far as who went where, with whom, in what order, and what did and did not take place, are so laden with controversy and conflicting first-person testimony, remote hearsay and general gold-rush legend that, if Nome's leading newspaper could not correctly sort it out within two years of the strike, it should raise eyebrows if today anyone claims he has settled it definitively, more than 100 years after the fact. I am confident in stating that it remains a confusion impervious to time and attempts at clarification.*

Erik Lindblom, a tailor, had been plying his trade in San Francisco when the steamship *Excelsior* docked there with its cargo of Klondike gold. Smitten with the fever that swept the nation but lacking cash for passage, he signed as a seaman on a whaler headed north. It was not until the voyage was well underway that the Swede, understanding little English, found that his contract bound him to chase whales around the Arctic Ocean for two long years! Seeing his chance to break free when the craft anchored at Port Clarence (near today's village of Teller) to take on fresh water, the little tailor jumped ship and made a run for it. He had gained the North free of charge and by good fortune had avoided going to the Klondike, where most of the productive ground was already claimed. By sheer luck, the direction in which he ran would

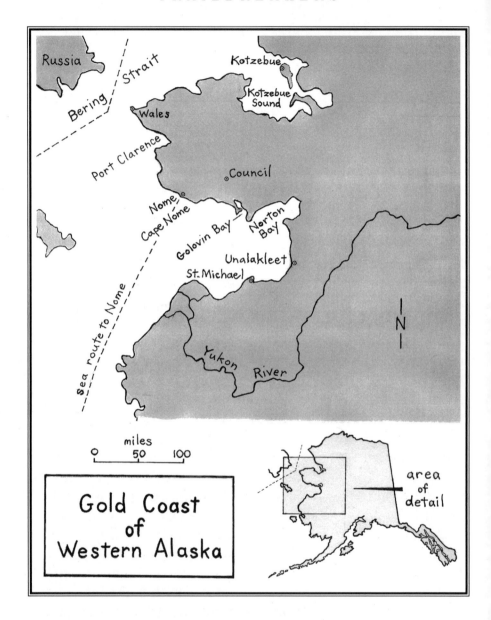

Russia

Bering Strait

Kotzebue

Kotzebue Sound

Wales

Port Clarence

Council

Nome
Cape Nome

Golovin Bay

Norton Bay

Unalakleet

St. Michael

Sea route to Nome

Yukon River

N

miles
0   50   100

Gold Coast
of
Western Alaska

area
of
detail

take him through the very area of his destiny, over ground
where he would soon become a discoverer of one of the
world's great gold deposits.

In a version of Nome's discovery attributed to him,
Lindblom later stated that during the flight south from Port

Clarence he ran into Blake as the latter visited the cabin of
Charley Garden and Sinuk Mary. There he was said to have
broken the news of the Klondike stampede to the others,
among whom he claimed there had been no prior knowledge.
In reality, the very reason the Libby party, of which Blake was
a member, had come north seeking gold was that news of the
Klondike strike had excited them.

Charley Garden and Blake gave the runaway directions
toward Hultberg's Swedish mission on Golovin Bay. As
Lindblom's way and Blake's return route to Council took the
same course for many miles before their paths divided, the
two were said to have traveled together. The way the story
goes, as they briefly paused to prospect around the area
Charley Garden described, Lindblom and Blake discovered
gold together, Blake panning while Lindblom looked over his
shoulder. Lindblom related that as soon as color began to
show in the pan, Blake dumped the contents, dismissing it
as insignificant, counting on Lindblom's lack of experience to
throw him off track and keep the naïve Swede from staking a
claim. Lindblom's story had them continuing together until
their ways split, whereupon he legged with all speed the
many remaining miles to the mission. There, he said that
he broke the news to Hultberg and others who were present.
The listening group included John Brynteson, who, according
to this version, first heard of Nome's riches (as, purportedly,
did Hultberg) as the exhausted man staggered in and semi
coherently began raving about finding gold. Brynteson was
said to have been the only one present to believe in and
desire to respond to the tailor's tale.

John Brynteson, like Lindblom, was a Swedish-born,
naturalized American citizen. A giant of a man for his day
at six feet, six inches, he had left the back-breaking physical
labor and low rewards of Michigan's coal mines in hopes of
unearthing something far more valuable in the North.
According to yet another discovery story, following the
aforementioned January trip taken by Blake and Hultberg

with Toorig Luck to the site of the Eskimo's find, in July the two white men boated back to the area, as planned. Their party included four others, among whom were the Swedes John Hagelin and Brynteson, both recently arrived at Golovin.

Later, Hultberg was to claim that he invited Blake and all four of the others. Blake, though, recorded that, as he did not want the party to be dominated by Swedes, he included two of his friends, Henry Porter and Chris Kimber (which apparently greatly angered Hultberg). If this did not confuse the record enough, Brynteson later stated that he and Hagelin were the ones who first organized the trip, and then invited Hultberg, who in turn included Blake and his friends.

As the party neared their Snake River destination at the end of their five-day voyage, a severe storm built. Striving to enter the river mouth, they swamped in the heavy surf. All of them made shore, but most of their supplies and gear were swept away.

Following the night around a bonfire, they made for the site Toorig Luck had shown Blake and Hultberg the previous winter. Reaching the watercourse later to be named Anvil Creek, four miles north of the future site of Nome, Blake and his friends stopped to work the lower streambed while Hultberg pressed on to look farther upstream. Later, when Blake hiked up to see how Hultberg was faring, the missionary, seeing Blake approaching some way off, hastily turned from his prospecting. Walking down to join Blake, Hultberg informed him that his investigation had drawn a blank, which eventually proved to be a blatant deception. By his following performance, it seemed obvious that Hultberg was hatching a plan to get everyone away from the area before anyone could stake. He would return to Golovin Bay and as soon as he could shake Blake and his cohorts, he would return on a better-equipped expedition including no one but the other Swedes and his mission friends.

The men, lacking everything required for a long stay, prepared to leave. Hultberg either actually became sick or

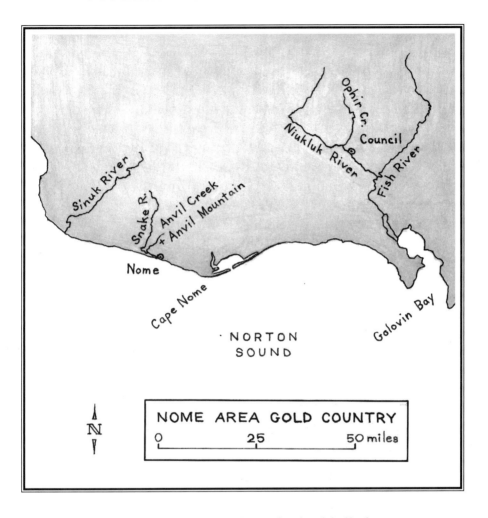

feigned illness, lying in a tent. Once he had lulled everyone, he sneaked away in the night, gaining a head start for his Golovin mission. Blake later testified that upon Hultberg's arrival there, the missionary (who actually was sick and exhausted by then) enlisted Lindblom and another "Swede," the Lapp-Norwegian, Jafet Lindeberg, gave them a small sailboat and a detailed map of exactly where on Anvil Creek to go and sent them off with not only his own power of attorney, but also that of every Swedish missionary in the Golovin area, wherewith they claimed, as Blake put it, "the whole country."

Prior to these events, Jafet Lindeberg had come to the North as part of the Reverend Sheldon Jackson's project in which 500 reindeer and 20 Lapp families were to be shipped in to teach Alaskan Eskimos how to tend and use the animals. Lindeberg had heard the siren call of Yukon gold and, chomping at the bit, had been looking for a way to get to Alaska. He had grown up in northern Norway where the Lapps brought their reindeer seasonally and knew just enough about the animals to gain a position in Jackson's enterprise. Just before he left Vardo, Norway, that winter, an old whaler was said to have found him and pressed the then-considerable amount of $2,000 upon the young man after securing his promise to "buy him a gold mine" with the sum.

By the time Lindeberg's services were no longer needed by Reverend Jackson, the project barge had taken him as far as the mission on Golovin Bay. By then he had learned that $2,000 was too little with which to purchase a paying mine. What it would buy, he correctly reasoned, was the necessary provisions and gear that it would take to look for one. He bought what the old prospectors called an "outfit."

Rod Perry: *There are, of course, many other versions of the Nome gold discovery. Another prominent variation had the Swedes, sent by Hultberg to work his claims at Council, overhearing Blake talking at the Libby party's cabin about the whereabouts of Nome gold whereupon they reported the information to Hultberg. But introducing other versions only makes looking into the issue all the more like staring into a tub of spaghetti. Whoever actually went where and did what with whom and when, remain questions, but it is fact that Eric Lindblom and John Brynteson teamed up, brought in Jafet Lindeberg for his outfit—food, clothing, shelter, tools, a few building materials, medicines—the basic supplies and equipment to live and work for a year—and the three sailed from Golovin Bay on a borrowed mission barge, leaving September 11, 1898 for the Snake River and Anvil Creek.*

Reaching the Snake, the trio of neophyte gold-seekers did not even seek a secure anchorage, but just splashed the hook as soon as they entered the unprotected river mouth. They grabbed a few essentials and quickly made their way over the tundra to Hultberg's spot on Anvil Creek.

Brynteson filled a pan from the stream bottom. In but a few moments of the usual swirling, shaking and tipping, the bottom of the pan gleamed. Looking at the others, he calmly stated, "We are millionaires."

A storm blew up that day. The Bering Sea off Nome is very shallow, allowing onshore winds to whip the waters into a seething fury. Exposed to the destructive breakers as they had left it, the barge with its contents was dashed to pieces and lost.

John Brynteson blew out of the site bound for Golovin to round up all the supplies he could quickly lay his hands on. As the huge miner quickly receded into the distance, his powerful, long strides must have given the impression he had donned the proverbial "seven-league boots."

Lindblom and Lindeberg threw themselves into building a rough cabin, staking a number of claims for the trio as well as their friends, relatives and backers. They quickly panned enough gold to buy winter supplies. In due time, presumably before Brynteson could return from Golovin, they, too, went back to the mission. The three quietly let Dr. Kittilsen and Gabriel Price know about their find.

Desiring to return to Nome in October, the men begged command of another of the seemingly endless supply of the Swedish mission's small craft, this time a schooner.

Rod Perry: *Though ice-up loomed, Hultberg would not allow them its use until they had built him a church! The finished product, complete with the steeple the missionary insisted upon, must have been some cathedral, slapped up as it was in but five days by the anxious-to-be-away miners, not one of whom possessed a lick of carpentry skills. With the structure* *finished, the men loaded the schooner with what remained of Lindeberg's original five-ton outfit, added to it some provisions purchased from a trader, piled on a small supply of lumber and weighed anchor for Nome.*

They beat the ice by just a few hours. The day after they arrived and laboriously wrestled the little schooner into the Snake, the river froze in solidly for the winter. Then the men bowed their backs to moving the cargo, as well as all of the driftwood they could collect for firewood, up to Anvil Creek.

With Dr. Kittilsen serving as chairman and Gabriel Price as recording secretary, on October 15, 1898, the miners officially created the Cape Nome Mining District. They went back and more carefully measured and marked the boundaries of Lindblom's and Lindeberg's original stakings. Then they located numerous other claims up and down Anvil Creek and the Snake River and on other likely-looking ground in the vicinity.

Leaving the ice-bound schooner locked in its winter moorage, the miners returned to Golovin by sled. Back at the mission, Gabriel Price sent a letter up to Council City hoping to quietly alert just a few of his closest friends. He bid them to slip away and stake claims at the new discovery but cautioned them to keep the information close to the vest to avoid a rush.

Rod Perry: *Leaning into the very teeth of a blizzard, miner after miner showed the suddenly shrinking burg a fast set of heels. However, one does not dare set off into an early winter storm on a round trip trek of 160 miles across the desolate Seward Peninsula for the purpose of locating and staking claims without having first assembled at least a skeleton outfit and loading the pile into a pack or onto a sled. That process would have been hard to hide. And be it mukluks, snowshoes or runners, they all leave tracks. Within one day of the letter's arrival, neither hide nor hair of even one Councilite could be found in the deserted town.*

The next stampede took place when Lindeberg and
Kittilsen arrived at St. Michael November 30 in quest of more
supplies and mining equipment, and their report swept the
town. That trading and transportation headquarters north of
the Yukon mouth held unsuccessful Klondikers who had
come downriver too late to catch the last ship to the States.
Most of them were so discouraged after finding that they had
arrived in the upper Yukon too late and that gold did not
simply lay under every rock, that all they could focus on was
boarding the next south-bound ship. However, among the
retreating hordes were numerous souls in whom still burned
a glimmer of hope. Another group in retreat that was
overwintering in St. Michael was made up of a small return
tide of prospectors whose enthusiasm, originally kindled by
Klondike gold, had led them on an unsuccessful search
around Kotzebue Sound north of the Seward Peninsula.
Mingling with that outgoing tide was a small flood of
incoming late arrivals from the States who had intended to
steam up to Dawson, but they had reached the Yukon mouth
too late to beat freeze-up. They would have to wait through
the long winter months for river shipping to commence the
following summer. Then there were the regular townspeople,
chiefly employees of the major transportation and trading
companies. The famed fight promoter, Tex Rickard was there,
too, running his gambling casino.

When St. Michael saw the Swedes' Seward Peninsula
gold, the place simply erupted. In frantic bedlam, men ran
to load provisions and gear on sleds. The big dog teams of the
trading companies pulled out first. Others, who owned no
dogs, raced hither and yon, making exorbitant offers for as
many Malamutes as they could secure. Soon, with the
almost-emptied town of St. Michael fading behind them,
these former inhabitants strung out in a lengthening line up
the coast, with the big, fast-moving teams stretching away in
the distance, the smaller teams following at a slower pace,
men pulling hand sleds helped by a dog or two behind them.

In the rear, stampeders in singles and pairs, necking their Yukon sleds piled with heavy loads, laboriously tramped toward Nome. All of the stampeders pushed their endurance to the utmost.

Rod Perry: *Shortly after the St. Michael stampeders had joined those from Golovin Bay and Council City, over 300 claims had been located inland from the Nome beach. With news of the apparently rich strike, almost everyone who heard of it quickly rushed to be among the first arrivals. Therefore, with the traffic flow almost entirely in Nome's direction, and with not many left with the wherewithal or inclination to head in the opposite direction, word did not quickly emanate outward. Someone, though, must have resisted the pull to become rich as Midas and started the news moving up the Yukon River Trail. By late winter, word of the find reached even Dawson, some 1,600 miles from St. Michael.*

The population and demographics of the Klondike area duplicated those commonly following all gold discoveries, major and minor. In the age-old pattern, once the stampede frenzy settled into the laborious process of extracting what had been claimed, for every fortunate finder who had struck it rich there were left multitudes who had struck out. Of those who came up empty, many returned home, their grand dreams of riches dashed. Of those who stayed, some with an eye for business saw the opportunity to "mine the miners" by providing services in high demand. They established sawmills, hotels, restaurants, laundries, gambling halls, brothels, freight-hauling businesses, newspapers and the rest of the infrastructure.

Rod Perry: *By far the majority who stayed, however, like Al and Alma Preston's old rest-home friend Anton Radovitch had in his younger days, settled for hiring out to the successful miners and business owners as menial laborers. As the* *venerable Mr. Radovitch told us, he was an example of this group, which being already positioned in the North, made up a restless horde ready to stampede to the next find.*

Not wanting to wait for more verified reports or for the opening of river navigation, some of the most optimistic, energetic and prepared individuals in the Klondike began the 1,400-mile-long odyssey to Nome. Like the exodus from St. Michael, those few with dogs led the way. Gold-seekers necking hand sleds, many equipped with sails, followed.

The first bicycles to be brought into the country were owned by a number of Dawsonites. Several owners, dubbed "wheelmen," began furiously peddling toward Nome on the hard-beaten Yukon Trail. Several hundred miles downriver, a native noted a strange site far out on the river. Not being able to see the thin lines of the bicycle so far away, all he could make out was the hard-to-explain posture and action of the cyclist. Shaking his head in amazement, he reported, "Crazy man go down river, sit down, walk like devil!"

Throughout the winter, gold-seekers, a few at a time, continued to arrive in Nome until by breakup as many as 1,000 populated the site. Most of the latecomers who made up the majority, looked around and, finding that the nearby creeks and gulches had been staked end to end, assumed to their frustration that all of the worthwhile ground had been taken. Adding to the maddening situation, with so many claims registered by the earlier arrivals through power of attorney for friends, relatives and backers who were absent, a high percentage of the locations were not even being worked. To the general anger was added a catalyst which greatly multiplied the confusion: more than a few claims were recorded for "phantoms," who did not even exist. The very last straw that broke the back of their sanity was that many of the claimholders were of foreign birth. Some, like the Lapp reindeer herders, were thought to be aliens. Others had so recently immigrated and gained U.S. citizenship that they spoke little or no English and were lumped with the supposed aliens as foreigners. Tempers flared.

Rod Perry: *The angry latecomers should have spent their energies combing the adjacent country in quest of new diggings. Though they trailed the very earliest stampeders, they had still arrived well ahead of the huge rush that would burst upon Nome as soon as shipping opened. As would be proven later, some of the very richest placers in the country were yet to be found, and many of them lay waiting virtually within sight of where the anger of the restless crowd boiled.*

In Canada's Yukon, the Mounted Police wonderfully upheld law and order. However, on the U.S. side, America had so ignored its farthest north possession that only the sketchiest of enforcement existed. In practice, what law existed depended upon the inhabitants themselves in the form of miner's meetings. In the very earliest days, in the 1880s and early 1890s, when few inhabitants lived in the upper Yukon Basin, almost everyone knew one another and largely coexisted in a spirit of good will and cooperation. They were sifted by the very nature of the difficulties of entry into the country and survival once there so that almost to a man, they were of high ethical character. In such a setting, miners' meetings had worked superbly. However, with the great gold strikes and the arrival of more people, the quality of the institution had deteriorated terribly. The Nome strike was so lawless compared to the Canadian Klondike, it was said that, just shaking his head, God had pulled out on the last boat.

The angered Nome population seethed. A small core of connivers hatched a plan to use the general unrest to their personal advantage. They called a miners' meeting intended to revoke the ownership of existing claims. Unbeknownst to the assemblage, the ringleaders had stationed cohorts on the heights several miles from Nome to watch for a signal fire from the town. The smoke would tell them that the meeting had made all of the so-called "foreigner's" claims illegal and that they were to swoop down and restake them.

However, they had not counted on the quick action and bravery of Lt. Spaulding, sent by superiors to Nome with a detachment of 10 troops from the barracks in St. Michael. Smelling a rat, he attended the meeting. Yes, indeed under federal law it was certainly not lawful for aliens to own claims unless they could show they had officially filed their intent to become citizens. However, no one had taken the effort to gain proof that the Swedes and Lapps had not at least filed that intent. Indeed, for all anyone knew, they may have already gained full-fledged citizenship with as many rights as those who fanned the flames of unrest. Therefore, the most illegal thing taking place was the way the miners disregarded due process and took the law into their own hands. So as soon as the motion was made to declare existing claims null and void and throw the country open to stake over from scratch, the lieutenant not only moved for adjournment, upon his order his troops cleared the hall with fixed bayonets.

Chaos had been averted, but order may not have prevailed for long had it not been for an amazing occurrence. Some versions say that it was one of Spaulding's idle soldiers, others say that it was a man sitting on the beach convalescing from an ailment, but whoever it was, someone took up a pan of beach sand, swirled it and found gold. Excitement over gold distributed seemingly endlessly along miles of beach sand available equally to everyone diverted attention far from the Three Lucky Swedes, the Lapps and the other "foreigners." As fast as Nome's idle population could appropriate almost nonexistent boards with which to fashion rockers they forgot all about claim jumping and swarmed to the beaches.

——◆—◆——

Al Preston: "Rod, that discovery of the Golden Sands made Nome unique as a double gold strike. First you had the rich upland placers where only those owners of staked and recorded locations or their assignees had rights to mine them. Then, second, there was the open-to-entry beach access where anyone was free to just pick a spot, set up a rocker and begin mining. The two-in-one strike once more set the North on end. It grabbed worldwide headlines like the Klondike strike so recently before it."

———•—•———

Salt water resists freezing more than fresh water and so it melts first. Moreover, tides and wind break up sea ice before river ice is ready to go out. Therefore, in the late spring of 1899, the pack ice opened and ocean-going ships filled with gold-seekers from the United States arrived in St. Michael well before the first riverboats could start up the Yukon. When word of the Nome find swept the fleet, instead of disembarking to take river steamers up the Yukon to the Klondike, where they realized they would be latecomers, almost every gold-seeker chose to remain aboard and continue up the coast to the new, ground-floor opportunity.

Upon reaching Nome, the deep-hulled ships had to stand offshore in the roads. Shallow-draft lighters then brought men and their outfits in to where the new arrivals waded through the surf right into the amazing beach mining pandemonium. Hurriedly offloading their outfits and securing them above high-tide level, they, too, dove headlong into the frenzied activity.

Far away, over 1,400 miles by sea and river from the golden sands of Nome, thousands of disconsolate Klondike have-nots eked out a mere living, working odd jobs in town or wielding pick and shovel helping wealthy claim-holders become richer. Their former visions of golden fortunes dashed, many were too destitute or too embarrassed to return home. As soon as the ice went out on the Yukon, verified reports steamed to the inland goldfields that the Nome find was much, much more than the unverified rumor that had reached Dawson by dog team earlier. Indeed, it portended to be the richest find, by far, yet made in Alaska. With confirmed news of the amazing new strike where, in truth, everyone could find gold, and as soon as those river boats could turn around, over 8,000 Klondikers crowded aboard and formed a huge outgoing tide, headed for the new El Dorado, Nome.

Al Preston: "Rod, the Nome beach was everyman's strike. It was so easily reachable compared to the strikes of the far interior. No long overland trips packing of a ton of gear over tortuous mountain terrain. No boat building or running deadly rapids. No need to be first or be left out. Just sail from Seattle, be lightered in with your gear, land on the Nome shore, and immediately begin mining the very beach sand. It was the richest tidewater diggings ever discovered.

"I'll tell you about the Nome Beach show. The beach gold was extremely fine, mixed with ruby sand. Miners dug holes between the high and low-water lines. They shoveled the gold-sand mix into rockers. Rockers were portable, easily moved between locations. A man worked his hole as long as he could stay with it. Each incoming tide displaced everyone and smoothed over the beach. As soon as the tide began receding, mining followed it out. Claims could not be staked below the high tide mark so men could only hold their spot by working it; the moment they quit, anyone was free to move in. For mile after mile the beach was a teeming swarm of 'hind ends and elbows' and swinging shovels. And often, swinging fists.

"Now, the owner of a rich gold claim inland could leverage himself and extract great wealth by setting up a more permanent operation including a crew of menial wage earners and elaborate systems for moving the overburden and separating the gold. But no one could get rich on the beach because miners were limited to one shovel length on either side of their rocker. That held every beach operation to a one-man show. And the tide made even those tiny "claims" temporary. But everyone who really worked at it could make excellent money on Nome's beach.

"Legally, the beach diggers were supposed to stop at the high-water mark. That's because holders of legal inland claims had staked everything from the beach edge of the tundra going inland. However, that didn't stop beach miners from burrowing under the tundra whenever they could get away with it. They dug under by thawing the frozen ground with driftwood fires.

"Leave it to those crazy miners! Here and there, Eskimos lived in sod igloos along the tundra just above the beach. One time a miner burned and tunneled his way so close to an igloo that his smoke came up through the floor and suffocated a bedridden old man. Another time, occupants of another sod house and the miner both were startled when the igloo floor dropped into a tunnel!"

———◆—————◆———

Naturally, it became almost impossible for the Three Lucky Swedes and other inland claim holders to keep hired laborers working their placers. After all, the going wage they paid was no more than $15 a day, while the beach miners could expect anywhere from $25 to $300 for a good day's effort. But lack of available labor soon became the least of the upland miner's concerns.

Rod Perry: *A new threat to displace them appeared on the scene, by far more dangerous than the disorganized rabble they had faced at the recent miner's meeting. What Nome's rightful claim-holders (particularly the newly naturalized Scandinavians) needed was security, relief from the threat of future mob actions. But what they got was a sinister, new conspiracy to "relieve" them all right, relieve them of their claims!*

District Judge Arthur H. Noyes and a small contingent of lesser officials sent to their rescue by the U.S. government did indeed keep their claims from falling into the hands of the mob. However, that protection was not for the Scandinavians, but for the shyster Noyes himself and his corrupt government crooks.

During "resolution" of claim-jumping that had become rampant, while supposedly sorting out the phantoms, foreigners and usurpers from the legitimate claim-holders, these outlaws in officials' clothing took advantage of the chaos and deluge of litigation. They twisted the law into a scheme to gain control of Nome's rich inland placers not for the rightful owners but for themselves. They counted on the great distance from higher government oversight to allow them to get away with it.

The Swedes and other lawful claim-holders found themselves up against the very might of the federal government. And the U.S. Army, which had so recently heroically saved their interests from the mob, now had to back the court in removing them from their claims.

If Noyes were not of despicable-enough character, he had come north accompanied by a treacherous, powerful civilian friend in the person of Alexander McDonald who held considerable influence over the judge. McDonald had friends in some the highest offices in the nation, including the presidency.

The Nome government lawfully (per their twisted interpretation) set about hiring crews and mining the rich ground for themselves. Day in and day out, as gold disappeared from their placers on pack horses taking it to the safes of Noyse, McDonald and their cronies, the maddened miners could do nothing but stand by wringing their hands. Since the shysters themselves were the highest authority in Alaska, and the Army was duty-bound to back up their actions, seemingly nothing could be done to stop them. Nothing locally, that is.

Charles Lane had bought out the interests of many of the original prospectors, making him perhaps the most powerful miner in the Nome Mining District. When the government deviants usurped his holdings, they fouled the wrong man. Lane, a man of wealth and political connection, was also a man of high moral character and action. Determined to stop the outrage not only for his own benefit but also for that of the rest of Nome's displaced miners, he slipped out of Nome in a small boat. The most accepted version of his getaway had him hiding in an empty barrel as the boat took him out to a southbound ship ready to weigh anchor.

Once he had made port on the West Coast and traveled by fast rail to the seat of his political connections in the East, Charles Lane's solid reputation and testimony soon got the process rolling that would clean up Nome, albeit only after the scofflaws ignored the federal government's initial mandate to right their wrongs. Eventually, Washington had to forcefully send in replacements. The crooks were ousted, given their legal comeuppance (though, it was widely agreed, not nearly stiff enough for the law they had thumbed their noses at and the financial harm they had caused) and the miners of Nome were returned to their claims. However, only a fraction of the treasure robbed from their placers ever found its way back into the rightful hands.

While the shyster Judge Noyes and his crooked pals were plying their shenanigans, every ship plying saltwater the nearly 3,000 miles between Nome and Seattle carried more news to the waiting media proclaiming the availability of Nome's gold. By the time the sea ice froze in the fall of 1899, the population of Nome stood at 10,000 people. Numbers froze around that level through the usual near-stoppage imposed upon transportation by winter conditions. But soon after the opening of navigation in 1900, the population of the Nome area exploded to between 20,000 and 30,000 gold-seekers.

The tent city became a temporary metropolis, stretching for miles along the beach. The more permanent structures of Nome proper went up almost as fast. Because building materials were shipped in so easily, right up to the beach in front of town, and sometimes within a few yards of their destination—some entire buildings even came north in prefabricated sections—the city sprang up almost overnight.

◆━━━◆━━━◆

Albert Hulse Brooks: "Remember that I explained how overflow from the Klondike spurred other gold strikes and development in Alaska? The overflow of which I spoke was both in men which were drawn North and excitement which stimulated exploration and development. That very Klondike bubbling over led directly to the Nome strike."

Next, the flow of Dawson-to-Nome stampeders really escalated winter use of the River Trail down the Yukon to Kaltag and heavy trail traffic between Kaltag and Nome.

Additionally, the timing of the first large wave of miners to the Nome strike, 1899, fortuitously coincided with the partial completion of the far-away White Pass and Yukon Railway. The swiftly developing transportation system from Skagway to Dawson was ready to fulfill Nome's winter communication needs.

◆━━━◆━━━◆

Old Ben Atwater: "The railroad builders finished the 56-mile-long stretch through the Coast Range as far as Carcross, Yukon Territory, that year. We dog-team carriers were then able to pick up the mail in the Yukon interior. That was an absolutely monumental advancement! It relieved us of having to go all the way to the coast to get it like we used to. Sometimes that mountain passage used to be impossible, but even when we could do it, the mountain crossing had always been grueling and dangerous."

◆━━━◆━━━◆

Alfred Hulse Brooks: "During the 1900 summer, construction crews completed the final 69 miles of the railroad from Carcross on into Whitehorse, the permanent end of steel. Coincidentally, in that summer of 1900, Nome's population hit its all-time peak. The timing was perfect. Because the Nome stampede did not become full-blown until two years after the main Klondike rush, the lag provided the Canadians with just enough time to finish their all-season railway connection."

———————•———•———

At the turn of the new century, Nome's post office boasted the largest general delivery address in the United States. Letters addressed to stampeders named Johnson alone filled several boxes. For a population of 20,000 to 30,000 the need for year-round mail delivery was monumental. Once ice-up closed shipping, the newly completed railroad allowed Nome to look east for its mail.

That year of 1900, the United States Post Office deemed the difficulty of the trip had been reduced enough, that they were persuaded to let contracts to run weekly mail from Dawson to the golden city on the Seward Peninsula. That decision was based upon several factors. First, completion of the railway to Whitehorse had further decreased the distance over which everything had to hauled by beasts of burden. Second, the rest of the way ran virtually level almost the entire, nearly 1,800-mile distance. Third, numerous gold-strike towns, native villages, steamboat wood-supply pick-up points and missions spread along the way could act as shelter and supply havens. The distance was long, but a city of 20,000 – 30,000 people could not very well go seven months a year cut off from communication with the rest of the world. And there was no other way, whatsoever.

Rod Perry: *Of course, just because mail left Dawson bound for Nome on a weekly basis, it did not mean that a letter leaving Dawson would reach Nome in one week!*

Old Ben Atwater: "Not many winter travelers or much winter freight went all the way over that long mail route.

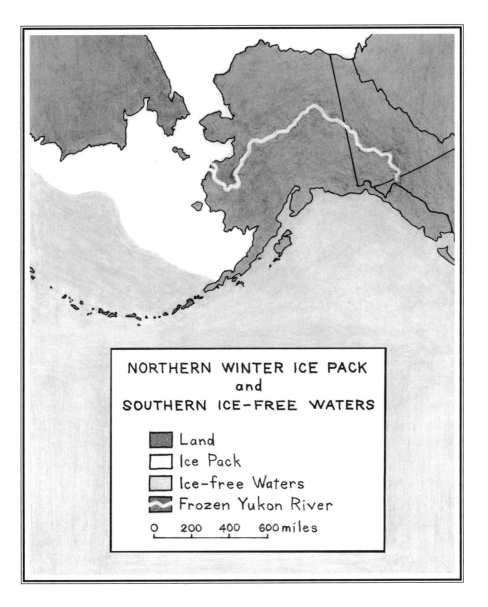

NORTHERN WINTER ICE PACK
and
SOUTHERN ICE-FREE WATERS

■ Land
□ Ice Pack
□ Ice-free Waters
≈ Frozen Yukon River

0   200   400   600 miles

After all, from the wharf at Skagway, through the Klondike, down the Yukon River Trail, over the Kaltag Portage and up the Bering Sea coast to Nome is about 1,900 miles. But if someone wanted to get in or out of Nome badly enough, he at least had some way to do it. Or maybe he just had to have some absolutely necessary item that couldn't wait for ocean

191

shipping the following summer to bring it cheap and easy right to Nome's beach. If he had to get it in that bad, at least penetration of the railroad through the mountain barrier into the interior in the far-away Yukon Territory made it possible. That is, if the traveler or shipper was willing to pay the considerable price."

———————

When the final upgrade came two years later with the building of the 12-foot-wide Dawson Overland Trail from Whitehorse to Dawson, the use of horse-drawn sleds and wagons over the stretch allowed freight by the ton to be brought into Dawson from the head of steel during winter. This new method of transport further reduced the distance—trimming 330 miles—over which mail, travelers and freight had to be transported in dogsled-sized loads.

In winter, everything heading the remaining 1,400 miles to Nome left Dawson and traveled down the Yukon River Trail pulled by sled dogs. The great "Inland Highway," already an ancient native travel and trade artery prior to Russian contact, had seen traffic gradually increase year by year. First it grew with the coming of white fur traders, later by miners and suppliers working the lesser strikes prior to the Klondike discovery. Then it further swelled with the great Klondike rush, the river seeing a huge boom in the summer steamboat traffic between the river mouth and Dawson. Winter traffic, however, remained relatively quiet until the fabulous Nome strike dramatically turned 1,100 miles of its frozen back into a hard-beaten thoroughfare. There were but two great cities in the north and the Yukon River Trail led most of the way between them. Not only dog teams carrying mail, freight and passengers, but hikers and even some on bicycles coursed downriver to get to Kaltag, within 290 miles of Nome.

At the Athapaskan Indian village of Kaltag, the Yukon bends closer to the sea than at anywhere else until nearing

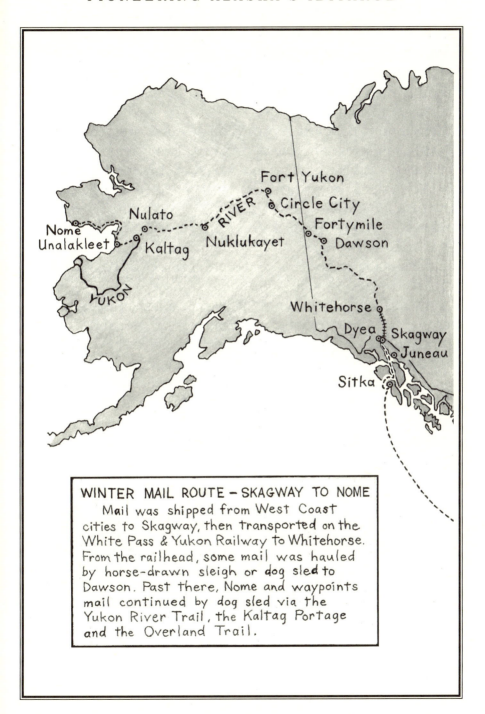

Fort Yukon
Circle City
Nulato
RIVER
Fortymile
Nome
Nuklukayet
Dawson
Unalakleet
Kaltag
YUKON
Whitehorse
Dyea
Skagway
Juneau
Sitka

WINTER MAIL ROUTE — SKAGWAY TO NOME
   Mail was shipped from West Coast
cities to Skagway, then transported on the
White Pass & Yukon Railway to Whitehorse.
From the railhead, some mail was hauled
by horse-drawn sleigh or dog sled to
Dawson. Past there, Nome and waypoints
mail continued by dog sled via the
Yukon River Trail, the Kaltag Portage
and the Overland Trail.

its mouth. There, fortuitously, lies a gentle, 90-mile-long pass, an ancient trade route, through the mountains. For untold generations, the Yukon Indians and Bering Sea Eskimos from the Unalakleet area had used the portage to rendezvous with one another.

The instant population explosion at Nome created a heavy demand to move mail, freight and travelers from the Yukon River over to the sea and up the coast to the Golden City by the shortest, easiest, safest route practicable. The Kaltag Portage offered a direct trail, and the way became a heavily trafficked highway. Upon leaving the Yukon Trail at Kaltag, Nome-bound travelers and freighters had about 290 miles to go, crossing over the portage, then following the sea coast north and west to Nome.

Nome still had no other viable winter mail and supply option. Anything coming into Nome over that terribly roundabout United States-Canada-United States course via Dawson had to come around 1,900 miles by rail and beast of burden after leaving Skagway on the Southeastern Alaska coast. It was a long, laborious, complicated way to haul a passenger, freight or a letter. Nomites wished for something more expeditious. They wouldn't have long to wait.

From the Trail:
Trip Progress Assessment

———— ◆ ————

Rod Perry: *Our long and winding trip through this Northland history has progressed to about the halfway point. When you climbed on the sled at my invitation, you didn't know your guide. By this time, however, we've become familiar, travel-hardened companions. Sharing a sled will do that.*

Now the trail toward our destination takes a turn that might surprise someone not familiar with the route: Geographically, the trail doubles back on itself! But not to worry, it is only geographical. Even though our sled will take us many hundreds of miles back over the same physical trail that brought us from the Klondike to Nome, historywise, storywise, it is as if we're not retracing our steps at all, but are heading into untraveled country. Trust the trail! It may twist and turn and even double back, my friend, but trust the trail. It takes us to Iditarod.

Before we turn the team, let's orient ourselves. The North has been unlocked. It booms in the east as the city of Dawson in Canada's formerly remote Yukon Territory has exploded into being. At its recent peak, the city on the Klondike boasted a population of 30,000. It is served by an efficient, year-round transportation system. The world is gripped in the age-old magnetism of gold. The yellow metal's irresistible force has drawn men from almost every nation on earth, not only to the Klondike, but to other regions of the North where they hope to unearth their own bonanza.

Now the great find to the east has precipitated Alaska's own blockbuster discovery. The North Country's West has blown wide open with the great strike at Nome! The Golden City has reached a peak population equal to that of Dawson at its recent height. Commerce, travel and communication between the two centers and through to "America" has caused a great increase in traffic up and down the Yukon River Trail.

But Nome has no close winter transportation link to ice-free shipping waters. That means, for seven months of the year, if it is to connect to the industrialized world, Nome must depend upon the Canadian transportation system to winter shipping. That constitutes a distance so far away that it approximates two-thirds the breadth of the contiguous United States. Because that so crimps Western Alaska's vitality and potential, it heads us surely toward Iditarod.

To get there, however, we must first turn the team back to a midway point. It is yet undiscovered and unnamed, but by the time we arrive it will be called Fairbanks.

Hold tight to the driving bow. Can you feel the energy of our spirited team transmitted through the tug lines, back along the towline and through the hickory of the sled to your mittened grip? Winding though the way might take us, our faithful huskies yet run strongly and our runners track true to the trail . . . toward Iditarod.

Chapter 15

———◆———

The Fairbanks Strike

IN THE SUMMER OF 1898, while the throngs who had arrived too late in the Klondike filled menial jobs or established service industries around Dawson, and while the Three Lucky Swedes were staking their claims at Nome, a savvy Italian prospector named Felix Pedro came upon the richest gold-bearing stream he had ever found. He did it while lost, out of food and trying to make his way back to Circle City. He marked his find but kept going, driven by hunger. Though he later searched for it, he never relocated "Lost Creek."

Rod Perry: *In Alaska, miners had widely prospected the country sloping north toward the Yukon River and had found gold in many drainages. Pedro and some others no doubt knew that Arthur Harper, two decades earlier, had found traces along the Tanana River, which gathers waters draining south away from the Yukon. They concluded that a good chance existed that over the height of land separating the Yukon from the Tanana drainage, stream beds running south toward the Tanana probably held gold as well.*

Al Preston: "You know, Rod, there are several versions of how Fairbanks was discovered. Old Ben Atwater couldn't very well run his mail route during summer so he went down and helped construct some of the first buildings in the town. He knew Pedro, Gilmore, Barnette, Wickersham, all of them. Here's the way he told me it happened."

———◆———

Old Ben Atwater: "In 1901, Pedro and his partner, Tom Gilmore, left Circle City with two pack horses. They wanted to look over the country around a Tanana tributary almost 200 trackless miles away, the lower Chena River. After miles of good going above tree line, they dropped down into heavy timber. That necessitated a lot of hard cutting to work their way through. Headway was slow. After a month afield, they began to run low on grub.

"A group of four miners, each with a horse packing provisions, left Circle City following Pedro and Gilmore. They hoped the pair's trail might lead them to a find, perhaps Lost Creek. With the trail already cut, those followers made excellent time. They swiftly caught up. Usually Pedro would have been unhappy over such a development. In that case, however, he and Gilmore were glad to partner with the others. It meant a resupply of food and a tripling of trail-cutting help.

"The group climbed Ester Dome to overlook the country. Scanning the Tanana Valley, the men saw distant smoke. Through binoculars Pedro watched as the steamer, *LaVelle Young*, turned back from trying to negotiate a stretch of the Tanana. It had been made too shallow by unusually dry weather. He saw them turn into the mouth of the Chena River. They ran a short distance upstream, and anchored. Pedro and the boys decided on the best course to reach the boat. Then the party dropped to lower elevation and camped for the night."

Rod Perry: *The majority of gold seekers involved in every major rush were newcomers, ignorant of how to effectively look for gold. They set out either under the impression that gold lay everywhere for the taking or assumed that finding a deposit was purely a matter of dumb luck.*

Experienced prospectors, however, tended to be fair amateur geologists; they intuitively knew what areas and land forms held the most promise and possessed an uncanny ability to visualize what lay below the surface. Many, when looking for

placer deposits, based their analysis upon the model of
a biblical, worldwide flood. Where would heavy, loose gold
most likely settle, they asked themselves, first amid the racing
floodwaters of the deluge and second, during rapid drainage
as the tremendous volume ran off in torrents?

Felix Pedro was a very competent prospector. However,
little did even he guess, so covered by wind-blown sediments
and hidden by thick vegetation as it was, that under his
very feet as he walked and camped on Ester Dome lay
unbelievable riches. Reportedly , the Ester Mining District
would eventually yield more gold than all of the other strikes
in Alaska combined.

Old Ben Atwater: "When they got to the *LaVelle Young*
the next day, they found the boat's owner and E.T. Barnette
arguing about offloading the cargo. The owner had contracted
to haul a large supply of Barnette's goods up the Yukon from
St. Michael, then go up the Tanana. Barnette planned to set
up a trading post way farther up river at Tanacross. Low
water had stopped them. Under terms of their contract, if
they couldn't reach Tanacross, they were to offload as far
up as they could make it.

"Pedro convinced Barnette that gold prospects in the
locality looked promising. Felix told him that other Circle
City prospectors were in the country round about. He said
to Barnette that if he were to establish a supply center at that
point on the Chena River, he could expect business. Pedro
explained that prospectors already in the country would
begin to base out of his place rather than waste themselves
on a several hundred mile round trip back to resupply at
Circle City. Furthermore, he said, other prospectors who had
stayed away because of the difficulty of the trip could be
expected to come. Barnette offloaded there, and the City of
Fairbanks had its beginning."

Two years later, in 1902, about 16 miles northeast of Barnette's post, Felix Pedro struck gold on Pedro Creek. Soon after, prospectors discovered Ester and a number of other locations close by. The main town of Fairbanks exploded in population, several outlying communities sprang up, and the new city became the territory's economic center. When Judge James Wickersham established his court in Fairbanks, it became the governmental center of Alaska as well. As with Dawson and Nome, the boom necessitated both summer and winter movement of vast quantities of supplies as well as in-and out-bound mail and travelers.

Since it was miners headquartered out of Circle City on the Yukon River who had made the Fairbanks discovery, the way between the two communities became well-beaten. Fairbanks business and government interests quickly improved the early prospectors' trail. Their approximately 200-mile-long branch trail gave them access to the great Yukon River Trail, the well-developed transportation line into Yukon Territory, Canada so that during winter, like Nome, they could take advantage of the dependable Canadian transportation system through Dawson. But Fairbanks interests wanted something shorter.

———

Alfred Hulse Brooks: "Back in 1898, well before the Fairbanks discovery, the United States government had seen the potential profit if a share of traffic to and from the gold fields could be attracted to course over U.S. soil. As well, they reckoned that if they were to stimulate development during a time when the imagination of the continent had been captured by exiting headline news flowing out of north almost daily, they could turn around the entrenched national mindset that the purchase of 'Seward's Icebox' 30 years before had been money thrown away on a worthless, frozen northern wasteland. Congress directed the U.S. Army to send exploration teams to Alaska to locate a practical way to the Yukon gold fields over U. S. soil.

"In command of the party exploring the Copper River was Lt. William Abercrombie. He had concluded that a trail should be built to the Yukon River not up the Copper, but beginning at the port of Valdez on Prince William Sound. Valdez was already beginning to grow as a port of entry and supply base for prospectors bound for the Klondike over a route discovered in January 1898, that led up the Valdez Glacier. Passage over the ice was extremely exhausting and treacherous, and many had lost their lives in the crossing. Abercrombie advocated an alternative route."

In the spring of 1899, construction of a pack trail had been started. Government work crews were supplemented by hundreds of destitute stampeders who had failed in their attempt to strike it rich in the Klondike. Now desperate for a way to earn passage to escape the North, they had hired on for $50 a month plus board. Progress on the 5-foot-wide pack trail had been so rapid that by fall, the first 40 miles including the most difficult section up the Keystone Canyon and over Thompson's Pass, had been completed. Ahead of the finished trail, 93 additional miles had been surveyed and cleared.

Alfred Hulse Brooks: "Coinciding with Abercrombie's 1899 work, the U.S. Army had also been progressing north in its laying of the Washington-Alaska Military Communication Army Telegraph System, termed WAMCATS. The next year, the last section of line was laid over Abercrombie's route and extended to Fort Egbert, at Eagle, Alaska, located on the Yukon River close to the Canadian boundary. In the process, WAMCATS workers improved Abercrombie's pack trail."

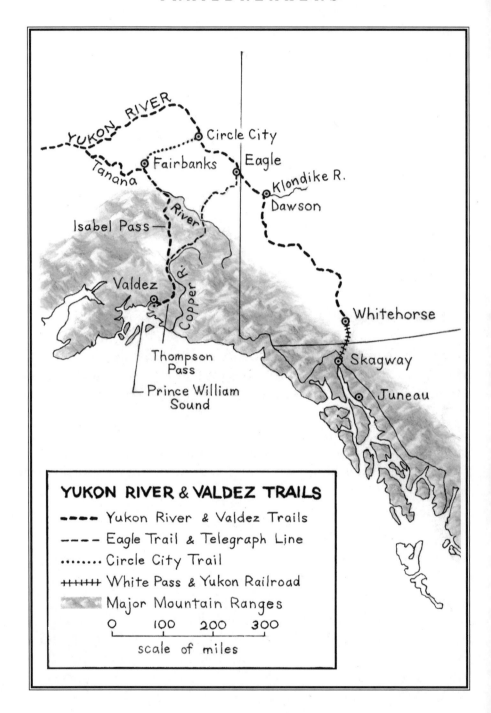

YUKON RIVER

Circle City

Eagle

Tanana

Fairbanks

Klondike R.

Dawson

Isabel Pass

River

Valdez

Copper R.

Whitehorse

Thompson
Pass

Skagway

Prince William
Sound

Juneau

YUKON RIVER & VALDEZ TRAILS
- - - - Yukon River & Valdez Trails
- - - - Eagle Trail & Telegraph Line
.... Circle City Trail
++++++ White Pass & Yukon Railroad
▨▨▨ Major Mountain Ranges

0   100   200   300
scale of miles

Rod Perry: *An energetic, young lieutenant worked on the project and, in the process, fell in love with Alaska and with driving sled dogs. Lt. Billy Mitchell would go on to gain fame as one of the pioneers of military aviation and would eventually go down in history as one of the country's great military thinkers and innovators. His portrait as a young dog driver hangs in the Dog Mushers Hall of Fame in Knik, Alaska.*

Alfred Hulse Brooks: "Fairbanks quickly grew in size and importance as a governmental and commercial center for the Alaska interior. As that took place, the town needed a shorter, more efficient winter supply line than going over 1,050 miles through Yukon Territory to Skagway. Simultaneously, the prevalent spirit of nationalism drove the city to push for an "All American" transportation line of its own through United States territory. To accomplish those ends, Fairbanks interests put in a trail heading south to link with the recently completed Valdez-Eagle telegraph and military pack trail. Their connecting trail ran up the Tanana and Delta Rivers, over the Alaska Range through Isabelle Pass, and down the Gulkana River to Gakona Junction. The port of Valdez boomed to serve Fairbanks."

Rod Perry: *For over two decades, until the completion of the Alaska Railroad, virtually everything that would enter Fairbanks during winter would come in over the 409-mile-long route.*

Once Fairbanks established its Valdez connection, much of Nome's winter transport shifted from running over the Canadian system to the new route. To reach Nome, it first moved from Valdez north over the Chugach and Alaska Ranges to Fairbanks. It then traveled west down the Tanana River to the Yukon and down the established Yukon River Trail-Kaltag Portage-Coastal Trail route. Though Nome valued it as an all-American route that was indeed shorter than going through the Klondike, the reduction in distance was somewhat offset. The Valdez-Fairbanks Trail had to cross two mountain ranges, whereas from Whitehorse the trail ran essentially level. At best, both trails were thought to be too time-, energy- and money-sapping. Nomites still yearned, like Fairbanks had yearned before them, for a shorter, more economical winter route of their own.

Rod Perry: *The problem keeping Nome from doing what Fairbanks had done in constructing a winter transportation route of its own to ice-free saltwater was two-pronged. First, the distance and physical obstacles separating Nome from the nearest ice-free port were far greater than what Fairbanks had faced. Second, whereas Fairbanks (like Dawson before it) had constructed its saltwater link while its boom was at its peak, Nome's cry for a trail did not become full-blown until its great boom was over and its population had diminished to one-tenth of its gold-rush size. Therefore, the length and degree of construction difficulty combined with a decreased demand forced Nome to continue to depend upon the winter transportation systems of Dawson and Fairbanks.*

From the Sled:
Progress Assessment and Overview

—————•———•—————

Rod Perry: *My friend, our journey has taken us to the northern subcontinent, paused on its east side, rushed across its wide span to its west coast, then reversed direction to travel halfway back to our beginning. You and I have traveled so many miles together through this northland history that trail and camp procedures now come second nature to you. By now we're quite a team.*

We've witnessed development of the transportation corridor to the east that so effectively served to develop the Dawson region. That Canadian system was vital, difficult as the great distance made it, to Nome's early life and growth. From Nome, our odyssey has taken us back eastward to Fairbanks. Even though the heartland city grew up hundreds of miles closer to Dawson and could thereby take advantage of transportation through the Canadian town far more economically than could Nome, Fairbanks saw the advantages of an even shorter transportation system connecting it to its own year-round port. It moved quickly to establish a trail link to Valdez.

Switching to use Fairbanks' new heartland corridor for its winter needs also gave Nome a significantly shorter route. Even so, Valdez to Nome is still a long, long trip.

It wasn't long before visionaries in Nome could see the possibility for an even shorter way of their own to winter shipping. However, as things stood, the great volume of transportation between the three major population centers of the North had so developed the winter trail system connecting them that it would only be by some tremendous, overriding developments that a new trail system could be created with enough logistical and economic advantages to induce professional dog drivers to abandon the established system and adopt a new one. That would be especially true when it came to allowing carriers submitting bids to haul U.S. Mail over a new route a chance to win contracts in competition with bidders using the well-established Yukon River route.

And so now, my friend, our journey must proceed back toward Nome. Our goal? To look into one of the most remote and almost unexplored regions left in Alaska, the distant country between the Upper Iditarod River and Susitna Station through the mighty Alaska Range. We'll see if such a trail is possible.

While I manage the sled, go on up and help our trusty leader turn the team. Once again, we're reversing direction and heading back over the Yukon River Trail toward Nome. Don't grow disoriented at this repeat turning about; instead, keep your eyes on the horizon. As before, this back and forth repetition is only geographic. As far as the trail through our history is concerned, we're once more headed into new country. Rely on your guide; he knows where he's taking you. Trust the trail. The way now slopes downhill. We feel new energy coming back through the sled and by the set of the dogs' head and ears we know that our surging huskies sense something ahead. Hang on! They pick up speed, taking us surely, now swiftly . . . . toward Iditarod.

Chapter 16

The Railroad Makes a Good Start

IT HAS BEEN SAID AMONG MARINERS that, along with New York and Sydney, Australia, Alaska's Resurrection Bay is one of the three most perfect natural harbors in the world. Seward, formally founded in 1903 at its head, also happens to be the closest ice-free port to Nome.

Coincidentally, a route running from Seward offered the best combination of an excellent, ice-free harbor, a gentle gradient and a buildable road bed for a railway through the Alaska Range to Alaska's commercial and governmental center, Fairbanks.

Not only the burgeoning city of Fairbanks, but also mining activity around Kantishna and other significant gold discovery sites located north of the Alaska Range depended upon transport along the Yukon River. On the south side of the range, prospecting and mining were thriving on the Kenai Peninsula and making starts in the Susitna Valley but had only primitive means of winter supply. Though all of these locations were far flung, a railroad from Seward north to Fairbanks would pass close enough to all of them to serve them. Even those strikes in locations along the Yukon and its tributaries that the route would not pass close to would benefit, for such a railroad would at least bring shipments much closer and greatly shorten their winter supply lines.

Those obvious advantages stimulated an investment group to begin construction of the Alaska Central Railroad. It started in 1903 from Seward. Although the effort went

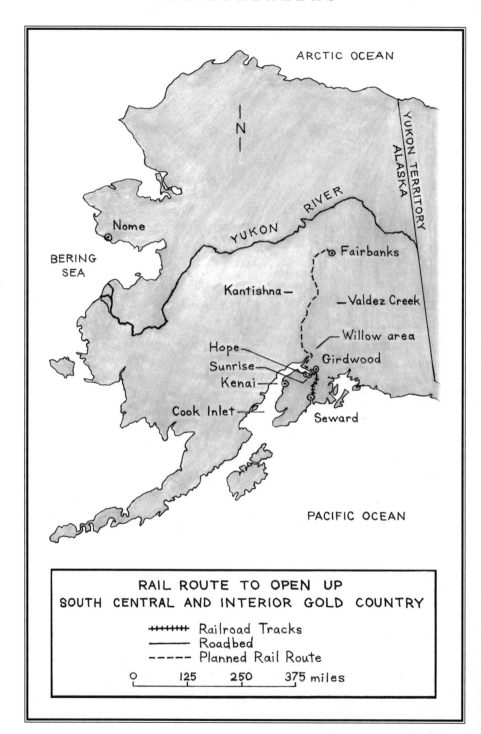

ARCTIC OCEAN

N

YUKON TERRITORY

ALASKA

Nome

YUKON RIVER

BERING SEA

Fairbanks

Kantishna—

—Valdez Creek

—Willow area

Hope—

Sunrise—

Kenai—

Girdwood

Cook Inlet—

Seward

PACIFIC OCEAN

RAIL ROUTE TO OPEN UP
SOUTH CENTRAL AND INTERIOR GOLD COUNTRY

++++++ Railroad Tracks
──── Roadbed
----- Planned Rail Route

o   125   250   375 miles

broke in the financial panic of 1907, crews had constructed 72 miles of road bed and laid 52 miles of track before the venture ceased operations.

Rail service or no, the quality and strategic location of its harbor quickly vaulted Seward to prominence as the main, year-round deepwater port for the Cook Inlet region. And though it was not used for train transport during Alaska Central's bankruptcy, the rail bed made a serviceable winter trail for 72 miles out of Seward. It particularly aided travelers where the railroad had blasted tunnels and built trestles to gain passage through an otherwise impassable stretch of cliffs and canyons in the Kenai Mountains. From the end of steel on the Placer River, the road bed extended another 20 miles, nearly to the mining activity at Girdwood on Turnagain Arm. Between Seward and Girdwood, foot travel became common and dog teams sometimes made the trip.

From Girdwood, the Crow Pass cutoff trail north over the mountains received less frequent winter use. Occasionally, mail carriers, miners and trappers entering or leaving the Matanuska and Susitna drainages during winter went that way. The path climbed almost too steeply to be negotiated over the pass and then dropped sharply into the Eagle River valley. Near the present town site of Eagle River, the trail rejoined the Alaska Central Railroad pack trail, which followed the future right-of-way that surveyors slashed out far ahead of crews preparing the road bed. The path led past the native village of Old Knik (present day Eklutna.) It continued around upper Knik Arm, crossed the Knik and Matanuska Rivers and what is now called the Palmer Hay Flats, not far from the future town of Wasilla, mile 160 on the 470-mile way to Fairbanks in the far away interior.

The developing railbed and pack trail gave northbound travelers a great advantage. Prior to that construction, gaining the Matanuska-Susitna Valley country in winter by foot or dog team had been terribly imposing. But the work of the Alaska Central crews presented those who had a compelling enough reason to go that way a doable, if difficult trail.

Chapter 17

Nome Desires its Own Winter Trail
Midway Gold Strikes Add Demand

FOLLOWING NOME'S BOOM, and once the easily discovered and mined upland placer and beach gold played out, Nome followed the predictable pattern of all of the great discoveries of the north: Mining went from being *labor intensive,* at the first stages during which gold was available with simple hand tools and manual labor, to *capital intensive.* It required capital to buy, set up and operate expensive hydraulic systems featuring huge hoses and nozzles to wash out and sluice less concentrated deposits that were harder to access, buried as they were under deep overburdens. Floating dredges, behemoths that cost even more to install than hydraulic systems, could economically operate where gold was even deeper and even less concentrated. Equipment replaced men.

As the tens of thousands of boomers folded their tents and left, Nome settled into an economically sustainable extraction mode based upon systematic development of the gold findings. The resident population dropped to a mere tenth of its gold-rush swarms. Therefore, though Nomites continued to yearn for a shorter, more economical winter route of their own to link to ice-clear saltwater, the demand of the few thousand remaining dwellers could not counterbalance the cost of building and maintaining a trail of such length and difficulty.

As already seen, all of the gold strikes in the Far North were linked by winter trails. Obviously, they were linked as well by the flow of humanity (often the same people) that ran from one discovery to the other.

During the Nome rush, the entire length of the Yukon River, the great Highway of the North became a hard-packed thoroughfare in winter as streams of the leftover "have-nots" of the Klondike Rush surged downriver from Dawson, using more than 1,100 miles of the river's frozen back on their way to the Seward Peninsula diggings. Then, with the Fairbanks strike, many "strikeouts" from Nome rushed back up the Yukon Trail into the interior. As well, some still in the Klondike stampeded down the Yukon River Trail to the Fairbanks discovery.

Alfred Hulse Brooks: "During the next few years immediately following the three great gold rushes, the north's primary population was situated either in Dawson, Nome or Fairbanks or in villages along the trail system of the Great Inland Highway. The three big towns were the only centers north of the Alaska Panhandle that could boast of anything qualifying as a significant infrastructure. Almost all winter travel, mail and freight moved along the connecting trails between the three bustling centers as well as along the branch trails which ran to minor strikes and habitations away from the main trunk line. The point is that the major population and activity of the North was confined to an area connected by Yukon River Trail system."

Rod Perry: *Thinking about Nome's hoped-for trail of its own, and looking at such a trail from both ends, it was plain that much of the route was already in place. From Nome, the first 300 miles as far as Kaltag had long been a heavily beaten thoroughfare from years of traffic back and forth between Nome and Fairbanks and Dawson.*

Alma Preston: "Here's the way things stacked up from the Seward end, Rod. The Alaska Central Railroad railbed and survey trail gave occasional hikers and dog drivers a great start. Following that beginning, just after crossing the Matanuska River the most-traveled trail left the railroad right-of-way to head off on its own. It went west across the Hay Flats until it gained the north shoreline of Knik Arm (of Cook Inlet.) The first objective of this branch trail was the tiny settlement of New Knik (now Knik.) In those days it consisted of George Palmer's store, an Alaska Commercial post and a few log buildings. Knik was visited by sporadic summer shipping. It served as a supply point for the nearby area.

"The second destination of the branch was Susitna Station, another Alaska Commercial post. It was a steamboat stop about 35 trail miles beyond New Knik. It was a snug little community nestled on the Susitna River. The population had grown to maybe as many as a couple of hundred people, enough to call for a school. There were perhaps 100-plus men prospecting and trapping in the region. It was really hard to keep track of such a shifting population. Su Station had gained its importance as a supply center serving that thriving little group of people plus the round about Indian population. Our trail from Seward had its terminus there. There was a fairly well-beaten trail out to a minor strike near the Yentna River. Other than that, beyond Su Station were found only the thin threads of snowshoe and hand sled tracks. They were left by individuals fanning out here and there to lonely prospects, traplines and native habitations and hunting grounds."

Rod Perry: *Obviously, from Seward north to Susitna Station, a distance of 200 miles, the trail was established. It was rough and lacking amenities compared to a trail such as the Yukon River Trail, but established. By the years right after the turn of the century, the dog teams of Seward pioneer and mail contractor Alfred Lowell and his son-in-law "Colonel" Harry Revell (Alma's employers) were carrying winter mail over the distance a few times each winter. Though seeing but a small fraction of the traffic that coursed back and forth over the winter thoroughfares of the Interior, and though the way*

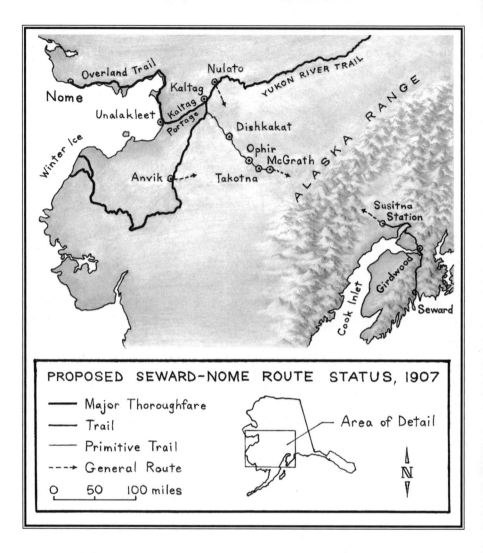

PROPOSED SEWARD-NOME ROUTE STATUS, 1907

——— Major Thoroughfare
——— Trail
——— Primitive Trail
---→ General Route

0   50   100 miles

Area of Detail

N

*featured little in the way of roadhouses or resupply points
except the Knik and Susitna Station posts at the far north
end, the way at least was defined and used enough to feature
a trail base of sorts that was intermittently rebroken.*

*With both ends in place, 300 miles from Nome down
to Kaltag and 200 miles from Seward up to Su Station, the
obvious, logical question must have been, why not just finish
the middle portion and connect the ends?*

Chapter 18

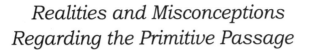

Realities and Misconceptions Regarding the Primitive Passage

Rod Perry: *One hundred years after Nomites were no doubt wondering why someone didn't simply join the hard-beaten first 300 miles south from Nome to the rough, but established 200 miles north out of Seward, some unknowledgeable Iditarod Trail Sled Dog Race writers and embellishers of gold-rush trail romance would claim that some ancient, native trade trail or system of such trails led from Cook Inlet over Rainy Pass into the upper Kuskokwim and on to Kaltag. They indicate that the Seward—Nome Trail essentially just fell in and coursed over it.*

Did the natives of the trail route at one time or another travel every foot of the country over which the trail passes? Of course. Did they trade with one another? Absolutely. But were any of their trails of a character to constitute ready-made, connected, serviceable platforms for a direct trail between Susitna Station and Kaltag? Any close look into the situation strongly indicates that that is a most fanciful stretch.

Al Preston: "You know, there was a guy up in Nome just up from America. He poked around a few months and all of a sudden he becomes a self-proclaimed authority on the country. He took up demand for the trail as his pet cause. He kept sounding off to everyone who would give him half an ear that the Indians had easy-to-follow trails they used to trade with each other, paths we could use to make it through.

"Did he just take us for fools? Did he think we were blind and stupid? If Indian trade trails through the middle country had been in place before gold-rush times, that would have meant the existing north and south ends of our longed-for Seward-to-Nome Trail were already joined! If so, all that travelers, mail carriers and freighters of the gold rush era would have had to do was to jump on the paths laid out for them and whistle for your team to get going. Convenient!

"Does it make sense that we Nomites would have wished so longingly for something that was already there? If what he claimed was true, wouldn't you think a few thousand residents and the professional trail builders would have quit pining for our connection and, long before, just started using it? The fact is, the guy was daft; there wasn't any such useable trail system.

"I'm no anthropologist but I had a friend, Mishka, who lived at Dishkaket. I spent quite a lot of time with him in the Bush. Within their own area his people knew the country like the proverbial backs of their hands. The various bands did trade with one another, but almost always only just with the band adjacent to them. The Kenai or Tyonek Indians would come over and trade with the bands living closest on the other side of the mountains. Those groups would trade with people farther along, like Mishka's group, the Innoko people. He said they were so involved subsisting they only took time to hook up with another group to trade maybe once a year; some years they didn't meet at all. One trip over the country a year does not call for building much of a trail.

"They were such tremendous woodsmen anyway, through trees and brush they hardly needed more of a cleared path than a lynx. They had priorities that far outweighed using their time to clear boulevards. If they could just readily make it through, the barest trace served. From what I found, Indian trails back then often went around obstacles we'd cut out. The result was, they were usually too narrow and twisting to be of much use for us. Mishka and the others I knew didn't have to get long sleds with heavy loads behind big dog teams through so, of course, they didn't require wide swaths and long, sweeping turns.

216

"Another thing was that trails that took Indians like Mishka here and there in the quest for food did not always lead directly between travel destinations of whites. We had different objectives. Winding through the country from a berry patch to a caribou fence to a fish trap was a lot different than bee-lining from one gold camp to another. Even their trade routes didn't give us what we needed. For instance, Mishka's people, when they traveled from over around McGrath north to the Yukon, their main trail came out at Nulato. From McGrath, we whites needed a main line toward Nome to come out at Kaltag. Last, our long trails needed to cut straight across the lands of several different peoples in one, unbroken line, something their trails didn't.

"Rod, when I came into Nome from mining, I had a little cabin I rented from a man named Ross Kinney who lived next door. Ross worked for the Alaska Road Commission. That's a branch of the Army that built and kept up roads and trails. One day at the post office, Ross and I heard that blowhard newcomer spouting off his Indian-trade-trail-through-to-Cook-Inlet bunkum. Like the rest of the crowd picking up mail, in fact, and like everyone else in Nome, Ross just rolled his eyes at that numbskull. He and I talked about it on the walk home."

Ross Kinney: "Preston, that guy must have never traveled the country in winter beyond the beaten track. If he had, he would know that it doesn't matter how many *summer* Indian trails crisscross the area. He obviously doesn't have any idea that through forested or brushy country, they have to be well slashed out to leave a defined corridor, while in open country, they have to be clearly marked well above ground level with something such as tripods that stand above the deep snows so that once the trail gets buried it remains distinguishable from the rest of the white expanses. An Indian knows his own country so well he can come through on snowshoes walking right above a summer trail he knows is there. All the summer trails on Planet Earth? If they're invisible to us, they're as good as nonexistent to the musher.

"There are a few other reasons I could elaborate on but they all add up to this: No Indian trail between Susitna Station and Kaltag was of the least use to us for our purposes.

"Now if that know-it-all would use the word *route*, that makes more sense. Some of the Native *routes* were useful. When the first white explorers like Spurr and Herron came over, they needed to know which drainages led them where they desired to go, and where the passes were and so forth. The Indians knew that perfectly and showed the way. But as you know, you can be traveling up the right valley but if you don't have a defined trail suitable for your method of travel, you're in for an ordeal. On Herron's exploration his men worked themselves to the bone struggling to move his pack train ahead only about three miles a day over a good share of the route. Although they were led by local Indians and going the right way, there was no trail through the woods and brush so they had to laboriously cut one.

"I've told you that with all the pressure the people of Nome are putting on the Commission, the inside thinking is we expect that the big brass are going to have to eventually respond and send us out to look the country over. You can make book on this, Preston, Colonel Goodwin and I have investigated it as thoroughly as the limited information allows and this is the layout: We have a fair idea of the way that proposed Mail Trail needs to take. When we get out there on the ground we're confident that all we'll truly find between the established north and south sections is nothing but a general *route*. A mere route is no good at all for commercial purposes like running the mail. What mail teams will require is a trail, and a good one at that, if it's to beat out the present Valdez—Yukon Trail system. Such a trail would have to be built completely from scratch."

JUST AFTER THE TURN OF THE CENTURY, at a time when the citizens of Nome first began calling for their own trail, there existed no white habitation over the entire distance between Kaltag and Susitna Station. Both the vastness and the fastness of the great wilderness between Kaltag and upper Cook Inlet made not only spanning the distance with a trail a formidable construction project, but even if built and presented to travelers as an option, travel over those (roughly) 400 miles with no source of resupply would present such a daunting barrier that few, if any, would so much as consider trying it.

Rod Perry: *Indeed, it truly would have been far, far easier for a Nome-bound musher sitting in Seward to catch a ship to Valdez and go all the way around over the Valdez and Yukon Trails. Even though he would be adding hundreds of miles to his trip he would find a hard-beaten trail with roadhouses and abundant provisioning conveniently spaced along the way. But while travel from Seward just as far as Susitna Station stretched a traveler a good deal, passage over the utterly uninhabited landscape between Su Station and Kaltag would require not only a full complement of camp gear, but also breaking trail at a snail's pace over the 400 miles. Such travel would take such a staggering mountain of food as to make such a trip nearly unthinkable. Counting on game tended to be iffy. No matter how much they wanted a trail, all rational minds had to dismiss such a project.*

But as if fate had ordained Nome's trail, a progression of seemingly unrelated developments began to take place that, as they stacked one upon the other, began to make the project increasingly worthy of consideration. Looking back, the first had been the 1903 commencement of construction of the Alaska Central Railroad. Although there had already been a trail out of Seward to the sizeable mining operation

of Girdwood on Turnagain Arm of Cook Inlet, it had been
a tough one in its ascents, descents and its winding course
roundabout through the mountains. The construction of the
railbed gave travelers an almost level roadway progressing
farther north with each year's work. And on beyond the
roadbed, the surveyor's pack trail that ranged north ahead
of construction greatly reduced the traveler's difficulty.

Then in 1904, the year after rail construction crews began
pushing steel out of Seward toward the Interior, hundreds of
miles to the northwest a steamboat churned far up the great
Kuskokwim, second largest river in Alaska. At a point where
the Takotna River flows into the Kuskokwim, related villagers
from Nikolomas, Big River, Telida and distant Lake
Minchumina had a traditional gathering place. There
Abraham Appel nosed his boat up to the bank and
established a trading operation. Not only was Appel's location
well-situated for native trade, it was well-placed because it
sat at the head of practical steamboat navigation on the river.
While he must have carefully considered those advantages in
positioning his site, it was only by pure luck that his chosen
location would be made far more strategic and profitable by
upcoming developments he could never have guessed were
right around the corner.

Appel's establishment happened to be close to the best
natural course for a Seward-to-Nome trail. Not only that, but
he had landed at the perfect position, about midway along
the proposed route. Nome's earliest trail visionaries could see
that the post offered wonderful future prospects as a strategic
shelter and supply waypoint. For lucky Abraham, a main trail
running through would obviously bring him even more
commerce than his trade with the far flung Athapaskan
villages his business had been founded upon.

But Abraham Appel's post was only a tiny pinpoint
in a great, desolate wilderness. Looking from there toward
Kaltag, though dotted with numerous seasonal canoe camp
sites of Old Shagluk, Holikatchuk, Dimenti, and Dishkaket

villagers, few white men had ever trodden the country of the Upper Innoko that lay between the Yukon and Kuskokwim Rivers. Since the Russian Lieutenant L.A. Zagoskin had briefly traversed it 60 years before, it had been almost untraveled and all but ignored by whites. It therefore remained largely unknown.

From Appel's post, looking the other way toward Susitna Station, the distance and difficulty of the country was so utterly daunting that Abraham probably shuddered to think about it—if indeed the slightest consideration of even the barest possibility of connecting with civilization in that direction so much as crossed his mind!

Rod Perry: *Though Abraham Appel probably harbored no thought of anything but maintaining his remote outpost for native trade, unconnected to civilization by anything but his summer supply by steamboat, his lucky streak accelerated.*

Only two years after Appel founded his trading post, in September of 1906, four intrepid prospectors—Thomas Ganes, Mike Roke, John Maki and FCH Spencer—boated up the Kuskokwim and hiked over the native portage to probe the remote upper Innoko River country. Stopping for a lunch break on a small Innoko tributary, Thomas Ganes tried a test pan and found gold.

After ascertaining that the find was substantial, the men hiked back to Appel's. Finding him short on supplies, they went down the Innoko to the Yukon. Sledding back with supplies in the winter of 1906–1907, they met a few others, telling them of their Ganes Creek find. Word spread, resulting in a rush of a few prospectors from the Kuskokwim side. By spring, news of the discovery worked its way out to the Yukon village of Nulato. From there it was telegraphed to Nome and Nome spread the tidings.

Over 1,000 stampeders rushed to the area, coming mainly from Nome and Fairbanks and the villages along the northern trunkline trail that ran between them. Ophir was struck in February of 1908 and other nearby discoveries quickly followed. The boom created the instant settlements of Ganesville, Moore City, Ophir and Takotna.

Rod Perry: *By great good fortune, Appel found himself close to the new strikes; none were farther than about 50 miles distant. In a country as big as Alaska, especially in the midst of one of the most desolate stretches of almost uninhabited wilderness in that wild territory, 50 miles was considered practically next door. Appel was right there, set to serve as a supply and transportation hub and his post grew in business and population.*

Prospects of the hoped-for Susitna Station to Kaltag trail continued to ascend. His outpost had originated as the only lone pinpoint of white activity for hundreds of miles. At first, his simple trade with the Indians had created but an almost unnoticeable stirring amid the silent spaces. But these instant boom towns suddenly interrupted the quiet of the vast wilderness with a growing little beehive of civilization. Now, instead of only Appel's lonely pinpoint, being rather lost out in the middle of the great wild between Seward and Nome, the small gold rushes transformed the area into a humming center of human presence and energy. This center was 50 miles across and expanding.

During the expansion Peter McGrath was sent into the area by the Nome court to keep order as sheriff and serve as U.S. Commissioner to record claims for the mining district. Upon arrival he noted Appel's perfect location and built a trading post of his own at the site. The place came to be called "McGrath's." The general area of the strikes became popularly known as the "Inland Empire."

Al Preston: "Rod, I knew Pete McGrath in Nome, and a fine fellow he was. He told me how it was when he first got to the Kuskoquim and how things developed in the early years.

Pete McGrath: "Coming from Nome, I had been interested in a mail trail through to Seward, in fact, highly interested. Mr. Preston, when I got to my location and got my feet under me as far as getting my bearings and a feel for the lay of the land, something became pretty plain to me. This understanding gave me all the more reason to construct my store at Appel's site. Boosting chances that a main trail might be built through the country, the first Inland Empire strikes were roughly aligned north out of our location right along the general course of the hoped-for trail. That spread the first third of the roughly 150-mile-wide distance between my place and Kaltag with connecting trails and rough settlements offering at least minimal shelter and supply. At least to the north that great wilderness stretch was being filled in.

"With these Inland Empire strikes, this area of the Upper Innoko that had been so ignored and almost unknown began to see exploration, travel and development aplenty. In summer, the only way to travel the country is by water, so stampeders used the Innoko River. It was hundreds of winding miles up that snake of a river from the Yukon but quite a few came that way to reach the diggings by steamboat or by poling boats or canoes. The briefest glance at the area reveals that with so many streams, sloughs, lakes, ponds, muskegs and swampy lowland, you'd find it unfeasible to travel overland in summer. But for seven months a year the reverse is true. When everything freezes solid, boats don't work so well. Trails do.

"We had some crude trails put in by the gold-seekers themselves. Planning, as far as building the best trail for future use, was not part of the thinking. From various points along the Yukon they were madly scrambling during the stampedes, trying to get to the new strikes the fastest way they could They just kind of beat the trails in as they went and they serpentined almost as much as the Innoko. One went in from near Anvik and another roughly followed the old Indian route from Nulato, but the main way emanated from Kaltag.

"As I mentioned, in their dash to get there, no one took the time to survey and cut the way to create the best possible permanent trail for the next traveler or for an eye toward future travel. You've been out there, Mr. Preston, and you know how such overland travel proceeds if no one has gone ahead to break trail. You just expediently follow meandering ways of least resistance. If the yards ahead show a relatively clear path, even if it takes you left of the desired direct line of travel, then that is the way to go. Then the next time you see a clear way that deviates right, you take it to make up for the left. You watch your compass, and a good navigator finds it's pretty easy to keep to the desired line of travel in an overall way. But man oh man, does it ever make for a snake of a trail.

"The next person, he wants only to get to the new diggings himself. He finds someone's broken trail and just follows his tracks. He might do something, cut out a log or lop off a branch, but he doesn't take much time to make the trail better. And no one in his right mind is going to be breaking a brand-new, straighter route when he has a hard trail base laid down for him. Therefore, the trails in from the Yukon were very rough and terribly tortuous. Even after the stampedes settled down into the extraction mode, travelers and freighters just continued to use the crooked trails to connect the strike with the Yukon River Trail and the Kaltag Portage. You can do most anything if you have to badly enough and dog drivers managed to make it in with mail and freight. But it was far from the kind of trail professional contractors needed.

"Like I said, the most heavily used trail out to the Yukon went between Ophir and Kaltag. Mr. Preston, how's this for falling into the hands of destiny? Along the trail lay the old Indian village of Dishkaket. It was inhabited by about 100 natives and a dozen or so whites. By 1907 it had two stores, a saloon and a roadhouse. Importantly, like Takotna, Ganesville, Moore City and Ophir, Dishkaket was strategically placed: it lay close to a direct line from my place to Kaltag. Not only that, but, roughly speaking, it broke the distance between Ophir and Kaltag in half. That meant that the 150-mile distance out to Kaltag was approximately divided into thirds, with two points offering shelter and supply out in the middle. How's that?"

———◆———◆———

Ross Kinney: "Making it even simpler for residents out there, someone with an eye for trail business slapped up a roadhouse near the mouth of Kaiyuh Slough. That divided the Dishkaket-Kaltag third in half. So by 1907 that whole 150-mile-long wilderness segment south from Kaltag had been relatively tamed. It was interesting to watch the whole segment just incrementally kind of fall into place on its own. Of course, we expect the Road Commission will get ordered to go out sometime and unkink it, maybe even completely replace it. But for now it'll get them by as is."

Rod Perry: *Yes, the McGrath's—Kaltag leg had been established, although not in a form someone with any other choice would have taken. One guy joked that it was so crooked that going around a tight corner, he ran into a musher coming the other way and to his shock realized the other guy was him! While that trail was indeed crude and overly long, the segment no longer offered any great obstacle; at least a beaten trail of sorts was in and reachable waypoints offered shelter and, much more importantly, resupply. Whenever travelers found that combination—shelter and resupply—they could go more lightly loaded, not having to carry much in the way of camp gear and dog and human food.*

That left only the stretch between McGrath's and Susitna Station as the last remaining trailless gap along the proposed Seward-to-Nome route. And what a gap it was!

Al Preston: "Standing out at Pete McGrath's front door shortly following the Inland Empire strikes, it was one thing to travel—or consider doing trail upgrade work—northwest out to Kaltag. But, Rod, turn and look southeast. Before you, that great, wild expanse toward Susitna Station was a horse of an entirely different color! Before you was the Alaska Range and hundreds of miles of trackless, empty wilderness."

———•———•———

Pete McGrath: "Until Ganes struck gold, no more than maybe a half dozen or so white men had ever been known to have made the trek between my post and Su Station. It wasn't merely almost untraveled; no, that way out was barely known at all to white men.

"Even after our Inland Empire gold strikes when that way of access became somewhat more understood, it remained merely a broad, vague description of wilderness landmarks. Once past the village of Nickolomas, nowhere along the way was there so much as one hint of human presence. That meant, of course, there was not the slightest chance of resupply. Looking from the door of my post east, if you were touched enough to even give going out that way the slightest consideration.... well, it's easier, Mr. Preston, if I just read you what I once wrote in my journal about it. 'All that lays before you to the east is a vast, trackless waste characterized by primeval forests, the winding courses of frozen rivers featuring every peril inherent of river ice, hundreds of miles of deep, untrodden snow, and a towering, imposing mountain range. It is a trek only seriously considered by fools!'"

———•———•———

A musher (from the French word meaning march) bound for Cook Inlet from the supply center of McGrath's on would understand that he must head up the Kuskokwim to where it flowed out of the mountains. By inquiring around, he could gain descriptions of landmarks and estimations of distances to accurately guide himself away from the main stream and up the correct side drainages that lead either to Rainy Pass or Ptarmigan Pass. The trekker would have learned that, after crossing the height of land, his descent would take him to a succession of Susitna River tributaries until he reached the main Susitna and then, Susitna Station.

Within those broad parameters, the path one took to get there was whatever way he snowshoed in himself. Immediate directional decisions were up to the individual. He took whatever way he judged as the clearest, least-obstructed way that he could see just ahead as long as it conformed close enough to the line of the general route.

Starting from the McGrath end, it was not all that simple to even find the way. The Kuskokwim is so wide, with so many braided channels, islands and side sloughs that two miners heading for Seward in the winter of 1908 became lost for 12 days before relocating the main channel. One superbly competent explorer opined, as he surveyed the Dalzell River below Rainy Pass, "I saw how one could easily get lost (at least temporarily) if coming upstream, as the canyons are so deceptive and the country so big." A major U.S. government expedition sent out to explore and map the country failed to even see several prominent rivers a later official reconnaissance party did record. The later party, on the other hand, entirely missed the mouths of the Dilinger and Tonzona Rivers, two major tributaries that the first government expedition had found and mapped.

If they were heading in from the Susitna side bound for the midway diggings, all travelers knew was that the way led up the valleys of successive Susitna River tributaries (the Yentna, Skwentna and Happy Rivers and Pass Creek) crossed

of the Alaska Range and a followed down the drainage of
the Kuskokwim River into the Interior.

Rod Perry: *Some modern writers claim that with the Nome
Gold Rush beginning in 1898, and even more so with the
1906 –1907 coming of mining to the Inland Empire, that
mushers immediately commenced whizzing back and forth
over the way through Rainy Pass.*

*That could not be farther from the truth. Such writing
demonstrates an absence of understanding of long-distance,
wilderness dog team travel and a lack of research into trail
history as well. Unknowing writers just repeat what they
read—that being written by some other unknowing writer—
and so it goes back and back and back. To one who knows the
subject, the constant errors and misinformation in newspapers,
magazines, books, brochures, tourist information, television
coverage and the Internet stand out like proverbial sore thumbs.*

*Few today have experience traveling great wilderness
distances over soft, untracked snow in sub-zero temperatures.
There is a vast gulf between the ease of following a defined
path, and the multiplied difficulties of having but a general
idea of the lay of the land and needing to make choices every
step of the way about which stretch of landscape immediately
ahead to take. Through wooded areas, there is a sea of
difference between traveling through a cleared swath, and
having to hack and saw the course through trees, brush and
blowdowns. And there is an absolute ocean of contrast
between moving at a brisk pace over a broken, hard-packed
trail and plowing through hundreds of miles of untracked,
bottomless fluff.*

*Carrying enough food and essential gear to support progress
and survival for the duration of such a journey stretched a
man to the limits. Snowshoeing ahead and helping his dog
team haul a mountainous load, or carrying a pack or necking
and gee-poling a heavily laden handsled ground a man
down, pushing him almost beyond limits of human endurance.*

For enlightenment's sake, make up a detailed equipment, clothing and food list that you would put together for a 30-day wilderness trek of more than 300 miles. Remember that much of the way will pass through bottomless deep snow, it will cross the greatest mountain range in North America, battling temperatures that will surely range down to 30 degrees below zero and could well plummet to 60 below; plus the short, subarctic daylight will limit your daily travel time. Carefully total up the weight of the gear and supplies. Though your list will include today's high-tech, light weight gear and freeze dried food, if you can shoulder it at all, your load will be staggering.

Take a pack and sled bearing a like weight to the nearest area of deep snow. Strap on the 50- to 60-inch-long, 8- to 10-inch-wide snowshoes required to hold you up in the dry, fluffy snow of interior Alaska. Now sample the work of hauling the load behind you. Consider, however, that if your test is performed anywhere that the snow is not at least waist deep, where the snow has greater moisture content than that found in northern Alaska and if the temperatures are much higher than those usually encountered on this stretch, you will not be able to gain a valid idea of the difficulty of dealing with bottomless fluff nor a sled that resists sliding through the cold, dry snow like you had mixed sand with it. Oh, yes, I almost forgot; instead of today's slick plastic, you must shoe your runners with the steel like they did in the old days and listen to it screech in protest when dragged over subzero snow! How long can you last at the task?

Think you could do it more easily with dogs? Not so fast; maybe, maybe not. Ask a seasoned Iditarod Racer about the weight of one dog's daily ration. Multiply it by the number of dogs you would take on such a 300-mile-long ordeal. Multiply again by the expected 30 days. Absolutely staggering.

Do you think racing dogs burn more calories? Maybe, maybe not. Racing dogs don't have to pull much. The sled is lightly loaded. Over a level, packed, fast trail, a team of eight or more flies along and the sled doesn't greatly affect their

229

speed. Like marathon racers, they primarily burn calories through the distance they cover.

So ask any Iditarod competitor to tell you what he thinks it would be like, even over the modern, fast race trail, to start from Susitna Station with the entire, just-calculated load of dog and human food plus the rest of your equipment— and haul it all the way to McGrath. One thing is probable: To bring it off he would have to go with a sled far larger than any he has ever driven, or probably, ever seen!

He is likely to tell you that even hauling that weight, he could make the trip in far fewer than 30 days. And he would be correct. Therefore, to make it more comparable with the old days we must perform the freight haul differently. Ask him to explain what he thinks it would be like to travel that 300 miles this way: never touching the trail, parallel it the whole way 100 feet off to the side. Travel through unbroken snow with no cut path through areas of trees and brush. While he is thinking about that, ask the racer how it would be, while on snowshoes, to manage his huge load in the bottomless snow he and his dogs will be wading through out there. And see what he has to say about the dogs' struggle to move such a load while they are virtually swimming in the fluff, able to gain almost no traction.

What is his opinion about how many calories dogs working like that might burn compared to a racing team? I really don't know, but it might close to the same, they're both big-time calorie burners.

Those who know the Su Station-to-McGrath trail know that on some parts of the trip dogs would speed you up, even hauling a big load. On other parts, though, they would hold you back and you'd be far better off to be on your own. You can see that making the trip using sled dogs might or might not be to your advantage.

Gear and food of a century ago were terribly heavy. Clothing and bedding were of wool and sometimes fur. Tents were of cotton canvas. Cooking gear was made of steel. Axes, saws and other commonly carried tools weighed a lot.

230

Dehydrated food, of course, was not nearly as light as the freeze-dried food of today.

The winter traveler always faced a conflicting choice: Should he risk going light, gambling his very life on a swift passage? The hindrance of carrying or pulling a heavy load through hundreds of miles of virgin snow and trackless, obstacle-ridden wilderness caused some risk takers to head out with a minimal pack or sled load, chancing their very lives that they would not be held up by route-finding difficulties, blizzards, snow and ice conditions, accidents, equipment breakage, injuries, sickness or exhaustion due to starvation.

The other choice was to prepare carefully to deal with contingencies. The more cautious traveler was inclined to consider the many possible difficulties and include more and heavier supplies and gear even if that meant going more slowly.

Difficulties stacked one upon the other. First, the energy expended in the Herculean effort and the calories required to combat temperatures that might fall nearly 100 degrees Fahrenheit below the frost point increased daily food intake far beyond requirements for summer travel. Dogs burn more calories under those conditions, too.

Not only was each winter day's ration heavier to carry, but also the problem was further compounded: the plodding nature of choosing the course immediately ahead, breaking trail on snowshoes, sometimes cutting brush and trees to clear the way, then, if traveling by dog team, going back to widen the trail and help the dogs wrestle the sled through the difficult stretches, all combined to slow the forward progress to a crawl.

Also greatly slowing the pace was that, in those times preceding modern flashlights, the short, subarctic winter daylight severely limited daily trail time.

All of those elements diabolically combined to add days to the trip and force a trekker to take a more mountainous load.

Only the most intrepid travelers—native or white—dared the passage, the nature of which was "make it all the way through on your own or die."

231

Today's "historians" who write that travel was common over the route during the era of those conditions reveal their lack of understanding of the nature of the primitive passage.

In those pre trail days, the crossing was obviously worlds apart from travel over a well-established trail such as the Yukon River Trail, which was hard-packed and studded with villages, roadhouses and shelters. If, back 100 years ago, the nature of the passage over an undeveloped, hardly travelled, mere "route" was so different than that over a developed "trail," it should go without saying that the nature of the passage between Cook Inlet and McGrath country during those pre-trail days of a century ago was so utterly disparate to today's dog-team racing as to have almost nothing in common save the dogs and mushers. And of course, today's long-distance racing is all that modern writers know.

To illustrate a comparison, say that early dog team travel over the trailless route could be thought of as akin to a solitary, heavily-laden freight wagon being pulled by plodding, hardy oxen over trackless country that would later become the Oregon Trail. In stark contrast, today's long-distance sled-dog races— staged over well-marked, beaten trails featuring many resupply points and help in case of trouble—are like a dash from St. Joseph, Missouri to Portland, Oregon over the old Oregon Trail route but on modern superhighways in an almost unburdened automobile. The comparison may be a stretch. But not by much.

Such travel as was undertaken over the route before any trail was put in is all but unknown, even within today's dog-driving community. Beyond a mere handful of the native drivers and a few others in the earliest Iditarod races (my brother, Alan Perry included) few other Iditarod Race finishers have taken winter trips by dog team, unsupported by a structured race organization, covering long distances in the arctic or subarctic far from human habitation or other sources of resupply and lasting as long as several weeks.

If one has to search far and wide among even today's dog drivers to find the rare musher who has experienced such travel, it stands to reason that among non-dog driving writers and historians it is unlikely any may be found with the experiential frame of reference to write with understanding and insight about primitive movement over the route before the way became a trail.

One isn't surprised by modern writers' and historians' mistakes, as they have not come within lightyears of experiencing what the old-timers did. They simply lack the background to write accurately about long-distance, unsupported, dog team travel in trackless wilderness.

In early 1977 I needed to get my team from our bush training location at Lake Minchumina out to the road system so that I could run the Iditarod. Accompanied by three others, and with my dogs split into two teams hauling long, heavily laden freight sleds by the indirect route we chose, we traveled approximately 175 miles, in much the way the early trailbreakers did. We proceeded as slowly as earlier travelers who found their own routes and made their own trails through the unbroken snow of virtually trackless wilderness. The arduous trip was one of breaking trail on snowshoes ahead of the team, picking and cutting the way, essentially a map and compass in one hand, an ax in the other. We traveled with no other means of support than the supplies carried on the sleds and we camped wherever night overtook us. It required 16 full days and parts of two others to reach the highway.

To emphasize how different that sort of mushing is from modern racing, today it is common for a middle-distance competitor skimming along on a lightly laden sled over a broken, well-marked race trail to cover such a distance within one 24-hour period.

To further emphasize how different travel over the primitive route was from the way it is now over an established trail we can go to the historical record.

Al Preston: "One explorer I knew from the Nome Alaska Road Commission office, documented that in late 1907 about 20 prospectors, disappointed with their luck in the Innoko

District, traveled (probably in pairs and small groups) over the mountains on their way out of the Interior. Walter said their trips were plagued with extreme hardships, including lack of food, and took, variously, *24 to 35 days—that's three and one-half to five weeks!*—amid early-winter conditions. It's probable that some of them "siwashed it," which means they traveled with minimal shelter—some may have done without even a tent to keep their load bare-bones light. Walter and my friend Ross Kinney said that all of those men managed to straggle in to Susitna Station. But upon arrival their condition was described as "pitiful." Several barely made it.

"Another account tells of what may have been the only carefully planned, commercial freight haul over the route before it was developed by the Alaska Road Commission into a real trail. It was a gold shipment. Rod, I knew the man who conducted it, Bob had the U.S. Mail contract at Nome. The length of time that trip took him sheds light upon how difficult it was to make it through before the ARC work. Even though Bob was one of Alaska's most well respected professional freighters and mail carriers, it took him a little more than five weeks to bring his "gold train" from the Inland Empire all the way out to Seward. I think I would be safe in saying that at least four of those five weeks must have gone into the section of the haul between McGrath and Susitna Station, the trackless part of the route. Once they got to the trail at Susitna Station the rest of the trip would have gone pretty fast."

Rod Perry: *Today, sled-dog racers would cover that stretch in as little as three days.*

However, formidable difficulties notwithstanding, as evidenced by the 1907 report from Susitna Station, occasionally there were individuals among the iron men of the day, trekkers who felt such a pressing need to travel during winter between the new diggings in the Innoko country and Cook Inlet that they were willing to take up the deadly gamble that one could make it through. So there was some traffic.

234

However, it is plain that until the trail was cut, marked and studded with roadhouses, the passage was so fraught with danger and difficulty that it took the strongest of travelers to the farthest fringes of endurance. So few made the trip that travelers of record seldom if ever found a broken trail.

Possibly the most succinct, well-known quote that has come down to us regarding this comparison of trail conditions came from the lips of the great adventurer, Archdeacon of Alaska Hudson Stuck: "The greatest gift that one man may bestow upon another in Alaska is a broken trail."

Chapter 19

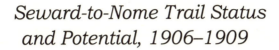

Seward-to-Nome Trail Status and Potential, 1906–1909

THE WINTER FREIGHT, travel and communication demands of the resident thousand souls of the Inland Empire continued to keep the way in and out in the direction of the Yukon beaten. As well, those demands, plus the punctuation of settlements lined up along the very trail route in the midst of the great Su Station-to-Kaltag wilderness, added rationale for those who continued to push for a main trail all the way through.

Al Preston: "With all of the desire of the people of Nome coupled with the demands and strategic position of those new midway booms, it still seemed worlds away from adding up to enough cause to outweigh all of the negatives that tipped the scales against starting trail work.

One night I got a new slant on the subject while having dinner at the Kinneys. Ross introduced some of his viewpoints on a slightly separate road building problem that explained a lot about why the Seward-Nome project was held back."

Ross Kinney: "Preston, let's forget for a moment that anyone ever thought of a trail to serve Nome emanating from Seward. Let's just isolate the problem of better transportation into the Inland Empire all by itself.

"OK, you have a thousand people roundabout in the Upper Innoko Country. Those settlements out there demand to be better connected for the flow of their travelers, mail and freight. I'm expecting our ARC office here will get our orders to put them in a decent trail. For discussion's sake, let's say the orders direct us to give them what we consider the best of two trail choices: north to the Yukon or southeast to Seward.

"Let's start with north. We could run them something much straighter and better than they have from McGrath's north to the Yukon River Trail. It would take a fair body of work, but it's very doable.

"One way you can think about that connection is it's about 1,100 miles from Valdez to McGrath's. That, my friend, is a long ways.

"The other way you can think about it is it's only about 150 miles from McGrath's out to the main trunk line where they could tap into all of the traffic and commerce flowing up and down the big river.

"Now let's consider going southeast to Susitna Station with a brand-new trail. Preston, It might be substantially less than half the distance from Seward to McGrath's than from Valdez through Fairbanks to McGrath's. But when I lay it out in an organized form, it will make it plain why we'd never go southeast. At least, not the way things stand now. We see four major differences between building a straighter, improved trail between the Yukon and McGrath's and connecting McGrath's southeasterly to Susitna Station. I told Colonel Goodwin I've named them the 'Four D's'.

"First, the Distance. From the McGrath's it's about twice as far southeast to Susitna Station as it is north to the Yukon.

"Second, is Difficulty. The work and logistics to build the trail southeast over the greatest mountain range on the continent is infinitely more difficult than the connection to Kaltag. Think of the expense, risk and backbreaking logistics. From what we can gather—and there's not a lot of information out there because just a handful of whites have ever made the crossing—it would be just barely doable. We figure it would require mounting a carefully equipped and heavily manned construction expedition.

"Then, even if we pour all of that expense and labor into building such a trail we still predict few will use it. Just because we cut and mark it doesn't mean we've made it easy. Remember, this second D stands for difficulty. Yes, it would make it better if we got it all slashed out and marked, but that doesn't take out the risk and backbreaking loads. Without roadhouses for resupply points along the way, it wouldn't be enough better to induce many more to travel it. It goes full circle. Without the traffic, no one will build a roadhouse out there. And without constant traffic, the trail doesn't stay broken.

"Up to now, even without a trail, the small number of men making the trek seems to make it through. But the rule seems to be the passage takes about three and one-half to five weeks from McGrath's to Su Station. A lot of them straggle in almost more dead than alive. Again, we don't expect cutting and marking alone to make it that much easier. That takes the combination of a cleared, defined trail plus roadhouses.

"Third, comes Direction. Preston, going toward Susitna Station is way outside the natural flow of winter traffic, which is from the Inland Empire out to the Yukon River Trail and on to Fairbanks or Nome. Think about it: our two big gold towns aren't just the largest population and commercial centers, they're the only Alaskan towns north of Juneau with an infrastructure amounting to anything. They're our only islands of civilization and culture and they supply about every basic we'd ever need, and even a few luxuries. In winter, Nome and Fairbanks (and especially Fairbanks) fuel the McGrath's area settlements with supplies and mail.

"Something else; most of those first to reach and stake the new midway finds came in from the closest populations— Fairbanks, Nome and the other gold strikes and villages located close enough to the main trunk line trails to use them to get there fast. Now when they go to and from the midway diggings, most want to head back north to the Yukon Trail or the Kaltag Portage to where they came from.

"Fourth, and lastly, is Demand. We just can't see enough human pressure, you know, people wanting to go by the route over the mountains between Seward and the Inland Empire. We can't see economic pressure either, at least not the way things stand now, to go to the considerable labor and expense of constructing a trail between Cook Inlet over Rainy Pass to McGrath's."

Al Preston: "Ross, those are some excellent points. Of course, it's easy to apply them to the overall picture of a more complete trail, one that not only serves the Inland Empire, but runs through that country on the way from Seward to Nome. If you guys do put in a trail from the Yukon through the Empire to McGrath's, you can bet all of the Seward-Nome Mail Trail advocates will jump right on it and ask, 'Hey, with a trail in as far as McGrath's, now you only have maybe fewer than 300 miles separating you from Susitna Station. Not even 300. Why don't you guys get after it and just knock it out? Then we'll have our complete Seward-Nome Mail Trail.' "

Ross Kinney: "Sure, Walter Goodwin and I know that bandwagon would get rolling. All of Nome is calling for a mail trail to Seward. But we think it would take a lot more travel than we can foresee to make it worth the expense of building not just a trail, but one of high quality that would allow fast enough travel to make it feasible for the mail contract to go that way. As you understand, Preston, if the trail didn't turn out a big improvement over the present route it would never wrest the mail contract away from the boys running it down the Yukon from Fairbanks. The colonel and I simply can't visualize a future increase in traffic big enough to make the construction of such a trail worth the effort and expense. We sure can't see much traffic coming from the few people living south of the Range around Cook Inlet. You can bet that no would-be mail contractor could ever win a bid for that route without roadhouses and traffic enough to keep the trail broken and fast."

———————✦———————

Alma Preston: "Rod, the Cook Inlet-Kenai Peninsula region as a whole had dwindled in population from its earliest gold-rush days. The number of miners and their families remaining at Girdwood, Hope and Sunrise totaled no more than a few hundred. A couple of hundred prospectors were poking around the Susitna drainage, especially concentrated around the Yentna, where a small rush got going in about 1905. Susitna Station had a little population that was growing. But all of that didn't add up to anything to speak of. When the railroad construction started, though, that brought the population right back up. For awhile, that is. When the Alaska Central went bust in 1907, it sank again like a rock down a well."

———————✦———————

Seward had a wonderful natural harbor and a strategic location. Those factors had started to make Seward the deepwater seaport of choice for the Cook Inlet area. Even at that, the town consisted of little more than the Alfred Lowell homestead at the head of Resurrection Bay until construction of the Alaska Central Railroad began in 1903. Since the early gold rushes around Cook Inlet had faded, the population of South Central Alaska had briefly decreased. That downtrend reversed when large crews arrived to begin building the rail line out of Seward. The construction boom jump started a thriving port town. After just four years, however, when the railroad builders went bankrupt and construction stopped, much of the town's boom populace drained away.

Therefore, at the time of the small strikes at Ganes Creek, Ophir, Moore City and Takotna, and McGrath's establishment of his trading post, there existed nothing in South Central Alaska remotely comparable to the developed infrastructures and trail and supply systems serving Alaska north of the Alaska Range. That meant that, as yet, Cook Inlet country and Seward had little available to contribute to the new settlements of the Inland Empire. So compared to travel between those midway gold settlements and the Yukon, there was little call for travel between them and the Cook Inlet region.

Halfway into the first decade of the new century, prospecting and mining activity and human populations throughout Alaska had already changed substantially since the great gold rushes. The wild, crazed stampedes of a few years before, with their frenzied hordes that instantly dropped everything upon first word of a strike and stampeded hell-bent-for-leather any way they could, overland or by water, to be among the first to stake claims at the new discoveries, had quieted down by 1906. Though the relatively small McGrath area strikes caused a blip in the trend, Alaska had mostly settled into a prolonged slowed-down pace of controlled extraction of the wealth.

———◆—◆———

Al Preston: "In that more staid, developmental mode, it made sense for most people to wait and take advantage of the easiest transportation. That usually meant waiting for summer to go by river boat and ocean-going ship. Almost always, if you intended to winter-over you planned ahead and positioned yourself before freeze-up where you wanted to be until the rivers started to run the following summer. Most who intended to leave the interior got out by boat before mid-September. Remember, as I've said before, very few besides professionals owned dog teams. If others decided they just had to travel during winter, it probably meant by shanks' mare. Outside of commercial hauling and periodic mail runs by dog team, there was just not much winter travel.

"Those few who desired to not only leave the new diggings, but also leave Alaska without waiting for spring, generally had two ways to choose: Option one was take the Yukon River Trail to Fairbanks, then the Richardson Trail to Valdez. Man, that was a trip of about 1,300 miles. The way was long all right—over two months for a hiker who could keep up an average 20 miles a day; its trail was almost constantly hard-packed, and that means the world. Combine that with its well-established roadhouse and supply system, and a man could hoof down the trail with close to nothing on his back or in his sled. If he took just one good dog, he could really pick 'em up and put 'em down, maybe making 30 miles a lot of days. And once he reached Valdez, he could count on passage south with all of the ships in and out. Choice two? Take on the tremendous rigors and risk the dangers of going the little-traveled way over Rainy Pass. Where did that get you? Into the comparatively thinly populated Cook Inlet region and Seward, that's where. Not quite nowhere, but close to it."

Chapter 20

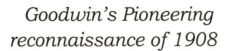

Goodwin's Pioneering reconnaissance of 1908

DESPITE THE NEGATIVES, planning for a Seward to Nome winter trail finally took on substance when Major Wilds Preston Richardson ordered the Army's Alaska Road Commission (ARC) Nome office to reconnoiter the country between Seward and the established Yukon River Trail at Kaltag. Their mission? To see if it offered a more practical alternative for hauling mail and freight than the Valdez-Fairbanks-Nome route.

They would evaluate existing trails for current usefulness and options for improvement. Possibilities for building new, high-quality trails and the degree of difficulty and expense to construct them would be assessed. Mileage, elevations and grades would be measured. Latitude observations were to be taken and adjusted for magnetic declination. Colonel Walter Goodwin, an engineer and the supervisor of the ARC's Nome District would lead the reconnaissance.

Rod Perry: *No doubt, as was common to all builders of quality ARC trails, Goodwin also considered of great priority the assessment of what percentage of the trail could be established in the timber or, at least, be kept off of the rivers. A woods trail offered increased safety, freedom from overflow, better footing, usefulness earlier in the fall and later in the spring, a windbreak resisting blown snow from filling the trail and a clearly defined course that reduced chances of travelers losing the way.*

The trek would consist of five parts. First, the party would travel the 72 miles of railroad grade out of Seward. Next, Goodwin would analyze, with a road-builder's eye, the existing trail between Turnagain Arm and Susitna Station to determine if all of it were suitable for heavy, regular usage and if so, how it might be improved. The third and fourth parts would be through trackless wilderness and would form the heart of the trip. They would explore the little-used passage between Susitna Station and the mid way, Innoko settlements. Then they planned to take a bee-line through the rolling country from Ophir to Kaltag to see if a high quality trail were possible. The fifth part would be over the heavily used trail between Kaltag and Nome. The usefulness of that final 290-mile stretch was not in question, but they would determine if and how the age-old portage might be straightened and otherwise improved.

Having had most of their outfit, including two 14-foot-long sleds and 18 dog harnesses assembled in Seattle, Colonel Goodwin sailed for Seward January 16, 1908 aboard the *S.S. Northwestern.* Accompanying him was expedition member Ross J. Kinney. Upon reaching Seward on January 25th, they were joined by George E. Pulham and Frank Jackson. They spent five days finalizing their packing and testing dogs.

Rod Perry: *It is highly likely that the dogs used on the trip came from the dog lot of the Alfred Lowell-Harry Revell operation, which since 1905 had held the U.S. Mail contract for the region. There is high probability Lowell and Revell were the only ones around Seward who could have rounded up 18 extra sled dogs their operation could get by without. Of course, that is only conjecture; Colonel Goodwin could have prearranged some other gathering of animals to be ready when he arrived there.*

On January 31, 1908, the four-man crew with (presumably) 18 dogs pulled out of Seward traveling the railbed. On their way to Turnagain Arm they encountered considerable difficulty crossing the many narrow bridges. Previous foot traffic had beaten in a canyon-like trench up to seven feet deep that had become so mushroomed over at the top as to almost form a roof. It was too narrow for their big sleds to pass. Therefore, they were forced to make their way above and to the side of the trench.

Goodwin wrote that sometimes above dangerous heights, that meant traveling upon cornices that precariously extended up to three feet out beyond the ends of the ties!

The men had to shovel their way in and out of the half dozen tunnels where snow slides had heavily blockaded the mouths. Once inside, as obstacle-ridden as the tunnels were with darkness, loose rocks, lack of snow, slick glaciering and large stalactites of ice hanging from the roofs, the men were thankful that railroad construction had given them those through-the-mountain paths because the canyon of the raging river below was absolutely impassable, even in its frozen state.

Between two of the tunnels the party encountered glaciering that would have been suicide to attempt without considerable improvement of the passage. Where the railroad had blasted a path along the sheer cliff face barely wide enough for the roadbed, seepage from the rock wall above had built up a deep layer of ice over the tracks. The flat road had frozen into a slick side hill sloping steeply toward the lip of the drop-off. The men had to chop a level, three-foot-wide, 500-foot-long trail in the ice along the cliff.

Rod Perry: *Although Goodwin did not chronicle the details, anyone who has freighted heavy loads with spirited sled dogs pictures what the men must have done once they finished chopping their trail across the deadly stretch. They no doubt disassembled the loads and carried parcels across piece by piece. Probably, the nearly empty sleds were skidded along by one man in front and another in the rear. Finally, the dogs must*

247

have been "hopped" over one at a time. For close control of the powerful, spirited animals, a man held the dog's head high by its collar, which kept its front feet off the ground, and the dog hopped along the ice trail on his hind legs. At the far end the huskies were staked out so they would not just run back and forth. That passage must have taken the better part of a day.

From Girdwood, the party ascended Crow Pass then descended to Eagle River. That was the only part of the entire course to Nome that they deemed impractical for heavy use. The ARC desired to hold to their standard of a maximum four percent grade. Goodwin noted how ". . . over Crow Creek Pass it would be out of the question to handle Nome mail with an ascent of 45 degrees for the last 1,500 feet and to an altitude of 3,550 feet and then down nearly as steep some places to Raven Creek and on down to Eagle River 9 miles below."

Rod Perry: *Apparently, as far as Goodwin was concerned, if regular Nome-bound traffic were forced to include Crow Pass, the whole idea of a Seward-to-Nome rail route might as well be scrapped.*

However, from anecdotal information he gathered, Goodwin reported that Indian Pass a few miles to the west was said to be shorter and gentler. It sounded like it offered good possibilities for a trail feasible for travel by heavily laden sleds and big teams. Although he thought it should be examined, apparently he did not have the supplies or time to do it during the 1908 reconnaissance.

The reason the party did not continue west along Turnagain Arm from Girdwood and travel over Indian Pass instead of Crow Pass was that the railroad bed stopped at Girdwood. From there to Indian, the steep mountainside with its many canyons, cliffs and rocky headlands falling into the swift waters and mudflats of the Arm formed an impassible barrier to dog-team travel.

Rod Perry: *Being an engineer and understanding Alaska's transportation needs, Walter Goodwin would have known that although the Alaska Central Railroad had folded, the idea of a railroad to the territory's political and economic center in the interior made such overwhelming good sense, somebody would eventually lay tracks to Fairbanks. Just fifteen more miles of blasting and filling around Turnagain Arm would extend the roadbed to the entry of Indian Pass, where a gentler route that dog teams could effectively and safely negotiate was available.*

Of course, once such a railroad could be pushed even beyond Indian Pass, just fifteen miles farther along the Arm as far as Potter, teams could travel the railbed to reach relatively flat going that extended beyond, essentially, for some 175 miles, all the way to the foot of the Alaska Range. As soon as that came into being, trails through the Chugach Mountains by either Crow Pass or Indian Pass would become obsolete.

An interpretive sign once located on the Crow Pass Trail spoke of the stretch being used by dog teams until the railroad was completed to Fairbanks in 1923. There appears to have been more priority placed on promotion of this stretch of trail by agencies, organizations and communities that valued a claim to a share of the famous trail's romantic past than on accurate scholarship.

Certainly, those who would make such claims demonstrate a lack of understanding of freighting by dog team. To climb 3,550 feet in a few short miles was grueling enough. But the final pitch to the top would have probably required either shoveling out switchbacks or unloading and taking small amounts of the cargo up in multiple trips. No dog team can haul heavy loads up a long, 45-degree slope, even on a hard trail. In deep, soft snow it is infinitely more impossible. And heavy sleds that cannot be held tipped up to carve on one runner cannot side-hill.

Neither could the drop down the other side have been negotiated safely except with small loads. Even with dog tie-out chains wrapped around the runners to "roughlock" them, a heavily laden sled could not have been kept from careening down out of control and overrunning the team, with the all-too-likely result of injured dogs and a damaged sled.

Although for foot travelers, going over Crow Pass was the better option because it was significantly shorter and they were not taking heavy loads across, no thinking dog driver would have hauled up the grueling ascent and risked disaster down the dangerously steep descent once there was a better option. As witness to that wish to escape the grueling and dangerous Crow Pass for something better, starting in the spring of 1908, right after Goodwin passed through, crews began laboriously building a trail along the Arm from Girdwood to Bird Creek.

The big breakthrough came in 1909. The railroad (under receivership) started work again out of Girdwood. By the time construction crews had barely roughed out the railroad bed around Turnagain Arm as far as Indian Creek, the much lower and more gradual Indian Pass, which led into the Ship Creek drainage, could be accessed.

Soon, even the switch to Indian Pass was left behind. When railroad construction crews took their work just 15 additional miles along the Arm from Indian to Potter, mushers did not even have to ascend Indian Pass. The dog men were no doubt glad to wash their hands of the mountains; after all, they were not in the business for exercise and scenery! From Potter, they had no more serious long assents—there were some short, steep climbs here and there through the rolling lowlands—until the beginning of the climb over the Alaska Range 175 miles farther.

Once the railroad became operational in winter as far as Anchorage and then Wasilla, years before it was completed to Fairbanks, dog drivers made use of every mile of rail transport possible. The end of the rails served as their advancing trail head as railroad construction pushed tracks closer to their destination. By 1922 most traffic did not even go through Knik and over the Alaska Range. Why do that, when travel could start from Nenana, beyond the mountains. On the north side of the range the trail ran over flat or gently rolling country all the way to Iditarod.

Goodwin and company continued around Cook Inlet country to Knik, where they left one of their basket sleds and added four Yukon sleds, the same conveyance referred to as "hand sleds" earlier on the Upper Yukon. The ubiquitous Yukon sleds were commercially manufactured Outside and were sold by the untold thousands throughout Alaska. They were a simple sled about 20 inches in bed width, and varied in length, but most were seven feet long. Four or five inches above the runner bottoms, short stanchions supported the bed. The stanchion bases were set into unique castiron sockets affixed to the runners and bolted to the cross bents or bridges by ingenious steel fixtures that allowed the sled to flex. Because the joinery was simple and they could be bolted together they were fast and cheap to mass-produce. Every trading post stocked stacks of them.

Rod Perry: *To refresh our memory, most of the sourdoughs "necked" their Yukon sleds without the use of dogs. From the front corners of the sled ran an eight or ten foot loop of rope that passed under both armpits and around the back of the neck. A long spruce pole was usually lashed to the right, gee side of the sled, most people being right-handed. The gee pole angled up and extended forward to the musher's hand. With the long lever he could steer easily. It also allowed him to hold the sled back on down hills. Yukon sleds were not designed to ride unless the driver sat atop the load, having no runner tails to stand on or structure above the bed to hold onto.*

Goodwin's basket sled, like most sleds of the day, had no runner tails extending behind the rear stanchions long enough for prolonged standing. Men handling working dog teams virtually never rode, but walked or trotted along.

Goodwin thought it a big mistake to leave behind the basket sled and switch to Yukon sleds, but Pulham had been placed in charge of transportation and the Colonel evidently chose not to pull rank. While at Knik, at the insistence of

George Pullham, they re-rigged their towlines so the dogs could pull single file. The party also bought more provisions.

On February 15, the men arrived at Susitna Station. Goodwin wrote, "Here a three-quarter-blood Cree Indian was hired to go through as far as McGrath's and then return, and we took on flour, sugar, bacon and other supplies as had been arranged for previously, and the real trip began as this was our last base of supplies."

Rod Perry: *Goodwin had obviously either shipped his own supplies to the trading post prior to freeze-up or communicated with the operator to make sure that when the post ordered its own stock it would include specified items that would be reserved, awaiting the group's arrival.*

One of the unnamed "other supplies" they must have taken on, which no doubt formed the major bulk of their cargo, was a large number of bales of dried salmon for the dogs. For additional dog food they probably added to their cargo several 50- or 100-pound bags of rice and an adequate supply of either lard or bacon (cheap in those days) in five-gallon buckets.

The load on every sled must have been absolutely mountainous. The powerful dogs used for freighting in those days averaged about twice the weight of today's streamlined racing sled dogs and, of course, ate a lot. In the old days, mushers figured four pounds dry weight of salmon and rice plus fat was standard daily ration per dog. Men and animals together must have eaten at least 80 pounds per day, even though most of the food stores—beans, rice, flour, sugar, dog salmon and the like—were dry. Fortunately, the sleds did not have to be carried, only slid.

Goodwin did not record whether the basket-sled runners were shod with steel or "ironbark," an extremely dense wood commonly used for runner shoes. Ironbark would be waxed or iced to run more smoothly than steel, especially in extremely cold weather. However, Yukon sleds came shod with steel

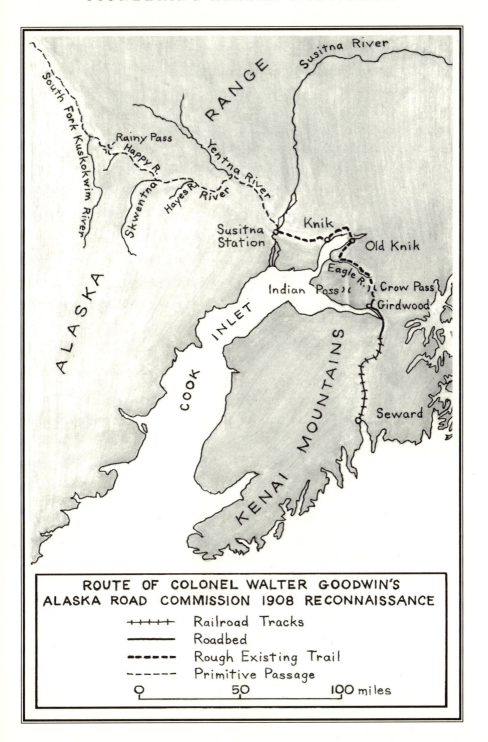

South Fork Kuskokwim River

RANGE

Susitna River

Rainy Pass
Happy R.
Yentna River
Skwentna
Hayes R. River

ALASKA

Susitna Station

Knik

Old Knik

Eagle R.
Indian Pass
Crow Pass
Girdwood

COOK INLET

KENAI MOUNTAINS

Seward

ROUTE OF COLONEL WALTER GOODWIN'S
ALASKA ROAD COMMISSION 1908 RECONNAISSANCE

+++++ Railroad Tracks
───── Roadbed
▪▪▪▪▪ Rough Existing Trail
───── Primitive Passage

0   50   100 miles

and Goodwin did not mention re-shoeing them during their equipment adjustment at Knik.

Good fortune smiled upon them when it came to moving their cargo. At the beginning, when their sleds were most mountainously loaded, Goodwin and his men traveled a gradient that climbed so gradually as to seem level, following the first hundred miles or so the twists of the Susitna and its successive tributaries, the Yentna, Skwentna, and Happy Rivers all the way to the base of the Alaska Rangel. And, of course, during that travel, the dogs were consuming 100 miles worth of their load.

Still, of course, it was not easy. Offsetting much of the advantage of level going were the deep snows that covered the river ice. Their way had to be laboriously snowshoed out.

Again and again, I read various writers (who have obviously never traveled raw country pioneering trails in the way of Goodwin) stating that during Goodwin's 1908 passage he "blazed" the trail. By tight definition, blazing indicates at least a rough marking of the way by cutting patches of bark from tree trunks, leaving "blaze marks." That process usually includes at least a rough slashing out of obstructions to allow passage, especially necessary to get a team and sled through.

In 1908, Goodwin did not "blaze" anything in this way. They were not sent out to build a permanent trail, or even decide upon precise positioning and marking. For heaven's sake!—at that point, the Road Commission did not even know whether or not they would eventually decide to build such a trail. Even marking the way would have required far more time and manpower—and dog food!—than they had. From his own account, Goodwin's trip was one of reconnaissance. Orders for the expedition limited the men to looking over the country in a very general way, not marking a precise trail. (When they built the trail three years later they did not even place two great sections very close to the same ground the 1908 trip traveled.) Although Goodwin knew that should their cursory assessment reveal that a mail trail should indeed be built, and that no

Walter Goodwin with Sled and Companion

permanent trail should ever run on the rivers, all that made sense for a one-time passage such as theirs was to travel out on the clear path the rivers gave them. They could make many miles on snow-covered river ice, winding though the course might be, for every mile they might have laboriously cut and slashed through the woods, brush and downed timber.

"Blaze" can be also used in a loose sense to describe the passage of the first pioneers through. Writers of Iditarod Trail history who use the word loosely in that way, use it wrongly as well. Addressing this use of the word, I repeat, "Goodwin didn't "blaze" anything. Many—not multitudes, but many— travelers had passed over the route before he and his crew journeyed through.

Properly, Goodwin's 1908 Reconnaissance "looked over" or "scouted" the route in a general way.

255

Alaska Road Commission (ARC) personnel reported in 1908 that they had heard of an Indian trail beginning within a few miles of Susitna Station that cut cross-country in the direction of the Alaska Range, ending somewhere near where the Talachulitna River empties into the Skwentna River. However, either because the trail was hard to locate, too difficult to follow or too narrow and twisting to accommodate dog team passage, the ARC men chose not to try to take it even though it paralleled their route and would have cut many miles of winding river travel from their trip.

Rod Perry: *Again, as they headed toward the Alaska Range they mainly traveled the rivers, Susitna to the Yentna, Yentna to the Skwentna, Skwentna to the Happy, just following the twists and turns, rather than taking shorter, but uncut portages through the forest.*

However, here and there during the trip they must have necessarily gone through stretches of woods and willow. Through such forested areas and brush they would have intently searched immediately ahead for paths of least resistance through trees, brush, downed timber and across or around terrain features. "Paths" may be misleading; what they would have usually found were just ways to get through the woods and thickets that were somewhat thinner than the tangle on each side.

Going ahead of the teams, some of Goodwin's men would have cleared the way just enough to get the sleds through. The second man in line stayed opposite the first in his stride so that his snowshoe tracks filled in the spaces between steps the first man's webs had left unbroken. During such going, the men in the lead would have had to return to the sleds time after time to help the dogs get them past especially difficult places.

Heading out of Susitna Station, the party began to enter the zone of progressively deeper snows as they made their way toward the mountains. Typical of mountain ranges near the sea, clouds moving inland drop most of their precipitation on the seaward side of the Alaska Range. Snows in the Finger Lake area can accumulate to over 10 feet in depth.

———————

Al Preston: "Rod, my next door neighbor, my A.R.C. employee pal I rented from in Nome was Colonel Goodwin's right hand man on the trip. Ross told me about snow conditions and getting the dog teams through that country."

———————

Ross Kinney: "The uninitiated tend to think that a dog team is somehow able to magically skim lightly over the snow like Santa's reindeer. Not so. A lot of people ask me about our expeditions, so this is how I explain it to them:

'A team pulling a load over a well traveled, packed winter trail is like a person easily pulling a loaded wagon while walking on concrete-hard beach sand just above the tide line.

'A team pulling that load over the same packed trail, but after a new snow has covered it, say, to the depth of the dogs' bellies, would be tantamount to a person wading hip deep, towing his loaded wagon in the water after the tide has covered his beach.

'A team hauling its load behind a man on snowshoes breaking trail through deep virgin snow, where underneath there is no trail all the way to the ground, may be loosely compared to the man drawing his burden unable to touch bottom while swimming in deep water.

"Preston, the latter is the condition we had to deal with on the reconnaissance."

———————

It is impossible for anyone reading the account of Goodwin's trip to fully understand the task or appreciate the difficulty of the party's accomplishment unless they, too, have pioneered long wilderness trails by snowshoe and dog team.

Rod Perry: *The almost 18-day, cross-country expedition I previously spoke of, the one I took with three others to bring my team from Lake Minchumina to the Parks Highway to run the 1977 Iditarod, that trek of some 175 circuitous miles on snowshoes breaking and cutting trail ahead of the teams, certainly equipped me with the background to appreciate Goodwin's feat. Others who have made similar treks by dog team, with no outside support, over such long, untracked stretches of the North, can picture with me what the passage was like for Goodwin and his men.*

February at those latitudes began with but about eight hours of useable daylight. March began with about 11 hours. Every evening they would look for a good stand of spruce in which to camp. The timber would have provided not only shelter from the wind, but also firewood, supports from which to string a ridge line for the wall tent and boughs for bedding. As every seasoned woodsman knows, it is appreciably warmer within a thick stand of trees. The forest canopy provides a barrier that reduces radiation as the north sky in winter (the dark side of the earth) pulls heat away from the planet into space. The crew would have pulled off of the river into the woods and found a suitable camp spot before it grew too dark to see. Camp routine was set; each man had his tasks and the work progressed with speed and efficiency.

The person experienced in winter travel by dog team can also visualize what the daily camping routine looked like. It went something like this: Two of the men set to stamping down a tent site, or, where the snow was shallow enough in the Interior, digging it out to ground level, using a snowshoe for a scoop. Quickly, they threw up a floorless wall tent, fired up the Yukon stove and began melting a large volume of snow for cooking. The cooks multitasked. While they readied the evening meal they probably worked ahead, pre-simmering beans or rice and reconstituting other dehydrated food for the following night. They would have made bannock (bread either fried in bacon drippings or baked atop the stove in a skillet with the lid on) enough to eat with the evening meal as well as the next day on the trail.

Simultaneously, they cooked for the dogs. Dog drivers then, as now, took a lot of pride in keeping their dogs in good shape, and that meant feeding them well. To a large cauldron of boiling snow water, the men likely added something such as rice and lard or bacon to go with one salmon per dog.

A third man cut and split enough dry timber for firewood to last the night and the next morning. A fourth man cut green boughs for beds for both men and dogs. The fifth man unharnessed the dogs, chained them out individually, put down some boughs for their beds and spread out the feed pans. As men finished their tasks they helped those who had not. The items from the sleds that needed to be brought into the tent were unpacked and carried in.

Wherever the way ahead did not require Goodwin to make route choices, and where it did not require daylight to still see enough to pick the way ahead (such as up the Susitna and its tributaries as far as the mouth of the Happy River), when the rest of the crew stopped to perform camp chores, he may well have had one of the men continue on to begin breaking the trail over the first part of the next day's march. Snowshoeing out a few miles, then turning around and widening the trail on the way back to camp, then having it set up while they slept would have given the men and teams a wonderfully advantageous start the following day. However, just as Goodwin did not include in his report many of the details of how they traveled and camped, he did not report whether he used such a strategy.

While the meals cooked and the stove heated the tent, by kerosene lantern or candle light the men made efficient use of their time, hanging clothing and harnesses to dry, repairing clothing and equipment, sharpening axes and saws and tending to whatever else demanded attention to keep them trail-ready. Goodwin would have worked on his journal,

*perhaps seated upon a salmon bale. Finally, with their meals
eaten, the dishes cleaned and the dogs fed, they spread a
canvas over the thick bough bed, lay down a caribou hide
apiece (hair up) over which each man spread his sleeping robe,
blew out the light and turned in.*

*Up in the predawn darkness, they built another fire in the
stove, dressed, ate, repacked the sleds and harnessed the team.
The tent and stove (filled with birch bark, kindling and small
dimension firewood) and stovepipe were packed last so they
could be unpacked quickly the next night. Each morning they
were back on the trail as daylight first grayed the eastern sky.*

The men would have piled even more food on the sleds
at Susitna Station had they not hoped to supplement with
game. "It is a veritable paradise for moose," Goodwin wrote
as they ascended the steeper gradient of the Happy River,
"and on the 28th of February, while some distance ahead of
the party I killed a big, bull moose. For the success of the trip
we figured on a moose or plenty of ptarmigan . . . the moose
dressed probably 650 lbs, and but for it we must have been
on short rations toward the end of the trip....We saw,
however, but about 80 ptarmigan on the entire trip and only
had four of them, these were all near timber line."

Along the way they had just come they passed three
parties totaling nine men, bound for the pass over the Alaska
Range to the headwaters of the Kuskokwim. All of them
were camping, killing moose and awaiting more favorable
traveling conditions.

Rod Perry: *Talk about something to create "favorable traveling
conditions." The five-man government party breaking trail on
snowshoes with 18 dogs and five heavy sleds packing down a
superhighway ahead of them must have seemed heaven sent!*

As the Colonel snowshoed ahead, he referred to the few
rudimentary maps available in that day such as those made by

the Spurr-Post expedition of 1898 and the Herron exploration of 1899 as well as the U.S. Geological Survey Reconnaissance map of the Mount McKinley region made in 1904. Some parts of the maps Goodwin found accurate, others in extreme error.

On March 2, the men and teams crested Rainy Pass south of Mt. McKinley. It was beautifully clear and calm at the summit. Goodwin noted with pleasure that he found Rainy Pass so easy of ascent and descent and near to a direct line of the desired route.

The following day, after having descended from the pass down the Dalzell River, they reached the Rohn River. There, the party met two men on foot. Bound for Seward to get medical treatment for one man's thumb, they had been virtually lost for a number of days, even though one of them had been out to Seward once before. The ailing man most happily received antiseptic tablets from Goodwin.

Rod Perry: *But the greater gift given them, the one that the two no doubt accepted with joy and relief, was the party's backtrail to Susitna Station! Nothing packs a trail like dog feet. The stamped-out campsites they inherited—and bough beds if they yet remained free of snow—would have been the heaven-sent frosting on the cake.*

Down the Rohn River and the upper Kuskokwim, the group rejoiced in some easy sailing of their own. Just across the summit, on the interior side of the range, is a region of light snows. There, almost incessant mountain winds usually keep the ice of the upper river blown free and the way clear except for patches of open water and overflow. On some stretches over polished ice with the wind at their back, the men were able to ride the sleds for the first and only part of the trip.

Continuing down from the upper Kuskoquim, as the reconnaissance party entered into the Interior, they left the mountains behind. Near the mouth of the Tonzona River

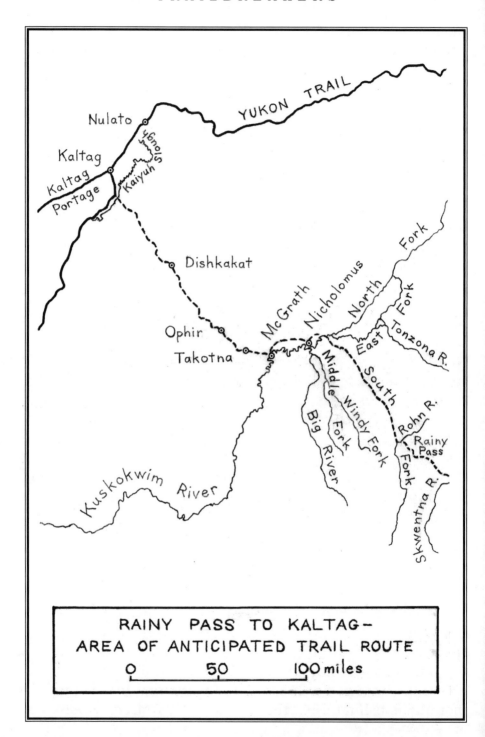

RAINY PASS TO KALTAG —
AREA OF ANTICIPATED TRAIL ROUTE

0   50   100 miles

they ran into Chief Nikolai with two women. Though the two groups had trouble communicating, the Natives guided the expedition 20 miles cross country to Nicholomas, a native village on the Kuskokwim opposite the mouth of Big River. At the village, they met a white man who had just snowshoed from McGrath's. After gaining useful information about the nearby country from him, they followed the man's backtrail to the post. They had finished the most remote, grueling and adventurous section of their reconnaissance.

The men halted for a day. There, as per their arrangement with him, they left "Johnson," the Cree Indian. If he could have hurried back, he could have taken advantage of the hard trail-base, but he was fighting a bad case of pleurisy.

Presumably, the party reprovisioned to whatever extent they could, but the recent gold rush in the nearby country had all but exhausted supplies at McGrath's trading post. They found damaged flour selling for $12 per hundred and sugar at 40 cents per pound. No other commodity was to be had.

At Moore City, a day's travel out from McGrath's, they found prices much higher because everything had to be laboriously brought there from the main river. Flour was $35 per hundred, sugar and beans both 50 cents per pound and dried fruits sold for 55 cents per pound. The going wage in that era back in the States was about $2.00 for a day's work.

They found as well that Moore City had been almost totally abandoned. Two weeks before, the miners had stampeded to a new strike at Ophir, 12 trail miles away. The group stayed the night with the U.S. Commissioner, still stationed at Moore City.

Goodwin gained a great deal of useful information about the country from him, including a hand-sketched map.

The next day the party traveled on to Ophir. Colonel Goodwin, as he had done every 50 miles, plotted the global position by taking observations on Polaris.

From Ophir, he would have preferred to take a direct line of travel cross-country to Kaltag which he calculated to be some 100 miles away. However, from the body of information

he had collected he knew that a beeline would require a
great deal of cutting through tamarack and brush. Not only
did he conclude that the season was growing late and they
were almost out of food, his orders were limited to looking over
the country and reporting route.feasibility to his superiors, not
investing time and effort in building—or even marking—a trail
the Road Commission still might decide against constructing.

The men and teams followed the beaten path, which
progressed in the most crooked, round-about way
imaginable, snaking through muskegs, around thickets and
over low, rolling hills to reach Dishkaket. There, about 100
Natives and a dozen white people dwelled at what was then
considered to be the head of navigation for supplies coming
up the Innoko River from the Yukon. It featured two stores,
a saloon and a roadhouse.

Keeping to the twisting trail, they traveled on to a
roadhouse near the mouth of Kaiyuh Slough amid plunging
temperatures, then reached Kaltag on March 19, at 43
degrees below zero, the coldest weather of the entire trip.
Forty-nine days had elapsed since they started from Seward,
43 days actually spent traveling. They had snowshoed ahead
of the dogs or walked on hard trails all but a 39-mile-long
stretch of incredibly slick ice on the Rohn and Kuskokwim
Rivers where they had been able to sit atop the loads.

It had been a veritable beeline. The distance, Seward to
Kaltag, Goodwin very roughly measured as 564 miles. The
winter route in common use, Valdez through Fairbanks to
Kaltag, was about 1,000 miles.

Parting with Pulham and Jackson at Kaltag, taking
on provisions and resting their dogs, Goodwin and Kinney
awaited arrival of the mail carrier, hearing that the trail was
obliterated ahead. On March 22, they left for Unalakleet. The
Kaltag Portage, even though it had seen heavy traffic for a
decade, looked to be so hard for the traveler to find in the bad
weather, with so many twists and turns that needed to be
eliminated, and over so much open, windswept, unmarked

country, that but for following the mail carrier and his dogs who knew the way intimately, they would have experienced great difficulty keeping the trail.

From Unalakleet, as the two men followed the coast north and west to Nome, they assessed the condition of the Overland Mail Trail, constructed off of the ocean to accommodate travel before freeze-up and after ice-out.

Goodwin and Kinney drove their dogs into Nome April 5, completing the "Winter Reconnaissance of 1908," 66 days after leaving Seward. By the pathfinders' estimate, the entire Seward-Nome distance was about 865 miles.

In his summary report, Walter Goodwin evaluated the condition of the route as they had found it from Seward to Potter and the way over Crow Creek Pass as entirely unfeasible for a mail route. He stated, however, that the route would become very practicable to put in and maintain if and when the railroad were constructed as far as the head of Knik Arm.

Goodwin further concluded that there was just not enough demand for such a trail yet. While it would indeed result in a fine trail, he said the effort and expense of cutting a 10-foot-wide swath hundreds of miles through trees and brush, building log bridges, erecting thousands of tripods to mark treeless stretches and accomplishing other construction would just not be worth it at the time.

"It would take infinitely more travel than is in sight at present to break a fast or feasible trail over the route, even were a trail cut through the timber the entire distance, and unless the new Innoko District shows up well, Goodwin wrote, *"or some big strike is made along the route*, it would be entirely impracticable to send Nome mail by this route, **as roadhouses would have to be built and maintained and the entire route is entirely too far from the line of travel under present conditions."** (bold italics mine)

No doubt, the Goodwin Survey excited Nome. But Fairbanks, by then the commercial and governmental center of Alaska, and Dawson, declining but still an important town farther up the Yukon, attracted a lot of summer shipping. The steamboat traffic not only caused villages along the great interior waterway to grow and thrive, but the steamers easily and inexpensively supplied the length of the Yukon River Trail. That readied the way for winter service to busy dog-team traffic. The well-supplied infrastructure explains a great deal about why government roadbuilders had kept Nome looking east up the Yukon for its winter connection to the outside world.

At the same time, when the Alaska Central railroad went broke in 1907 and construction crews left, the combined populations of Seward and the rest of the Cook Inlet region had bottomed out and the economy was a far cry from that found north in the relatively bustling heartland. And how could a trail through hundreds of miles of desolate, unpopulated wilderness ever duplicate the infrastructure of the Yukon River Trail?

Obviously, Alaska Road Commission would not have sent Goodwin if they had not at least entertained the possibilities of building the trail should his reconnaissance prove it immediately practical. However, with a sizeable workload already, once Goodwin's assessment opined that rationale against the undertaking outweighed rationale for it, it is doubtful the ARC would have ever begun work on the project without some major shift.

Little did anyone guess in those waning days of the 1907–08 winter following Goodwin's passage that the very shift that would break things loose was beginning. Partners John Beaton and William A. Dikeman, dissatisfied at their fortunes prospecting the Innoko River, decided to probe far up an almost-untraveled tributary river, a navigable waterway which, they reasoned, probably had its headwaters in the virtually unknown and unprospected area of the Kuskokwim Mountains. Along with a non-prospecting partner, Merton "Mike" Marston who worked a town job to gather money for their ventures, they bought a small steamboat and laid plans for a thorough look into the remote country the following summer.

As the snows of the winter of Walter Goodwin's passage melted into summer and his ARC report was filed, Beaton and Dikeman, accompanied by Beaton's young brother, Murdock, began steaming their way up the tortuously serpentining Innoko tributary.

Summer passed into fall, and once hopeful Nomeites saw that not only was their pet trail project no closer to becoming reality, for all they knew possibilities had all but disappeared since Goodwin had turned in his assessment.

The Beatons and Dikeman, having taken their small steamer as far up the small river as they thought practical, beached their boat. Having secured it for the coming winter, they built a small cabin on skids, thinking that they might need to move it later. Ready for the winter, they shouldered heavy packs of camp gear and supplies and picks, shovels and pans, left the cabin and prospected their way south toward the unknown Kuskokwim Mountains.

Through the early winter of 1908 as snows again whitened the land, Colonel Goodwin's reconnoitered route between McGrath's and Susitna Station lay dormant except for the occasional prospector possessed of some powerful need to dare the passage and take on the cruel vicissitudes. Out on that desolate stretch, nothing had changed. As far as anyone knew, nothing would.

Near the foothills of the Kuskokwims, Beaton and Dikeman, with the help of Murdock, sank test hole after test hole, probing the unknown country for the yellow lure. November passed into December. Ten test holes . . . fifteen test holes . . . twenty test holes . . . twenty-five test holes, twenty-six . . . Christmas was approaching, the work was terribly taxing, should they take the day off to rest and celebrate in some simple way?

Back in the Nome office of the Alaska Road Commission, the entire substance of Goodwin's reconnaissance might well have remained as it stood: just 14 pages consisting of his expedition report and negative needs assessment, perhaps gathering dust in a file under some heading such as, "Ideas Investigated and Found Wanting."

Then it happened!

Chapter 21

———◆———

IDITAROD GOLD!

In the distant recesses of the remote, unknown Kuskokwim Foothills Country, far back near the headwaters of a small stream, Otter Creek, On Christmas Day, 1908, John Beaton and Henry Dikeman, assisted by Murdock Beaton, working 12 feet deep at the bottom of their twenty-seventh test hole, strike gold!

In Alaska, a land of fabulous paystreaks, the find would turn out to be the widest paystreak ever discovered there.

THE FIND IS IN SUCH REMOTE SURROUNDINGS that the country remains silent; nothing whatsoever is known about it because the men don't leave the distant, uninhabited discovery area for some months. They prospect further, thawing and sinking test holes upstream and downstream in an effort to locate the richest deposits. By ice-out, the men have staked close to a mile of Otter Creek , as John Beaton would put it, "For ourselves and a few of our friends." Of course, not forgotten is their supporting partner laboring back in town, Merton "Mike" Marston.

Finally, the men skid their steamboat down the ways and head for distant Ophir to record their claims. During the hundreds of miles of descending the "Haiditarod" (Athapaskan for, variously, "distant place" or "clear water") River and ascending the Innoko following the unending bends, they encounter another steamboat with prospectors aboard. True to the miners' code, the partners freely tip the others off.

Even after that, due to the isolation of the area, Iditarod Country still holds word of the strike close to the vest. Finally, however, in the fall of 1909, the clarion cry rings out once more across the North: **GOLD!**

The better part of a year after the Christmas Day strike, Nome and Fairbanks get the tidings first. The Seward Gateway reports "The people of Fairbanks are simply wild over the reports recently from the Iditarod . . . , the scene of the latest stampede. The steamer Martha Clow is billed to leave tomorrow and will be the last boat of the season. Miners and others are so anxious to engage passage that they are simply fighting for the right to be taken on board.

So the stampede was on! Hordes by the hopeful thousands charged into some of the most remote real estate in Alaska, bound for Haiditarod (which quickly becomes known as Iditarod) country over any route they could. It turned out to be the last great, old-fashioned, hell-bent-for-leather gold rush on the North American continent.

The first town established in the Iditarod Mining District was Flat, in 1909. It was located on Otter Creek, seven miles east of its junction with the Iditarod River.

As winter froze the waterways, some continued to venture in overland, but most of the would-be stampeders chose to wait until the following spring to head for the new diggings by water.

Rod Perry: *If winter conditions so held up the thousands of stampeders who were desperate to enter the gold country over the much less difficult trail from the populated side—the Yukon side—how much more was immigration into Iditarod virtually stopped from coming in over the infinitely more difficult, sparsely populated side—the Seward-Su Station side.*

In May of 1910, almost one and one-half years after the discovery, thousands boarded steamboats bound for remote goldfields, some following outgoing ice down from Fairbanks. The first craft, the steamboat *Tanana* arrived June 1 with others hard in its wake. The *Tanana* progressed as far as it could up river, reaching a point eight miles west of Flat. There, where it offloaded its cargo, the town of Iditarod sprang up.

GREAT RUSH TO IDITAROD

Ten Thousand Gold Seekers Arrive and Confusion is Great.

Special to the New York Times

TAKOMA, Wash., June 26 . . .In the last week 10,000 goldseekers have been landed by steamers at the mouth of Otter Creek, on the Iditarod River, the scene of the latest Alaska gold stampede. Between 3,000 and 5,000 more are on the way. The landing of the thousands of newcomers with their baggage and thousands of tons of freight in the Iditarod wilderness has created confusion surpassing anything Alaska had previously experienced.

Several thousand "sourdoughs" who have mined in the Klondike and Alaska camps know exactly what to do. They are spreading out on Otter, Flat, Willow and other gold-bearing creeks. Merchants from Nome and Fairbanks are erecting temporary buildings and starting business. The best of order is being preserved by Deputy United States Marshals Wiseman of Koyukuk and Sheppard of Ophir. These were sent to Iditarod by Marshal Crossly of Fairbanks on his own initiative. Otter City, at the mouth of Otter Creek, the metropolis of Iditarod, is being surveyed.

The New York Times
Published June 27, 1910

By August 1910, 3,000 people lived at Flat. Soon the communities of Flat and Iditarod were joined by a tramway.

Within one year Iditarod grew to become, briefly, the territory's biggest city. It boasted banks, newspapers,

IDITAROD GOLD FIELDS

a theater, hotels, electricity, telephones, automobiles, and, of course, the usual boom-town establishments crawling with practitioners of iniquity plying their specialties, saloons populated with gamblers and confidence men and houses of ill fame where ladies of the evening plied "the world's oldest profession." The towns of Willow Creek, Discovery Otter, and Dikeman sprang up nearby.

One result of the Iditarod Gold Rush and the accompanying population increase in the Last Frontier was that in 1912, Congress elevated Alaska to Territorial status.

Chapter 22

---◆---

Constructing the Iditarod Trail, Winter of 1910–11

THE ARC QUICKLY ACCEPTED that Goodwin's qualifier, **". . . or some big strike is made along the route. . . "** had become reality. And then some! The strike was not exactly along the direct route, but it was close enough.

During ice-free months steamboats served Iditarod by churning up the Yukon, turning up the serpentine Innoko, then winding up the tortuously twisting Iditarod River to the city located at the extreme end of high water steamboat navigation. Though not all that far in a straight line, Iditarod lay almost 1,000 river miles from the Bering Sea.

No other way than by water was practical in summer. The beeline overland was too obstructed by streams, shallow ponds and lakes and passed over tussock-ridden muskegs spread over permafrost that would have quickly turned into an impassible quagmire once summer use destroyed the thin vegetative covering.

Once winter set in, though, and ice had stopped steamboat traffic, freeze-up not only left overland freighting and travel the only way possible, but also it made it practical. However, there were yet no direct, high-quality trails to take advantage of the beeline possibilities west to Anvik on the Yukon or north to Kaltag. Alaska Road Commission wheels began to turn.

In June of 1910, trail work began because some work could be more effectively done in summer. The greater part of trail construction, however, would have to wait until after freeze-up. A few months later, early in the winter of 1910–11, the

ARC again sent Colonel Goodwin out, this time to build what they officially labeled The Rainy Pass-Kaltag Trail. It would lead from Kaltag to Susitna Station. From there they were to continue on to Seward over the existing trail and railroad bed.

———————

Al Preston: "Between Colonel Goodwin's two expeditions, the emphasis had changed as far as where the main route was to be located as it passed through the area of the Inland Empire. No longer was the priority making a trail that would most expeditiously carry mail straight through between Seward and Nome by the shortest route. The main objective had become building a trail primarily for the purpose of best serving Iditarod and secondarily serving Nome. Remember that, for a brief time, Iditarod was much bigger than Nome. Creation of a straight, beeline between Kaltag and McGrath's would have to wait. So Colonel Goodwin was directed to work on the trail by way of Iditarod, a long side-swing west from the straight line of the anticipated mail route that he had looked over three winters before.

"I want to clarify an important point to us old Nome miners. The historically correct orientation, that of Colonel Goodwin and everyone else in our day, was that what would eventually become known as the Iditarod Trail was properly limited to the new route only, the route that branched from the long established trail at Kaltag. Of course, everyone called the side loop to the west through Iditarod the Iditarod Trail. Some called the route going straight through from Kaltag to McGrath the "Mail Trail" and some just lumped it with the side loop and called it the Iditarod, too. Absolutely everyone called the long trail from McGrath over to Su Station and on to Seward the Iditarod Trail.

"But get this straight: none of us old trail hands called the old trail between Nome and Kaltag the Iditarod. For heavens sake, everyone had been calling the Nome-to-Unalakleet

274

stretch by their old names, the Coastal Trail or the Overland Trail for more than a dozen years since the beginning of the Nome Rush. And the Kaltag Portage had been the Kaltag Portage for who knows how long before Nome became Nome. Thousands upon thousands of trips had been taken over the route to connect us with the Yukon River Trail at Kaltag and men had known the beaten thoroughfare between Nome and Kaltag so well by the old names. I tell you, it never so much as entered the mind of anybody I ever heard of to rename the whole, doggoned, way from Nome to Kaltag.

"Now, Rod, standing on your brake in Nome with your dogs yapping and ramming into their collars anxious to get going, you might say you were *headed for* the Iditarod Trail. But no one on the trail right out of Nome said they were *on* the Iditarod. Not yet. Naturally, we Nomites were proud of our old trails that we'd put in long before that upstart strike at Iditarod. No, we didn't consider that we'd reached the Iditarod Trail until we'd first mushed 300 miles over the old trails to Kaltag.

"That applied both directions. Travelers going northwest from Seward thought of their trip as having come to the end of the Iditarod Trail when they reached the junction of the new trail with the two old ones, the Yukon River Trail and the Kaltag Portage Trail.

"Goodwin and other travelers of the day who were familiar with the Territory flat out did not think of the Iditarod Trail as connecting Seward to Nome, but only Seward to Kaltag. After all, look at the name they gave the project: The official, government name was the Rainy Pass–Kaltag Trail."

From Dishkaket, Goodman's orders were to depart from the southeast-heading main line that headed straight through to McGrath to work on a direct, high-quality trail 67 miles south to Dikeman, the head of Iditarod River low-water navigation. His party would then continue on south the remaining 40 miles to Iditarod over the already heavily traveled, well-placed and marked trail along the east side of the river. From Iditarod they were to travel the 10 miles through Flat to Discovery Otter, then turn east 74 miles to rejoin the Kaltag-McGrath trail at Takotna.

As stated, in the overall scope of the general project planning for the Seward to Nome Mail Trail, this out-of-the-way loop of about 192 miles to better connect Iditarod with the Yukon Trail, Nome and Seward had grown to take on even more importance than that of shortening of the mail route to Nome. Evidence for the relative priority lies in the fact that following directions Goodwin would leave bypassed the greatly needed straightening and marking of the 78-mile stretch from Dishkaket to Takotna on the direct Seward-Nome line. It is easy to see why the route from Seward to Kaltag became known as the Iditarod Trail, not the Seward-to-Nome Mail Trail or the Kaltag-to-Rainy Pass Trail when the focus of so much of the travel was the new gold-rush town and the bulk of the traffic took the long, Iditarod side loop.

Pulling out of Nome on November 9, 1910, a nine-man construction crew and 42 dogs divided into six seven-dog teams accompanied Goodwin. Stage one involved three weeks of trail work on the established Overland Trail between Nome and Unalakleet. They measured distances with a cyclometer, a measuring wheel attached to the rear of one of the sleds. They started with two, but one broke off and was lost on Thanksgiving Day. The remaining device had been tested for accuracy over the 47.2 mile-long surveyed road leaving Nome. It had checked out perfectly, and functioned well the entire way. On November 30 the group reached Unalakleet. The route taken measured 206.8 miles, correcting the 222 miles claimed for years.

From Unalakleet on the Bering Sea, the second stage took but one week to straighten and upgrade the heavily traveled portage to Kaltag. Arriving on December 7 at the Yukon River

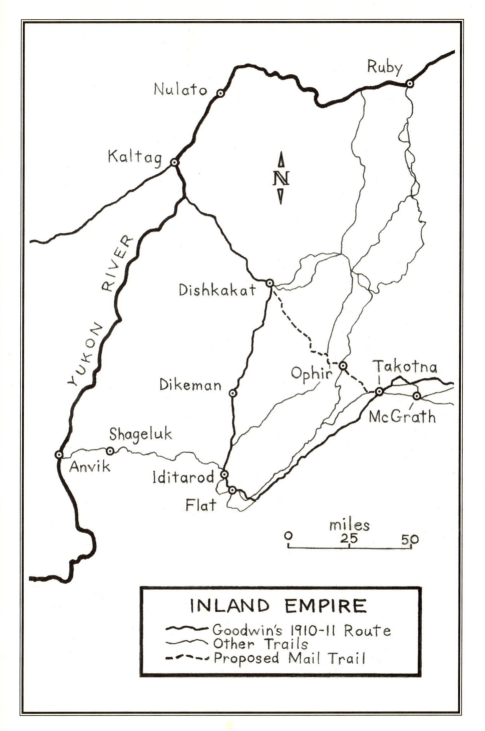

Ruby

Nulato

Kaltag

YUKON RIVER

N

Dishkakat

Dikeman

Ophir

Takotna

McGrath

Shageluk

Anvik

Iditarod

Flat

miles
0   25   50

INLAND EMPIRE
—— Goodwin's 1910-11 Route
—— Other Trails
- - - Proposed Mail Trail

village, Goodwin recorded their newly straightened trail as a significantly shortened 73.9 miles. Nome to Kaltag was henceforth known to be 281 miles when the Overland Trail was taken.

The third stage began when they crossed Yukon ice and started over the newly straightened Kaltag to Dishkaket leg of the mail trail. A Foreman Giddings (almost surely an ARC employee directing a work crew) had done extensive work on the stretch, possibly during labor beginning the previous summer. Goodwin found the trail to require almost no work and reported that it was the best-marked trail he had ever traversed in Alaska.

Giddings' marker tripod design particularly impressed Goodwin. The colonel adopted the model. It featured two, eight-foot poles with the third pole, one of ten or eleven feet, fastened so that the longest leg extended beyond the others at the top. The tripod's long end could hang directly over the trail. The men placed such tripods close enough together across all treeless expanses that, even in a blinding blizzard, a driver could see the next marker.

One unique and important feature between Kaltag and Dishkaket were the windlasses and ropes that had to be established at several trail crossings of the Kaiyuh Slough. The high banks were too steep to either take a laden sled down safely or for the dogs to pull it back up on the far side so they had to be lowered into the gulch and raised out mechanically.

Three days out from Kaltag the 10 men and their teams finished the leg to Dishkaket, and none too soon. The bottom fell out of the thermometer. After a four-day layover, the mercury rose to a balmy 36 degrees below zero, so on December 14 they moved out. On December 20, they reached Dikeman, having marked the 67 miles with more than 1,300 Gliddings tripods.

The way from Dikeman to Iditarod required no work. It was the only well-broken length of trail encountered on the entire expedition. The work crew took two days to make Iditarod over

the easy stretch, and again, arrived at shelter just ahead
of a plunging thermometer. From December 22 through 27
they holed up while temperatures plunged to between
60 and 70 degrees below zero.

On December 28, they hit the trail by way of the mining
creeks and smaller villages and during the next few days
accomplished trail work the next 84 miles to Takotna.

At Takotna they rejoined the direct Seward-Nome route.
The long-dreamed-of through route to Nome, the direct Mail
Trail, if all eventually went as planned and it was put in,
would make its way straight from Dishkaket through Ophir
to Takotna. That distance was but 78 miles, 114 miles
shorter than going around the side loop Goodwin had just
traveled through the Iditarod district.

From Takotna the trailbuilders revamped the way to the
mouth of Big River on the Kuskokwim River, widening,
marking and straightening it to save three and one-half miles.

Beyond Big River, the fourth stage began and the
complexion of the trip changed. All the way from Nome they
had been either doing touchup work or relocation work on
well-established trails. From Big River on to Hayes River,
their way would be over trackless, sparsely traveled country
with, but for a scant five miles, no cut or marked trail. This
stage actually fell into two parts: First, a cut-off they would
laboriously build from scratch from Big River to Mount
Farewell, and, second, from Mount Farewell on over the
divide to Hayes River.

From Big River, on February 21, the men began cutting
a 7- to 10-foot-wide trail through trees and brush.

Al Preston: "That country usually gets lighter snow
than any other section on the whole way to Seward. Being
close behind the inland side of the Alaska Range away from
saturated ocean clouds, it's in what they call a rain shadow.

What I don't know, and I never thought to ask Colonel Goodwin, is whether he directed the men to shovel down to ground level to make their cuts. I think he must have, or they would have been putting in a trail useless except in midwinter. Sleds just have an eight- or nine-inch clearance under the cross bents. No one would attempt to use the route in early fall and late spring if there was an impassable sea of harness-tangling, sled-wrecking stumps in their way.

"Of course, it would have added greatly to the work to make ground level cuts and you can imagine what must have been going through Colonel Goodwin's head: 'Should I add to the complexity of such an already time consuming task? Especially when time itself adds to the complexity because of the increased provisions consumed by men and dogs that have to be hauled? Or should I leave the stumps, depending upon the ARC to either send out a crew later or contract with someone from the area to clean up our work during snow-free months?' "

———◆—◆———

After the first five miles out of Big River, Goodwin kept to the single tangent he had noted as the best way on his 1908 passage, with slight modifications in places where the most direct line would not make the best trail. The cut-off took 21 days to clear through woods and willows, and to mark with tripods across open flats, but when they had finished, they had created a 56-mile-long straight shot with all the advantages of an overland trail. The old way that followed the bends of the Kuskokwim had been 108 miles, Big River to Farewell.

Along the entire way game had been plentiful. The party added spruce grouse, sharp tailed grouse and ruffed grouse, ptarmigan, snowshoe hares, and caribou to their fare whenever they came by them or they could afford the time to hunt. At Fairwell Mountain a halt was called to wait out a blizzard. With provisions dwindling, two men set out, weather notwithstanding, to hunt moose. It took but two hours to down a huge animal, a Godsend for both men and dogs.

From Farewell Mountain they reversed the course of the 1908 reconnaissance to Susitna Station without stopping to do substantial trail work except for one very notable exception: They set tripods over the treeless 12-mile expanse from the end of timber on the Dalzell River over Rainy Pass to timberline on the Pass Creek side.

Today, the last remaining tripod from this part of the trail hangs in Rainy Pass Lodge near the old trail route. Although Goodwin did not elaborate, a look at the size of the "poles" (small logs better describes them) and a reconnaissance to determine how far the poles/logs must have been hauled from the sources of timber draws one to the conclusion that marking the treeless stretch must have occupied the trail-builders for several very hard days.

If the men placed markers at the same interval they had over the Dishkaket to Dikeman stretch, almost 200 tripods per mile, locating and cutting and limbing the 7,200 individual poles (3 poles/tripod x 200 x 12 miles) carrying each pole by snowshoe from the stump over to the trail to stage them for pick-up, then freighting them uphill with the teams would have been no light work. Then there was the joinery. The two eight-foot poles were cut at about 65-degree angles at their top end so that when standing spread-out they could interface the 11-foot pole sandwiched between them with fairly long, flat surfaces. All three poles were drilled with a brace and bit and a long, two-inch spruce dowel tapped through the holes to join them.

The cyclometer declared the distance from Nome through Iditarod to the summit of Rainy Pass to be 669 miles.

As Goodwin snowshoed his way down the Happy and Skwentna Rivers, he again scrutinized the country with a view to creating an overland trail pursuant to the anticipated act of Congress appropriating $50,000 for work to begin the following winter.

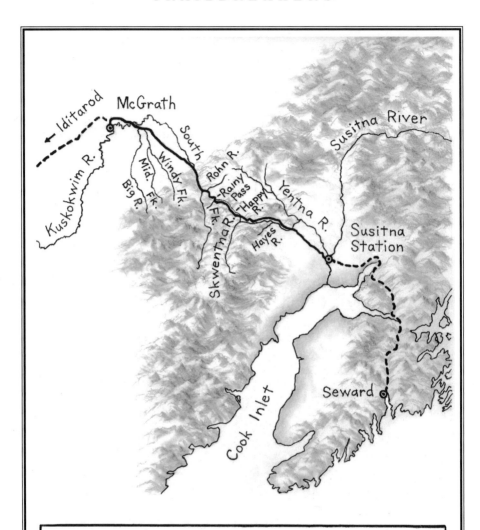

IDITAROD FINALLY COMPLETED IN 1911
This section of the Iditarod—Susitna Station to McGrath—was heretofore nonexistent as a cut and marked trail. Prior to this date, few risked it. Now, trail conditions encourage and support heavy use.

0   50   100 miles

A new ARC cut-off beginning six and one-half miles below Hayes River and leading straight cross country to Susitna Station appears on the map showing their trip route. That trail project—somewhat equal in difficulty to Goodwin's Big River-to-Farewell work—had previously been built by another work party sent out from Seward under the direction of Anton Eide to perform upgrades and construction all the way to the Alaska Range.

Between Goodwin's two treks, the Alaska Central Railroad had been reorganized and the new operation was called the Alaska Northern Railway. The new administrators had extended the right of way much farther and winter sled and foot traffic had increased. These developments created not only a longer roadbed but the increased use kept the trail over the roadbed broken better. The party could pass over the country much more quickly than Goodwin had before.

The Colonel was no doubt happy not to have to cross Crow Creek Pass. He found that terrible climb had been made unnecessary with the option of a much gentler route over Indian Pass that most dog-team travel was taking. Even counting a one-day holdup at Glacier Creek (Girdwood) to wait out a blizzard, over Eide's refined trail, they required but nine days to cover the last leg of the trip, Susitna Station to Seward.

On February 25, 1911 they arrived at Resurrection Bay. To the great pride of the expedition members, all 42 of their sled dogs trotted into Seward in prime condition. Goodwin's cyclometer had measured the route as 958 miles. Actually, 957.95 to be exact.

Rod Perry: *Most writing about the old trail has been poorly researched, if researched at all. As a result, there is so much absolute hooey out there that is commonly repeated about the state of the Iditarod Trail and about its use prior to Goodwin's work. As previously mentioned, many writers today have made it sound like some thoroughfare existed and traffic simply whizzed back and forth over it since antiquity. Again,*

*even after the 1906–1907 Inland Empire strikes, very few
headed for the interior from Susitna Station. In fact, Colonel
Goodwin himself commented that the entire use of the route
was limited to only about 20 travelers, total, the winter of his
reconnaissance, 1907–08. Correctly speaking, it was not until
Walter Goodwin's construction trip the winter of 1910–11, that
there was truly an Iditarod Trail,—if one's definition of a trail
is a definite path that may be followed fairly precisely— and it
wasn't until the winter of 1911–12 that roadhouses were first
in place, that all of the conditions were finally combined that
allowed the way to become well-trafficked.*

*Let's go over it again to clarify the chronology. It should be
abundantly clear that until word of the Iditarod strike became
known and the trail froze up the last couple of months of 1909,
there had not been much reason to head over the route. The
draw of the small midway strikes apparently wasn't that
compelling. Only a few going between Cook Inlet and those
minor diggings around Ophir had been risking the passage.
Even after the big strike at Iditarod, even with an increase in
numbers that wanted to get there, there wasn't much travel the
winter of 1909–1910. Even the winter of 1910–1911, the
winter Goodwin cut and marked the trail, there wasn't much
use of the trail because he didn't finish the work until most of
that winter was over. And trail or no trail, mushers still had to
mound their sleds with enormous loads, everything they would
need to take them all the way through. It wasn't until the
winter of 1911–1912 that enough of a trail infrastructure was
in place in the way of a roadhouse system offering shelter and
food for man and beast that significant travel commenced.*

*Because of the sheer mountain of erroneous thinking and
writing out there, I feel compelled to state it one more time:*
***Let it be firmly reiterated that it was not until the fall
following Colonel Walter Goodwin's trail work, the fall
of 1911, that the Iditarod Trail truly had its beginning
as a real trail, a cut and marked path, not merely a
general, barely known and hardly traveled route over***

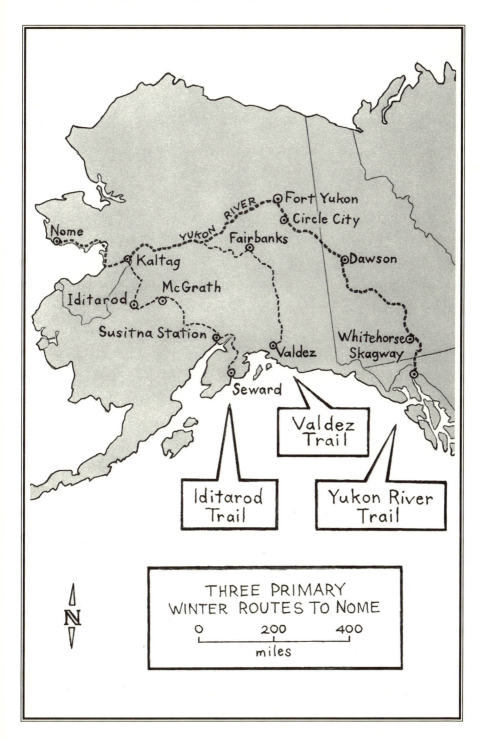

Fort Yukon
Circle City
YUKON RIVER
Nome
Fairbanks
Kaltag
Dawson
McGrath
Iditarod
Susitna Station
Valdez
Whitehorse
Skagway
Seward

Valdez
Trail

Iditarod
Trail

Yukon River
Trail

THREE PRIMARY
WINTER ROUTES TO NOME

0   200   400
miles

N

deep, unbroken snow. Let it be repeated that it was not until that fall of 1911—with the roadhouse system newly established—that route use turned from risky and occasional to sure and heavy.

Chapter 23

Use of the New Trail Skyrockets

ALASKA ROAD COMMISSIONERS had given Walter Goodwin the additional directive to locate advantageous sites for roadhouses along his way. Because stretches of trail between locations varied in difficulty, which affected traveling speed, the most important criteria was that they be spaced a typical day's foot travel apart. His usual spacing was about 20 miles between sites.

Enterprising folk who ventured into even the most remote locations to set up places of food and lodging jump started heavy use of the trail. In anticipation of the traffic to come, a few would-be purveyors of shelter, sustenance and supply followed hard on Goodwin's heels. They hardly allowed his trail to set up, using prime spring freighting conditions during the tail end of the 1910–11 winter to reach and claim their site before breakup and take in tools, building materials and supplies to begin work. Others intending to locate near a navigable waterway probably awaited the opening of the river transport season to move what they needed as close to their little piece of heaven as possible. Some of the new businessmen spreading over the trail built on Goodwin's sites, some set up shop at locations they thought were better. Pat O'Cotter reported in the July 1911 edition of *Alaska-Yukon Magazine* that by the time of his writing (four months after Goodwin finished his trip) roadhouses were already spread all along the trail, one-half to one day's travel apart. Hikers covering 20 miles a day would not only be able to buy meals—for 50 cents to $1.50 and sleep in beds—50 cents to

$1.00 each night, but also they would often be able to stop midway between for lunch.

Once the roadhouses were built and supplied, the terribly backbreaking and inhibiting do-it-all-yourself, make-it-clear-through-or-die nature of the former primitive passage was but a memory. The route was tamed.

The ground had hardly frozen the next fall and the first skiff of white had barely covered the way when teams by the hundreds began pouring over Colonel Walter Goodwin's trail. During one week alone in November of 1911, some 120 teams pulled out of Knik bound for the gold fields of the interior.

Because of the constant traffic it began to receive, the fall of 1911 also marked the first time a traveler could count on finding a trail with a hard base. Beginning then, even if it had snowed in or blown over in a storm, the dog driver or hiker could be assured that, at some distance below the soft surface, there was a packed foundation so that man and dogs would not have to wallow through bottomless fluff.

Rod Perry: *Only a dog driver who has floundered days through a ground-to-surface accumulation of unbroken snow can truly appreciate the value of a hard trail bottom!*

It was the cutting and marking of the way, the establishment of a set-up trail base and the rest and resupply points every 20 miles or so that jump-started trail use, turning the Iditarod into the thoroughfare of gold-rush renown and legend.

About the time Goodwin's party passed through in 1910–11, prospectors found more gold in the country between Ophir and the Yukon River village of Ruby. Quickly, new settlements of Long, Poorman and Cripple Landing sprang up. The finds not only added to numbers traveling the trail, but the new finds necessitated the building of several branch trails connecting Goodwin's trail with the new settlements.

Trappers—termed "cat stranglers" by the miners—comprised another sizeable group who used the new trail. It gave them a beaten path and supply support leading deep into territory that previously had been too logistically difficult to effectively work. They quickly established myriad side trails of up to fifty or more miles in length, opening up thousands of square miles to the fur industry that ranked in importance only behind gold and fisheries in the territory.

The anticipated Mail Trail planned take the most direct, Seward-to-Nome route had not been finished because the Takotna-to-Dishkaket leg had not, so far, been relocated to take a straighter line. Also, until 1914 the U.S. Mail contract still ran through Fairbanks. Therefore, most traffic heading north out of Seward and south from Kaltag was not traveling Seward to Nome or Nome to Seward, but bound for the new gold finds of the Inland Empire and Iditarod, chiefly the latter. Again, no wonder that the route between Seward and Kaltag quickly became known as the "Iditarod Trail."

The Dogs Were Big! Alma with friends.

Chapter 24

＊＊＊◆＊＊＊

Dog Days: Trail Life in its Heyday

ANYONE CONTEMPLATING A JOURNEY by dog team from Seward over the trail to Iditarod country planned on a trip of two to three weeks; all the way to Nome could take four to five weeks. Travelers were of a wide description: freighters, miners, mail carriers, Natives, trappers, business people and gamblers, to name a sample.

Those who wanted to travel as passengers could do so if they had a deep enough pocket. They usually went with the freight teams and hardly ever got to add their weight to the already heavily laden sleds. They had to walk most of the way, and they were usually expected to help muscle the sled through tough passages. Passengers paid about $1,500 to go clear through to Nome and $275 was standard fare, Knik to McGrath. Most drivers had their own teams, but a team complete with a sled, towline and harness setup—and even individual dogs—could be rented.

Rod Perry: *Dogs of the day were large. My old sourdough friend, the late Carl Clark of Hope, used to freight for the trader at Tanana, where that great river joins the Yukon. The trader had two teams, Carl told me, the "little yappers," 80- to 90- pound native huskies used for lighter loads and faster going, and the heavy freight team of 120- to 150-pound Mackenzie River Huskies.*

The true origin of the fabled Mackenzie River husky is— arguably—lost to time, retelling and lack of actual records many can agree with. Most agree that the breed was the creation, long before the Klondike Rush, of early Hudson's Bay Company freighters in the Canadian Arctic around the Mackenzie delta. The genetic mix that made up the breed draws heated argument today. Some have said the great dogs resulted mainly from a cross of the large, native huskies of the Canadian Arctic with the Saint Bernard or some other giant working breed, and with perhaps a touch of wolf blood added. Whatever they were, they were not fast, but at their pace they could really yank the slack out of a towline.

Today, it is not uncommon to encounter an Alaskan who claims that their dog is a MacKenzie River Husky. Maybe it is, but if so, it may well be something substantially different from dogs of that designation during gold rush times. The late Raymond Thompson, inventor of the famous Thompson locking steel snare, who trapped in the Athabaska country of the Canadian subarctic as a young man in the early years of the 20th century and wrote the "Sled Dog Trails" column in the *Alaska Sportsman Magazine* as an elderly one, knew the old breed well. He once spent an entire summer in the 1960s traveling the Yukon and Northwest Territories searching to see if any of the breed still existed in a form he recognized. He found not one.

Freighting over the Iditarod Trail, most of the large dogs, when pulling substantial loads, traveled at about four and one-half miles per hour, an aggravating, "too fast to walk, too slow to trot," in-between pace for a man.

By the time of the Iditarod Rush, dog-team gear, sleds, hookups and methods had evolved substantially from what had been used far to the east along the Upper Yukon in the years leading up to and immediately following the Klondike strike. Russian and Eskimo dog driving methods and gear began to exert a strong influence when thousands from the interior rushed to the Arctic west coast during the Nome Rush.

Just in front of the sled were the wheel dogs, or wheelers. These were often the biggest, strongest dogs in the team because from the position they not only had to pull, but had to counter the influence of the towline and sled. If, say, the majority of team ahead had already gone around a bend to the left, the towline would be pulling with great force left across the turn before the last dogs and sled had yet reached it. The driver would do all he could to "run the sled out" by running and vigorously shoving the sled to reach the corner before the power from the towline pulling left could haul it off the trail over the inside of the curve.

Not only rounding sharp curves but just the common meandering of the sled over the usual unevenness of the trail continually jostled the wheelers. They had to be nimble because good wheeler work on a winding trail required that they continually had to jump the towline to pull from the opposite side in their effort to keep the sled on course and keep themselves from being swept from the trail by the towline cutting a corner. Obviously, a dog of level disposition fit the job description best. It helped to rotate wheelers to give them periodic breaks.

Between the wheelers and the front of the team were "team dogs," the common working animals. The final two just behind the leader were the "swing dogs." Swing dogs were usually some of the fastest, most spirited animals on the team. A team somehow receives its pace signal from the dogs up front so speedy swing dogs helped keep the team moving faster. Most swing dogs knew the driver's commands to the leader, and were often themselves backup leaders or young leaders in training.

At the head of the team was the very extension of the driver himself, his leader or leaders. A well-trained leader could follow commands to start, stop, accelerate and decelerate the team, steer it left and right, and turn back to reverse direction, as well as smoothly pass other teams without interference. Besides those things that leaders learned from their drivers, some leaders possessed unique natural abilities, some of them downright uncanny and amazing.

Togo, the great leader of the immortal driver, Leonard Seppala, hero of the world-famous 1925 dog team relay to race diphtheria serum to epidemic-stricken Nome, led his team across the sea ice of Norton Bay in the black of night during a raging blizzard on their leg of the life-saving dash. Seppala felt secure in entrusting his own life as well as the fate of Nome to Togo's uncanny ability to hold unerringly to an absolutely straight line of travel once he had been put on course.

Rod Perry: *Following Togo's death from old age, Seppala had a taxidermist mount him. The mount may be viewed at the Iditarod Trail headquarters building on Knik Road out of Wasilla, Alaska.*

Some lead dogs could sense thin ice and turn the team to avoid the danger. The late Lester Bugsby, who seemed to strike it rich wherever he turned, be it in gold, salmon or land, told me that with a newly purchased team and a young leader hauling a big sled weighted with his entire winter supply, he pulled out from the trading post at Tanana just after freeze-up, bound for his diggings on the Koyukuk.

———◆———◆———

Lester Bugsby: "Rod, I'll tell you about the value of a leader. Heading out of the Tanana mouth onto Yukon ice, I come to a place where maybe the mixing of the two currents is causing some extra turbulence that slows ice formation. Whatever's going on under the ice, it makes for a thin spot.

"With no warning, the sled breaks through! The load weighs hundreds of pounds so it goes down like so much stone. As the current starts to suck me under with it, I have barely an instant to kick off from the cargo and reach the edge of the hole. Even as I just get my arms above the edge to hang on, the sinking sled caught by the strong current drags the poor dogs backwards. They're desperately scratching and clawing, resisting for everything they're worth, but with all their power they're nothing compared to the current's drag on that huge, sinking load. I'm having all I can do to hang on and not be pulled under. I can't come close to getting to my knife or moving over to cut the towline. So they just disappear pair after pair into the hole and under the ice.

"I'm getting more and more numbed and can't hang on much longer. The tug of the current is terrible. Just about when I'm about to go the way of the dogs, an Indian man shows up. He'd been traveling with his family and they'd seen us break through. They live there and know the ice so he leaves his wife and kids back and drives his team and empty sled up as close as he dares. He moves fast, lines his team out away from the hole with his leader facing back toward his wife. He walks carefully closer with a line attaching him to his sled so the team can pull him out if he breaks through. He throws me another rope with a couple of loops at the end so I have something to grab. A real smart fellow and a quick thinker. I owe that man my life.

"Fifteen minutes later, old John, the trading-post owner, and Carl Clark, his freighter, are mighty surprised to see me stumble through the door with my rescuer's help, half frozen and caked with ice. They get me in dry clothes, and sit me almost on top of the roaring barrel stove. They put hot water bags next to my back and belly, between my thighs and over my head. I'm halfway to my knees in a tub of hot water. They keep hot blankets coming to throw over me. As soon as I can, they get me to start swallowing hot soup.

"As soon as he thinks I'll be OK he tells me to just gather up a whole new outfit from his shelves and warehouse as soon as I'm ready. He loans me one of his big sleds. Then he sends Carl around the village to buy dogs from various owners and put together a whole new team. The way it was in old-time Alaska, he trusts me to settle up when I can.

"Rod, we were talking about leaders and their talents. With my old leader, the breakthrough would have never happened. I could trust that savvy old river dog to sense thin ice. I don't know how he picked it up, but he had a real fear of it and he'd steer me well away. It was an uncanny ability the new leader lacked."

———◆———

Little wonder that drivers valued top lead dogs like gold, and drivers and their leaders grew especially close. Roadhouse operators commonly allowed drivers to bring their leaders in to sleep beside them. Some of the greatest lead dogs gained fame that spread throughout the north. One such dog, a huge, handsome animal owned by enthusiastic young dog-driver, Army lieutenant Billy Mitchell, became the envy of the Upper Yukon.

Valued lead dogs that grew too old for hard duty in harness but were still able to trot along sometimes had their careers extended as "loose leaders," trotting free in front of the team.

The great gold stampedes created a huge demand for dogs. It was said that no large dog wandering the streets of San Francisco, Portland or Seattle was safe. Many were snatched up and brought north. With such a premium on large dogs, many of the working and guarding breeds that were fierce defenders of herd and home came into common use and often mixed their genes with some of the large native dogs that fought at the slightest provocation.

———◆———

Rod Perry: *The late Native leader and sagacious dog man Fred Stickman told me that his people along the Yukon sometimes mixed some wolf blood into their working dogs, but most selectively, only if they could catch a wolf with just the right rather streamlined build. Some famous sourdoughs such as Slim Williams and Frank Glazier—the latter with whom*

I had a couple of lengthy visits—bred teams of half, or even three-quarter wolf blood.

My old pal, Ron Aldrich, the only man to run both the first Iditarod Trail Sled Dog Race and the First Yukon Quest race from Fairbanks to Whitehorse, once asked tough old-time miner and freighter, the late Rocky Cummings, "Rocky, back in the old days when so many men drove teams of big, fighting dogs, did you ever have any problems on the trail around other teams?"

Rocky Cummings: "One time I'm freighting out near McDougal, north of Su Station. While coming down a steep hill, the dogs prick up their ears and step up the pace. A moose or another team has to be close ahead. Immediately, we see a team coming up toward us. The trail's narrow, with only room for one of us. The downhill driver has the right of way because he has less control. The guy's not making any move to give me the trail. So I look for a trailside tree to snub off on to give him time to move his dogs and sled off. I can't figure him out, he doesn't do anything. He just brakes to a halt and stands there like an owl on a tombstone.

"My team's surging. I have all my weight on the brake. But with my heavy load and the power of my dogs dragging me down the slope I can't hold them back. As we try to pass, things happen just like I expected; a huge battle blows up. I yell to the guy to grab his dogs and help me bust up the fight. He just stands there, looking dumb. I get out my heavy shot whip (leather sewn in a long, tapering tube filled with number-eight lead bird shot) and go through his team. I use the butt like a blackjack to tap his dog out. When all of them are laying there unconscious I straighten out my team—some of them are pretty chewed up—and get them going. The guy had never done one single thing to help and I'm boiling mad. As I pass by I swing from my heels. I land the nastiest, hard right cross you ever saw square on his temple and drop him like a bad habit!"

"You ask me what happened to him? I don't know, Ron. There's a big open flat starting at the bottom of the hill. When I get to the far end, I turn and look back. He's still lying there."

———◆———◆———

Drivers carried a whip and used it the way teamsters did while driving teams of horses and mules, almost invariably using it exclusively to crack for noise to reinforce voice commands. They had to keep absolute discipline and order. Sled dogs naturally take eagerly to trail work like a Labrador retriever takes to water; neither has to be forced to perform. Dog mushers understood that happy dogs perform enthusiastically and energetically, but whipped dogs grow discouraged, even to the point of lying down. Almost ironically, using a whip like Rocky did to break up a fight was humane. It was better than allowing the animals to maim or even kill one another.

Men streaming north into Gold Rush Alaska came either from farm and ranch backgrounds or cities where most transportation was still horse-drawn. Naturally, sled-dog harness construction drew heavily from horse and mule harness design. Work dogs leaned into neck encircling, leather collars filled with hair or other padding. Singletrees (spreader bars) behind the tail allowed the pulling force to be transferred to the tug lines while keeping the dog's legs free of inward pressure from the traces that would otherwise interfere with movement.

Unlike earlier and far to the east in the Canadian north where dogs were lined up single file, later Alaska dog teams were usually lined up in pairs. A towline stretching the length of the team ran up the middle between the dogs in each pair from the sled bridle forward to the leader(s). Three-foot-long tuglines connected the towline to each dog's singletree (a spreader bar at the rear of the harness.) Coming off the towline beside each pairs' heads, foot-long neck lines connected the main line to the dogs' collar. Each pair of dogs took up six feet of towline length. That gave them room to work and maneuver, yet kept the overall towline length as compact as possible. Old time teamsters calculated "draft," figuring that the closer they could keep the load to the power source, the more efficiently the load could be drawn.

Freight sleds typically had basket lengths of 10 to 14 feet and usually measured 24 inches wide, outside to outside of the runners. Runners were usually shod with steel, the harder the better, with band-saw steel being best. New steel ran relatively slickly but should the runners be dragged over a bare gravel bar, common on the upper Kuskokwim, the steel would be scored and thereafter pull very hard, cutting the freighter's speed and unduly tiring the dogs. The colder the weather, the harder the steel dragged. Hot dog manure dropped on the run froze instantly to the steel when run over, creating a drag.

Some drivers built their own sleds during the off season, but, as few had access to carpentry shops, many were built commercially, either Outside or in Alaska. Shops often turned out many sleds of stock design but would build to custom specifications. Designs varied widely depending upon their intended use, the conditions of the country, and the biases of the driver.

Though sleds built by Natives and some old sourdoughs were often constructed of native white birch, most sleds were built of much stronger and more long lasting hickory, ash or white oak. At the turn of the 20th century, eastern hardwood forests still held many old-growth trees, tall and straight with boles reaching far above ground to the first limbs. Long, quarter-sawn boards of straight-grained, knot-free sapwood (live, outer wood is more flexible than heartwood) were commonly available by order from suppliers Outside or from the stacks stocked by every general store and trading post in the territory.

The mark of a cheechako (newcomer, ignorant to the ways of the north) sled-builder, especially if he were an advanced carpenter who took pride in his work, was that his joinery would be too tight and he would use bolts, screws and nails to put his entire sled together. Such a sled had no give to it over uneven trails. When wood and steel became brittle in the intense cold, his sled would break apart. Sound basket-sled construction required joints featuring an "engineered sloppiness," not poor joinery, but a sizing of the parts with enough ease to allow movement in those mortise and tenon joints that needed to flex. All but the very few non flexing parts were lashed together with babiche—long, rawhide laces cut from moose, caribou or seal hide.

Cargo sleds commonly came with plow handles, most useful but nefarious features, extensions of the top rails that the driver could grab to help manhandle the load from the rear of the sled. Nothing worked quite as well for working a heavy cargo, but, as they pointed directly at the driver's abdomen or groin when he leaned to the side to muscle them, should the sled hit anything and suddenly stop, the man could be badly injured. Or worse. A driver was killed in such an accident while freighting near Lake Clark.

It was extremely hard to influence sled direction from the rear of the sled, even with a load much lighter than the freighters carried. In contrast, steering even the heaviest load could be done with relative ease from the front of the sled with a long lever called a gee pole. The driver often trotted in front of the sled, straddling the towline to steer when traversing level ground.

Over hilly going, however, that was impossible for a lone driver. The steeper the incline, the more the heavy sled would tend to pick up speed and overrun the man and team ahead. On downhills, someone needed to hold the sled back by standing on the big hinged brake at the rear of the sled. Therefore, heavy freighting often required two men, one on the gee pole, the other back on the plow handles and break. At the brink of extremely steep pitches, freighters often stopped to roughlock the runners, that is, wrapping them with dog tie-out chains. And up the climbs or down the drop-offs that were impossibly steep for huge loads, such as up or down the benches of the Happy River Canyon, the Alaska Road Commission installed windlasses.

In smooth going, when the effect on the team was judged negligible, the gee poler often attached a pair of short skis or a short toboggan called a Ouija board to the towline and rode as he steered. Rarely, the driver got to ride as well, though runner tails of that day usually extended behind the rear stanchions only far enough to accommodate the front half of a man's mukluk.

Another piece of specialized equipment found on many large sleds was a slew brake. Sleds slinging around corners on fast going, sleds encountering glaciering (seepage from underground springs that built up a thick layer of ice over the trail) that formed side slopes or sleds struck by side winds on slick ice, tended to slew sideways. To keep them tracking straight, the slew brake, consisting of a single- or double-blade mounted to straddle a runner tail for side support, was depressed. Like an ice-skate blade, it offered almost no resistance in a forward direction, but carved and greatly resisted sideways movement.

When freighting an extra-heavy cargo, two or even three sleds were drawn one behind another. To keep the whole train tracking as true as possible, the sleds were "cross lashed." The right rear corner of the leading sled pulled with a short rope or chain on the left front corner of the trailer and vice versa on the opposite side so that the short, attaching lines formed an "X" between the sleds. The trailing sled followed with just enough clearance to avoid contacting the rear of the forward sled. When managing such a procession, the gee pole man still worked right behind the dogs and the brakeman moved to the rear sled, treating the two (or three) sleds as if they were one.

Multiple sleds had several advantages: They reduced the risk of sled breakage under extremely heavy loads. They spread the load out to lower the center of gravity. Items that did not have to be unloaded until reaching their destination could be packed once and the lashings left alone on one of the sleds. And the sleds could be detached to singly negotiate steep climbs and downhills and other difficult passages.

Cargo of every conceivable description—anything that could be piled onto a sled and for which someone was willing to pay a dollar per pound to be delivered, was hauled over the trail. In 1910, Bob Griffis —a former Black Hills stage coach driver and a respected mail carrier serving Nome—received a contract from the Miners and Merchants Bank of Iditarod to transport much of the season's gold out to Seward. On November 10 (one day after the Alaska Road Commission's Colonel Walter Goodwin and his work party left Nome to improve and mark the trail), Griffis began his trek over the raw, unmarked route to Susitna Station. More than five laborious weeks after pulling out of Iditarod with over 700 pounds of gold [then] worth a quarter-million dollars (today worth $10 million dollars) secured under the canvas on the bed of his sled, he arrived in Seward, mission accomplished.

Having seen that such a haul could be successfully completed even over the primitive, uncut, unmarked, unbroken route, the bank felt even more secure after Goodwin's trail improvements resulted in the system of roadhouse support and heavy traffic that kept the trail broken. For the following eight years, Griffis' gold convoys became an annual institution, and some years he conducted more than one "gold train."

In 1912, four teams delivered 2,600 pounds of gold. On December 31, 1916, the Griffis caravan came into Knik carrying 3,400 pounds of gold behind 46 dogs. (For perspective, gold in those days sold at $20.67 per ounce. The dollar back then could buy about 20 times more than it can today. Those sleds resting outside of the roadhouse at Knik carried about $15 million in Year 2000 dollars on their beds!)

Only one major robbery ever took place on the Iditarod

Trail. In 1922, the owner of Schermeyer's Halfway Roadhouse plotted with a shady lady of Iditarod's red-light district to relieve a mail carrier, who was attracted to her favors, of his burden—$30,000 in payroll cash. After being tracked down and found hiding in California two years later, Schermeyer confessed. Also brought to justice was his partner in the crime, the shady lady professionally known as The Black Bear. Acquitted in 1927 at her second trial in Fairbanks, she afterward married the dog driver she had allegedly helped rob.

The U.S. Post Office was a major player in the establishment (and, finally, abandonment) of thousands of miles of winter trails crisscrossing Alaska Territory. The late Iditarod racer, Don Bowers, well described some of the gold rush mail service history and the mail carrier's importance. (See *An Informal Background of Mushing in Alaska, the Alaska Trail System, and the Iditarod Trail*, by Don Bowers.)

Don Bowers: "The U.S. Post Office . . . contracted for its first regular long-distance Alaskan mail route in 1895 with the son of the chief of the Taku Tlingit tribe, Jimmie Jackson. He received $700 plus $1 per letter to deliver the mail from Juneau to the gold fields on the upper Yukon River near Circle. He and two Tlingit friends went up the Stikine River in a canoe as far as they could and then went by dog sled the rest of the way to Circle, more than a thousand miles. The Indian mail carriers delivered mail year-round on the Juneau-Circle route, receiving $600 per trip, until the completion of the White Pass and Yukon Railway from Skagway to Carcross, British Columbia, in 1899.

"From the other end of the Yukon, in the winter of 1897–98 Jack Carr carried the mail from St. Michael on the Bering Sea, up the Yukon to Dawson, and over the Chilkoot Trail to Dyea. He arrived in Dyea after 82 days on the trail, covering more than 2,000 miles.

"Jimmie Jackson was the first of Alaska's legendary mail drivers, starting a tradition of 'Contract Star Route Carriers' that endured for decades. (The last dog sled mail delivery in

George Adams with U.S. Mail Team

Alaska was in the 1960s by Chester Noongwook to Savoonga on St. Lawrence Island, which until then was one of the few remaining Alaska communities without a suitable airstrip.)"

"By the early 1900s the mail driver reigned as king of the winter trail. Don Bowers helps us understand the circumstances of such travel, explaining how, " . . . winter traffic along the trails had a well-established hierarchy. At the top were the mail drivers, the parka-clad Pony Express riders of the north. They ran on schedules and usually had the biggest, fastest, best-trained teams, sometimes more than 20 dogs. They were highly respected, often opening trails after storms and pushing through hazardous conditions. More than a few mail drivers died when their sleds went through the ice or they were caught in avalanches or became trapped in blizzards.

"By law, mail teams had the right of way on all trails. The drivers always received the best seats at roadhouse dinner tables, the first servings at meals, and the best bunks. In addition to the mail, they hauled some freight and passengers, and kept their loads to about 50 pounds per dog. For the most part, mail by dog team was limited to first class, meaning letters and small packages. Like most mushers of the day, they often spent more time walking or running alongside the sled than riding it, but mail drivers were usually able to ride the runners much more frequently than other teams on the trail."

Rod Perry: *The stature of the drivers and the vital nature of their deliveries cannot be overstated. In the wonderful book by Jim Reardon about the life and times of venerable Native leader, Sidney Huntington,* Shadows on the Koyukuk, *painted this picture of the Koyukuk mail run from Tanana to Wiseman, which lasted from 1906 until 1931:*

"The monthly mail run was the sole contact with the outside world for miners and prospectors who lived in the Koyukuk in the early 1900s. There were no airplanes. Dog teams carried everything in winter . . . Letters from loved ones, magazines, and newspapers were treasures beyond value for these isolated men. In remote villages and mining camps, I've seen magazines with loose pages, the print worn from handling, treated as if they were valuable documents, as they were handed from man to man. Small wonder that mail drivers were considered special."

Alma Preston: "Some of our drivers had some, umm—let's just call them "unusual"—experiences while on their mail runs. See this snap shot here of George Adams with his team? I dont know whether his or Al Ferrin's experience was the most unusual but I'll start with George's, just the way he told it to me."

George Adams: "The Iditarod Trail wasn't just used to go straight through, but, also, to get to where we could branch off to run the mail into places off the main trunk. Like Hope. I pulled into Hope one day and if a bunch of the bystanders hadn't rushed out to help control the team by grabbing my dog's collars, I hate to think what would have happened. Right there in the middle of the main street was a man on his sled. And what should be pulling it by a chain from the sled to his collar but a two-year-old grizzly! I don't know whether the man was in town on serious business, maybe to pick up supplies, or on a bet, or just to create a sensation. But there he was.

"I found out more about the man and his bear later. Seems he was Nate White, a miner from Sunrise, six miles away. That fall he had loaded his belongings on a big sled to move his family over to Hope for the winter so the kids could go to school. The wife and kids were perched up on top of the load.

"Now the wife was quite a load all by herself. I don't know whether she was fortifying herself for an expected famine or laying on a thick layer of insulation against a long, arctic winter but she was packing maybe a couple hundred extra pounds. And disposition? Sour as spoiled milk, and a nasty temper she had, too.

"Here they come approaching Hope, the dogs really leaning into it to pull all that tonnage. From 10 feet of chain attached to the rear bent, the grizzly is trotting along behind the sled as nice as you please. Well, when they reach the edge of town, every dog in Hope cuts loose in an excited din.

"That bear just panics. As strong as the team is and as heavy as the load, that darned grizzly drags them backwards to a big cottonwood. He's still young enough he can climb and he goes up until he has the back of the sled leaning up the tree way off the ground. The kids bail off and think it's high, good fun. But the round lady rolls down the load 'til she whacks her noggin and bloodies her nose on the head board, and lands all tangled up with the wheelers. While she's wallowing and thrashing around like some beluga gone dry on a sand bar, just bellowing and screaming and cussing, all wrapped up in the tug lines, the terrified dogs start to fight and bite her. Her husband's been there from the start trying to get her free of the bedlam, if she'd only let him. When she's finally unwound and picks herself up, she's blubbering and swearing at the bear and her husband, and then she lights into her kids and the village onlookers who think it's one of the best shows they've ever seen. Alma, you couldn't *buy* entertainment like that!

"Well, they get settled into their cabin and start village life. Now that they're living in the big city they can't just let a grizzly go wandering around wherever his bear desires would take him. So he's kept on his chain that can slide along a cable running between the cabin and the outhouse. The doggoned bear's eyelids are getting pretty droopy, it's that time of year. The critter doesn't think very highly of the digs under the outhouse so the only other natural place he can reach to den up is beneath the cabin.

"He burrows under, curls up and snoozes off. You'd think everything would be fine 'til spring, but if you do, you haven't counted on the creativity of the fat lady to find something to get herself all aggravated about. From down below the floor comes this slow snoring. The husband and kids think it's kind of nice because it reassures them their friend is contentedly doing what snug bears do. But the old lady builds up a good rage. She just keeps jerking the poor critter awake by his chain, pulling him out and making him drink extra strong coffee.

"Well now, Alma, my lass, I don't know about the effect on a grizzly bear if he's awash in caffeine in the best of times during summer. But while the lady is screaming at him to guzzle concentrated brew, everything in this bear is screaming sleep and he's getting as irritated as she is. It's plain the critter's sense of humor is just used up. One day

May 1917
Hope, Alaska

Sled Grizzly

when the husband is off on some errand, the bear just gives his tormentor a cuff and sends her rolling half way across the yard. She's got plenty of padding so just picks herself up. But then she takes one look at the mad animal and scampers for cover, making it to the outhouse just a half step ahead of the grizzly. Every time she tries to escape back to the cabin, the bear rushes at her and she barely makes it back into the outhouse and slams the door. By the time her husband returns, she's been trapped for two or three hours and so mad she's spitting nails. Well, that spells doom for the bear; she shrieks that it's either the bear or her.

"That wouldn't have been much of a choice for me, but the husband was a better man than I am."

Alma Preston: "You couldn't make up stories as crazy and bizarre as some that actually took place. Al Ferrin, told me about this one."

Rod Perry: *Examination of the sign over the business establishment in the background of the grizzly and sled photo show Ferrin as one of the owners.*

Al Ferrin: "I was on the Hope run, when along the trail down Sixmile Creek I stopped at one of the trailside cabins to deliver mail to the old miner like I always did. Ol' Anthony was no where to be seen, no smoke coming up from the chimney, no answer to my halloo, nothing. Long story short, I found him dead around behind the cabin. He'd obviously had a heart attack while splitting kindling. He'd just dropped his axe, sank down on his knees, leaned over with his chest on the chopping block and died. It had been near zero for days and he was frozen solid. I had quite a time wrestling the body around the cabin and was wondering about the best way to load it when it occurred to me he was frozen into a perfect sitting position. I just rearranged some of my mail and sat him up on one of the bags like he was a proper passenger. The only thing that was in the way was his arm reaching out with the chunk of wood still frozen so tight into his hand I couldn't pull it out.

"We must have been a sight to behold coming into Hope. I suppose it might have even been humorous, in morbid sort of way, if we all weren't good friends of ol' Anthony. At the roadhouse they helped me offload and carry him around back to a shed where nothing could gnaw on him until the marshal could get there, maybe a week or two. I went on to the post office to make my delivery and get the dogs settled in for the night.

"From quite a ways off as I walked back to the roadhouse I could hear quite a hullabaloo going on inside. You know what a bunch of Anthony's old miner friends had done? They had gone back and brought him out of the shed and into the roadhouse. There at the bar on a stool sat ol' Anthony with his arm outstretched. They had tapped with the back of a boy's ax on the end of the chunk until they had it driven out from his grasp. In its place they put a glass and filled it with whisky. Those crazy miners!

"Well, we old mail drivers were never *supposed to* drink when we're working, but I figured this occasion called for at least a small shot. Maybe a couple. Well OK, several, I guess. We told our favorite stories about the deceased. Then someone brought out a mouth harp and another guy went and got a fiddle. We gathered around ol' Anthony, sang every song we thought he'd enjoy and just gave him the best sendoff we knew how. It went on through the night until he commenced to slump. We sure laughed a lot, and I guess we shed a tear at the end, but all in all we thought we did ol' Anthony proud."

———◆———◆———

The Northern Commercial Company (N.C.) bought out Alaska Commercial and operated the most prominent system of general stores and warehouses throughout the Territory. N.C. won the biggest postal contract, the Yukon mail run, as well as other contracts to deliver mail during a 31-year span over thousands of miles of trails elsewhere in Alaska. The company prided itself on the professionalism of its drivers and its well-trained and cared-for teams. Most of the men who, while the very world held its breath at the 1925 drama, ran legs of a dog team relay of life-saving serum, battling through blinding blizzards and temperatures down to 40 degrees below zero to rescue epidemic-stricken Nome from diphtheria were N.C. mail teams and drivers.

Rod Perry: *In 1969 my father (whose picture graces the cover of this book) and I worked on the brickwork of the final, major N.C. store construction in Alaska. It is now houses Nordstrom on 6th Avenue in Anchorage.*

Besides the freighters and mail drivers, individual travelers in great numbers used the Iditarod. Some of them drove full teams, some used just a dog or two to help pull a Yukon sled as they walked, and many walked carrying back packs, some accompanied by pack dogs carrying loaded panniers.

———•—•———

Al Preston: "Rod, people of all descriptions used the trails. This is a rare one. A veteran dog driver, Will Fentress told me this bizarre tale. Ol' Will had an obvious flair for a story, and he could color it up, but I never knew of him to lie.

———•—•———

Will Fentress: "Al, I know you might find this account hard to believe but I'll tell about an encounter with the strangest trail user I ever saw or heard of. I was freighting with my team of big, hundred-pound, mixed-breed malamutes that I really had to lean on hard to keep from picking a fight whenever we passed another team. What I'm saying is that that bunch of dogs didn't back down from anybody.

"Way out along a remote stretch, as I started across a long, open flat, my dogs began to act queerly, kind of fearfully, and all but stopped working. Then, as I halted the team, all eyes turned toward the far side of the flat where the trail came out from the timber.

"Out of the trees appeared a big team, long sled and driver traveling at a fast pace. The closer they came, the more upset my dogs became. Once, the oncoming driver wielded a long, blacksnake whip, cracking it above his team.

311

He was still 200 yards off but it was like a rifle shot, and my dogs jumped. Other than that, he stood stock still on the runner tails.

"As the approaching team drew closer, I just stared in amazement at those swift, lean, striders. Each one was a full half a foot taller than my own big freight dogs and every one a matched jet black. The animals looked like huge, gaunt wolves, yet not quite like wolves either. I've simply never seen their like. The contents of the long sled they pulled were shrouded by a black canvas.

"I'd been working my sled off the trail. As I got my dogs off to the side to let the oncoming team by those warriors of mine laid their ears back and began to whimper.

"As remarkable as the black team looked, they couldn't compare to the appearance of their driver. He was a giant of a man clad in a full-length, black, wolf-fur parka. He wore a huge Cossack hat of black -bear fur pulled low over his ears. His face was real swarthy and his great, black, full beard framed it. Heavy, black eyebrows accented the giant's dark, grim visage.

"As the black team passed, some of my dogs tried to bolt away farther out into the deep snow. But they couldn't because of the anchor of the others that froze there laying on the ground, just cowering pitifully. The black dogs hardly looked right or left. They payed almost no attention to my groveling team.

"Now came the strangest part of all. I tentatively raised a hand in greeting. Though we two were alone miles from the nearest other person, and though the grim traveler passed within three feet, the giant in black glared straight ahead. Al, his expression was just so cold and foreboding it still chills me to think about it! He never so much as acknowledged my presence, like I wasn't even there.

"I just stood there with goose pimples all over me, kind of dumbstruck. My dogs and I followed the forms of that mysterious train of dogs, sled and driver as they grew smaller in the distance. We watched until they vanished from the flat into the far timber. I'll tell you, Al, I couldn't have felt weirder if I'd seen the very hounds of Hades pulling the death sled driven by the Grim Reaper himself. Shoot, for all I know, that's who it might have been, hell-bent on his way to collect on a debt!

"My terrified dogs just couldn't tear their eyes from the point where those hell hounds had vanished into the woods. Minutes later, we heard the far distant, rifle-shot crack of the blacksnake."

———◆——◆———

With the likes of the Dark Rider possibly abroad, neither Will Fentress nor his team would have wanted to bed down alone by the trail that moonless night. But if they could not have made it to the sanctuary of a roadhouse before dark they might have had to do just that. Before the advent of flashlights, there wasn't a lot of travel on moonless nights. Most travelers put in at a roadhouse until daylight.

Dogs were either chained out singly or, at the more developed roadhouses, sheltered in dog barns sectioned off in individual cubicles. Some of the better-constructed barns featured openings on both ends. Heavily loaded, big teams could drive in under cover, stop, unharness and tether and feed their dogs, leaving the towline and harnesses strung out in front of the dogs in their hay-filled stalls but out of their reach. In the morning it was easy to harness up and drive out the open door at the far end.

Often, when fast-moving teams reported that slower travelers had been passed on the way, the roadhouse owner hung a "widow's lamp" out where it could be seen from as far away as possible. It only came down when the last traveler had arrived safely.

Salmon fishermen along the rivers did a brisk business supplying dog drivers with dried salmon. The premium product and most coveted were Yukon chums (dog salmon) and kings (Chinook) caught below the mouth of the Anvik

Bird Creek Road House

River. Since salmon cease feeding once they enter fresh water, the Yukon river fish that were bound for the upper river had to carry tremendous energy reserves to fuel their 1,000- or even almost-2,000-mile-long fight against the current. Lower river fish selected with a practiced eye were not "used up" like fish caught upriver near their spawning beds. Dog men knew the rich nutrients translated into performance, for "it can't come out through the feet unless it first goes in through the mouth."

Many roadhouse owners, freighters, mail contractors, a few forward-thinking individual dog team travelers as well as the many trappers who used the Iditarod to reach the points where their trapline trails branched off, contracted with salmon fishermen to deliver the dried bales to roadhouse locations. They were stored high above the ground in dry, bear- (and loose dog-) proof caches.

During summer many dog drivers left their teams to be boarded, freeing them to go about their summer work such as prospecting. Commonly, dog-boarding operations were run by the same fishermen who supplied the driver with winter dog food. As they caught and dried their catch, they fed the boarded dogs part of the resource.

Many of the initial roadhouses began as mere heated tents. Some of them survived, many went quickly out of business. Some that died out had set up in poor locations, perhaps out of sync with the regular 20-mile, day's-travel spacing. Others earned negative reputations. These were weeded out by natural economic elimination. An operator who turned a profit and saw a future in the business usually invested in better and more permanent structures and stayed in business as long as there was enough traffic to provide a good income.

Most of the roadhouses provided welcome havens and some gained widely recognized reputations for the quality of their accommodations and service. Cox's Roadhouse at Poorman featured a 22- by 30-foot central building with a lean-to kitchen attached. It boasted a dining room plus running water and an "outside white porcelain bathtub." Both a cache and an outhouse stood nearby. For the entertainment of patrons, the roadhouse had a pool table, card tables and a phonograph "with 40 records." The nine single beds were topped by springs and mattresses. Henry Cox took pride in his establishment as a resting place of comfort and leisure.

Famous church leader and intrepid dog team traveler, the Reverend Hudson Stuck, claimed that the finest roadhouse on the Iditarod Trail was the Bonanza Creek Roadhouse near Iditarod, praising the fresh meat and roomy bunks as luxuries.

Anyone familiar with Stuck's adventures and writings will vouch that the Archdeacon was no whiner. So when we read that he stopped at a filth-ridden, low-ceilinged roadhouse at Shaktoolik where he disgustingly noted that the inhospitable proprietor went on with his card game, ignoring his patrons, we know it was far below even the rough standards of a long, exhausting trail dotted with rugged outposts frequented by hard men.

However, it seems that Stuck's record of the lack of a quality reception at that coastal village roadhouse expressed a mere aggravation. His experience there could not hold a candle in shock value to accounts some of the other encounters that have come down to us through the pens of travelers who, though taken aback, had no choice but to endure whatever conditions they found where they stopped at day's end.

Al Preston: "One trail waypoint was described by an old friend as run by two 'low-lifes' who were indescribably despicable. Their scraggly hair and filthy beards looked like they had never been cut, combed or washed. Their mouths were ringed with grease. Their yellow teeth were so coated they appeared to be growing sweaters and their breath would so set you back on your heels, it smelled like they had a case of the 'zacklys' ('zackly like the bottom of the hen house!') The only thing shiny about those guys was their too-short mackinaws that shone with impregnated grime and let their bellies hang out.

"When they'd go outside to scoop up buckets of snow to melt for water, they took no care to watch what they were dragging off the ground. It was a toss-up if you got sicker from the water or from looking at the bucket contents which usually could be counted on to include sawdust, rabbit droppings, urination (animal? human?) and maybe more. My friend said they carved moose meat off a carcass lying right on the floor and when you went near it the shrews gnawing on it scattered in all directions. It was so old, it was black. As the steaks bubbled in old bear grease that had been used over and over, in a pan that had possibly never been washed, you could see dirt coating them. Anyone starved enough to eat them had to be careful not to break a tooth on the gravel from the floor imbedded in the meat. This whole insult cost my friend $1.50 and he felt lucky to survive.

"I know that tended to be pretty typical of bottom-of-the-barrel waypoint stopovers. The worst of the lot were always dirty and you didn't know what kind of vermin might lurk there. You got soaked $2 a night even if you didn't get a bunk and had to bed down on the floor with the rodents. The grub? It could be anything from red squirrel tasting like spruce pitch to scrawny rabbits, greasy beaver, grizzly that was half-raw, or tough old bull caribou shot during the rut with a taste and odor that would make a starving dog run and hide. Breakfasts often ran toward flapjacks that maybe had been cooked the week before and recycled from other guests who pushed them away, the coffee might be nearly cold and taste like poison, and you didn't even want to consider eating the dark looking, foul smelling eggs. Or maybe I should have said, 'fowl' smelling because some were fertile with baby chicks rotting in the yolks. Their canned goods were usually just left to the elements so the cans were rusted and bulged from being continually frozen and thawed with the contents turned to mush.

"The proprietor of one roadhouse I stopped at kept picking tobacco out of his yellow teeth with a fork, then he'd use the fork to stir his cooking. I'll tell you, you might pull into a place like that hungry and you didn't even have to eat; just one look at the cook, his habits and what he called food was all it took to take care of your appetite! You'd just lie in your bunk praying for the hours to fly by so you could get up and make a run for it. We used to joke that some of those operators had to post an armed guard to make sure no one escaped before morning."

Alma Preston: "During the very peak years of the Iditarod boom, The Iditarod Trail route couldn't wrest the mail contract away from the old Valdez-Fairbanks-Yukon River

Trail route. At first, mail bound for Iditarod left the Yukon at Nulato and mail bound for Nome kept on over the old, traditional route. But finally, in 1914 we won the contract, or I should say, my boss did. But the "Colonel"—he was known far and wide by that name but he actually held no official rank—made us feel like family so I say we. Here's a picture of him taking a picture of me, and here's another one of him with his favorite mail sled and lead dog. I used to ask Colonel Revell questions about his early days in Alaska and life on the trail, which I seldom got to see since I was so busy tending his dog operation along the railroad between Moose Pass and Spencer Glacier."

"Colonel" Harry Revell: "I stampeded into Cook Inlet country back in '96 looking for gold. Instead I found a wife, Eva. She was the daughter of Frank Lowell who was the real pioneer of Seward. Eva and I married in 1903 in Seward.

"Beginning in 1905, my father-in-law and I had the winter contract to run mail to Hope and Sunrise, Girdwood, Old Knik (Eklutna), New Knik (Knik) and Susitna Station. As soon as Walter Goodwin cleared the trail and roadhouse operators rushed in to set up shop, I began thinking about going after the big contact to Iditarod and Nome. I'd already been running up to Su Station for several years so I knew the first 200 miles out of Seward. I used make that run when it was really tough. We had to start all the way back in Seward; there was that horrible Crow Pass climb and descent, not much in the way of shelters along the way, and very little traffic so we were always breaking trail.

"But things were getting better. A huge improvement happened in the fall of 1908 following Goodwin's scouting trip of the winter before. They started building trail from Girdwood around toward Bird Creek. Then the next year while the railroad was being reorganized they did some

"Colonel" Harry Revell

work and pushed the grade farther around Turnagain Arm. Whether trail or roadbed, the upshot was that we gained the use of Indian Pass. What a breakthrough! After that we didn't have to use Crow Pass which had been close to impossible.

"Let me stop and tell you about that. When you climbed Rainy Pass, you were crossing the height of land over the greatest mountain range in all of North America. You started slowly gaining elevation maybe a hundred miles before you got there. The last 30 miles, you started picking up height a little faster. Then at the last, you had a steeper climb to the summit, but it wasn't bad at all.

"But when you tackled Crow Pass you had to start at sea level, and in a scant handful of miles climb 150 feet higher than Rainy Pass! The whole ascent was torture enough. But right at the last it was nearly impossible. For the last third of a mile, the climb was 45 degrees. Even with a hard-packed trail and perfect footing, no dog team ever born can pull even a light sled straight up an angle like that. Well, if you know that country around Girdwood, you know it is a deep-snow area, always snowing. That usually meant that every time you got there, you couldn't find any trace of a trail from the last traveler before you. We had to do things like go up and shovel out switchbacks the day before and let them set up overnight. We'd usually break down the load and make several trips. Going down the other side we would wrap tie-out chains around the runners to roughlock them and still not be able to keep the sled from overrunning the dogs. We usually did things like drag the sled down on its side. And Crow just brimmed with avalanche danger.

"But when we got started using Indian Pass, we found a nice, long ramp to the summit and the pass itself was 1,200 feet lower than Crow Pass. No one who hasn't hauled heavy loads with dogs can imagine the difference that change made.

"Another thing which started making the trail better was an increase in traffic into the Susitna Valley. In 1905 there was a small rush into a strike on the Yentna. A pretty sizable community sprang up around the Alaska Commercial store at Susitna Station. I think they counted about 200 men living there at least part time, and enough families with kids they built a school. Then another community began up the Yentna. Several men established roadhouses along the trail from Knik all the way past Su Station to the Yentna. The increased traffic meant the trail got broken out ahead of us more often and we didn't always have to do it. And the roadhouse operators made some trail improvements.

"When they struck gold at Iditarod, the first winter after word of the discovery went out, that would be in '09–10, a few more people *wanted* to go over the range from our side. But that didn't mean they did. As much as the Iditarod strike built up desire for trail use beyond Su Station, not many tried it because, gold strike or no gold strike, the trip was still hardly doable, just as bad as before.

"Most kept going into Iditarod from Nome and Fairbanks, because that's where the population and good trail was. That continued the next year, too, the winter of 1910–1911. Nothing changed that winter, even after Goodwin and Eide went through, cutting and marking the way. By the time their crews got done, most of that winter was shot and a musher would still have to carry the same, old, mountainous load.

"But then, at the tail end of that Goodwin-Eide winter and on through the spring and summer, businessmen hurried out there and worked like madmen to get roadhouses ready by the next fall. Then, with the first snows the fall of 1911, the flood gates burst open and the trail almost melted down from the traffic. We figured we were already hauling mail to Su Station, so why not go after the Iditarod and Nome contract?

"At that point, I started to prepare bids to try to win the mail contract. But no matter how I sharpened my pencil, I just couldn't compete with the slick operation and might of the N.C. Company, who seemed to have a lock on the contract. It might have been a lot longer to go from Valdez to Fairbanks and down the Tanana and Yukon River Trails, but they had it easy compared to us. There was so much traffic over their trail the way was being rebroken every time you turned around. Harder trail means easier, faster going which equals cheaper overhead.

"Then you consider the overhead of the roadhouses, and how that affects their fees and the quality of their service. Up on the Yukon and Tanana a steamboat capable of carrying hundreds of tons could pull right up and offload. Even between Valdez and Fairbanks they could haul in a ton or more at a time by horse-drawn sledges. Compare the economy of that to a lot of the roadhouses on the Iditarod, where you had to wait for winter and stock them piecemeal, one sled-load at a time. Freight by the pound that way is anything but cheap.

"Now consider something like dried salmon for the dogs. The best feed in the world is Yukon fish that are selected by their fat layer. The fattest ones are bound for Canada, a thousand miles away, and have fuel stored up to fight their way up there. Those salmon swim right up to the dog lots of those Yukon Trail mushers. That means a lot of them don't even have to buy them, which reduces their overhead. Now compare that with a remote roadhouse on the Iditarod, which has to buy them from a commercial operation then transport them hundreds of miles, the last way on a dog sled. By the time they get there, and you buy them, you wonder if they're made of gold. Just buy Kuskokwim fish? If you don't have anything else, they're OK, but think about it: They're pretty close to their spawning beds, and can't compare with the Yukon fish to fuel your dogs. You've got to maintain the machinery.

"For three years I tried to outbid those guys. The thing that kept edging me closer to the advantage I needed was that the railroad kept making things easier on my end and cutting down the length of my haul by dog team. Shorter trips cut our expenses and made us more and more competitive. Finally expensive as our route was per mile compared to the route up north, when our way got short enough it tipped the scales in my favor. Especially when the federal government bought out the old railroad interests, set up a new headquarters at Ship Creek, (now Anchorage), and employed thousands to really get construction rolling. We won the contract and ran the Iditarod and Nome mail for four winters, 1914 through 1918.

"But you know what? Those three years we missed, 1910 through 1913, turned out to be the biggest years of Iditarod and the most profitable for a mail contractor. By the time I was able to win the contract, Iditarod was starting to slide. That meant three things: First, as traffic tailed off, it made it harder for the roadhouses to stay profitable. Second, we had a tougher time with the trail because it didn't stay as constantly broken. Third, with the population dropping, there wasn't as much mail.

"Funny thing, the straight trail running from McGrath (in 1910, the Post Office dropped the 's') straight through Ophir and Dishkaket to Kaltag, the way the people of Nome had dreamed of, and the path of the route that Goodwin and the ARC first intended to cut, well, that never did become the most heavily used way for the Nome mail. Our main mail route went around the big, side loop to Iditarod. We also took mail through the other new Inland Empire communities that had sprung up with discoveries that followed hard on the heels of the Iditarod strike: Cripple, Poorman, Long and Ruby. So when our drivers got to Takotna, the Nome-and-way-points mail bags left on a spur that went through all of those new mining settlements and connected with the Yukon River Trail at Ruby. From there it went on down through Nulato to Kaltag, then on to Nome.

"Finally, our mail runs just got overly hard. We had too much trail to break and most of the drivers got sick and tired of it. As the conditions worked against us, slowing us up, the measures we had to take to keep to the schedule got more laborious, and that eroded the profit margin. The mail contract that had been such a lucrative opportunity was golden no more. I could see that all of the factors eroding the profitability were only going to get worse. Finally, after 1918, I just chucked it to 'em and let the contract go back to the boys up north."

Rod Perry: *1918 saw a decline in the fortunes of not only Harry Revell, but in those of John Beaton, co discoverer of Iditarod's gold. In one of Alaska's most famous tragedies, on October 25, 1918 the ship Princess Sophia sank with all 343 aboard after grounding on Vanderbilt Reef in Lynn Canal near Juneau. On the ship were John Beaton's first wife and two children. Coincidentally, lost as well was William Harper— youngest son of Arthur and Jennie Harper and the first to stand at the top of Mount McKinley—and his wife. The only survivor of the worst maritime accident in Alaska history was the Beaton's family dog, Golddigger.*

Chapter 25

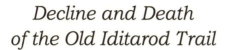

Decline and Death of the Old Iditarod Trail

THE IDITAROD BOOM HIT ITS PEAK from 1910 to 1912 after which gold production began to taper off. The Guggenheims and other big companies with the resources to mine deeper, harder-to-reach gold with bigger machinery such as huge, floating dredges bought up the best claims. The efficient techniques replaced men with machinery and out-of-work miners moved on. Iditarod faded until neighboring Flat was left the bigger town.

By 1920 Iditarod had but 50 residents. Many buildings and even Iditarod's telephone system were moved to Flat. A flood in 1922 delivered the final blow, cutting a new channel that left Iditarod marooned on an isolated, shallow side slough. The once-brawling town saw its post office close in 1929 and in 1931, it became disincorporated.

Peter Miscovitch, an almost unschooled Croatian immigrant who had arrived penniless in the great Iditarod rush, married, raised a family at Flat, and through shrewd analysis and business management ended up with most of the claims. Pete was quite an innovator and inventor and his use of new machinery and methods allowed Miscovitch and Sons to profitably mine for decades ground that had already been turned over—and sometimes twice turned over. But it was primarily limited to a Miscovitch-family show.

Rod Perry: *For all of Nome's early hopes and dreams for its own, shorter mail route, even after they got their trail, except*

U.S. Mail teams come through at Mile 54

*for those four short years of Colonel Revell's contract, the
U.S. Postal Service continued to deliver Nome mail during the
Iditarod Trail's history via the Valdez-Fairbanks and Yukon
River Trails.*

As the Alaska Railroad extended its rails northward,
the trailhead for Iditarod-bound traffic moved along with
construction, first to Anchorage, then to Wasilla. Eventual
extension of steel through the Alaska Range to Nenana
eliminated the reason for the old route over Rainy Pass for
there no longer remained any need for dog teams to laboriously
climb over the mountains to reach the Interior. In 1922, dog
drivers switched to a route over flat country north of the Range.
The northern trail to Iditarod left the railroad near Nenana and
proceeded through Lake Minchumina, Telida, and Nikolai to
connect with the former trail at Big River. Most of the few
remaining roadhouses on the old Knik-Rainy Pass-McGrath
route that had managed to stay open for the already-

dwindling traffic shut down. As roadhouse proprietors quit their operations, the government established a system of shelter cabins in the Inland Empire area. Although those cabins did not provide nearly the level of support service the roadhouses had, the unmanned, unsupplied shelters at least supported travelers to some extent. To enhance safety, the cabins featured a sign-in-and-sign-out system to track travelers. It is likely that the flow of traffic the shelters kept going, though reduced, allowed the last of the die-hard roadhouses to stay in business as long as they did.

On February 21, 1924, Fred Milligan, a dog driver on the northern route heard the distant drone of an approaching engine. At first, he may have been puzzled as to the source so deep in remote wilderness. However, it must not have taken him long to deduce that it must be emanating from an aircraft. In a few minutes he watched the plane pass almost directly overhead. It was legionary pioneer aviator, Carl Ben Eielson flying a government-owned, ski equipped de Havilland DH-4BM following the dog team trail on an historic flight, the first delivery of the U. S. Mail by air in Alaska.

Eielson had contracted to conduct 10 Fairbanks—McGrath flights to test the feasibility of mail delivery by air in Alaska. He flew one way in 2 hours, 49 minutes, and after laying over several hours, had time to make it back to Fairbanks by dark. It was the first time McGrath residents could get an answer of mail originating in Fairbanks back to its sender the same day. The Nenana-to-McGrath round trip by dog team took 10 days to two weeks. The $2 per pound rate by air was half the dog team rate. Though the Postal Service cancelled the contract after eight flights gave them all the information they needed (they could see there was potential but did not think Alaska was quite ready) Eielson's successful Fairbanks-to-McGrath delivery ushered in one new age and signaled the beginning of the demise of another.

Interestingly, in the evolutionary progression from ancient to modern transportation systems, from simple trails traveled

by foot and beasts of burden to air transport, Alaska was—
and is—unique. It skipped the usual step of covering the
country with a well-developed web of highways and rails.
Alaska went from the dog team directly into the air age.

Rod Perry: *Co discoverer of Iditarod gold, John Beaton played
a prominent part in Alaska's transition into the air age. Wealthy
through his Iditarod earnings and an astute businessman, he
invested in Star Air Service, which grew into Alaska Airlines. He
also provided key early money in the development of Bethel Air,
which evolved and branched into Wien Airlines and Northern
Consolidated Airlines. Alaskan aviation industry pioneer, the
late Ray Peterson flatly stated, "He started both those airlines.
Back then he was the only one who could have."*

The coming of the airplane brought down the curtain on
most of the old trail and roadhouse systems that had catered
to dog-team travel. So ended the most picturesque period of
Alaska's history that had begun with the great gold rushes.

As the old trail fell into disuse, the undisturbed, cleared
swath provided a perfect environment for seeds to sprout and
trees and brush to spring up. Only a few stretches near
villages and remote hunting lodges continued to be kept open
by use. Year by year, more of the marker tripods rotted, fell
and returned to the soil. The roadhouses succumbed as well.
Those built with sod roofs went first. Then, one by one, even
those structured with more lasting roof construction had
their covering cave in, leaving walls, floors and the rest of the
once-snug havens to be obliterated by nature. And so, just as
the great dogs and grizzled travelers who had frequented its
miles waned in vitality and disappeared over the final, Great
Divide, the last great gold rush trail in North America faded
into silent memory.

From the Sled:
End of the Trail Overview and

Epilogue

C.K. SNOW OF RUBY, ALASKA, who during 1915–18 represented the 4th District in the Territorial House of Representatives, offered this perspective from the end of the trail in Seward, February 15, 1919: "If you love the grandeur of nature—its canyons, its mountains and its mightiness, and love to feel the thrill of their presence—then take the trip by all means; you will not be disappointed. But if you wish to travel on 'flowery beds of ease' and wish to snooze and dream that you are a special product of higher civilization too finely adjusted for this strenuous life, then don't. But may God pity you, for you will lose one thing worth living for if you have the opportunity to make this trip and fail to do so."

Well, my friend, after just having completed a journey several times the distance of that of Snow's, we couldn't agree with him more. Together, and with the help of my old sourdough friends Al and Alma Preston, we've traveled the trail of McQuesten and Harper, Henderson and Carmack, The Three Lucky Swedes, and Pedro and Beaton and Dikeman. Now you know why this trail of ours had to start so long before and so far away from Iditarod. You've examined, first-hand and in-depth, the meanders of the greatest of the gold rush trails, how one flowed into another, and now you can comprehend how vital the transportation corridors were to the birthing and life of the Far North.

Covering the thousands of miles behind our tireless team, you got to briefly share in how Old Ben Atwater, The Goin' Kid and the rest of the old ones traveled and moved loads. On our way, many's the night under the glittering stars that the malamute chorus serenaded us, lifting their heads and pouring out their souls, perhaps compelled by an ancient urging to respond to the plaintive, drawn-out howl of a distant wolf. Through it all, the trail took us onward, ever onward . . . to Iditarod.

I couldn't have asked for a better traveling companion. You never complained, you kept your sense of humor in the heaviest going and always pulled more than your weight with the camp chores and dog care. I'll never forget you—it's tough right now to bid you farewell. Before you go, will you help me put away the dogs and sled? Just go up and unharness old Baldy there and then . . .

Wait! . . .

Shhhh . . .

Look . . . do you see him?

Close your eyes. . . . Now do you see what I see . . .?

It is a day in early March, 1973. A very old man, slightly bent from his four score years, stands alone in fastness of the northern wilderness. The old-style, pull-over, knee-length, ticking parka, recently taken from a trunk in his attic, keeps the cold at bay. He surveys the surroundings hopefully. Towering above him rise the shimmering white peaks of the Alaska Range. The stark beauty is as he recalls it, but the landscape appears lifeless. Not so much as a passing raven does he see. The thick silence begins to disappoint him. This is not the uplifting return he anticipated. Maybe Thomas Wolfe was right, "You can't go home again." Maybe he was foolish to think otherwise. He wonders if the old trail, which seems so devoid of life, is truly dead. Or might it be only dormant, like nearby Pass Creek hibernating under its winter encasement of ice and snow?

Final U.S. Mail by Dog Team Leaves Anchorage, May 28, 1917

Dead or dormant, this is not at all like the bustling trail he knew. He closes his eyes and remembers. In a clip from an old movie that has replayed so many times, yet again his mind's eye sees a man trotting up the trail toward him. Clouds of blowing snow somewhat obscure the image, but the man is obviously in the full vigor of youth, ramrod straight and strong, clad in a parka identical to the one the old onlooker now wears. Stretching out in front of the young man is a long team, 11 pairs of mighty draught dogs following an old loose leader. Their heads and tails are low, their ears are laid back, they are digging hard to pull their heavy load toward the pass. The man's mittened right hand reefs on the spruce gee pole that steers a long sled, its 14-foot-long basket heavily laden with freight. Coupled to the rear of his sled trails another of like length, similarly loaded. Behind the rear sled jogs a venerable sourdough, seemingly as aged as the mountains themselves. Every exhalation adds to the icicle buildup on the weathered old driver's long, gray beard. As the team trots by and the young man draws close, he turns to stare straight into the eyes of the trailside observer.

The old, familiar vignette has played so many times before, but this time, out beside the very trail, it seems so real. The old man at trailside wants so badly to connect to the two, engage them in trail talk, anything, just to bridge the gap. As the drivers and team draw away and a strong gust sends a dense cloud that begins to hide the image, the old man reflexively reaches out to them and opens his mouth to bid them stop.

That he went so far as to almost actually call out jolts him back to reality. Feeling foolish for allowing himself to enter so fully into a fantasy, he jerks himself out of his reverie and sees that, of course, the drivers and team are not there, not so much as an apparition. He grows angry at his lack of good sense, cursing the notions that brought him here. It was nothing but pure, unadulterated, ill-conceived idiocy for him to have expected anything uplifting to reward him for the trouble and expense of all it took to make it back here to reminisce. He closes his eyes again as dull disappointment deepens and a heavy sense of melancholy weighs upon him. No use to indulge in imaginations, they are vain. The old trail is dead. And it won't be long before he, too, crosses that last great divide.

But wait! Something begins to register on his consciousness, this time on his hearing. He catches his breath to hear more clearly. Is it? Could it be? It indeed sounds like the banging of the front end of a swiftly moving sled as it bumps over trail moguls. Now comes to his ears the unmistakable, approaching, quick panting of a working dog team . . . The old man fears that the sensory treat will fade if he opens his eyes. Yet the old familiar sounds seem so real. And they are growing closer. Then he hears the driver whistle to his team and the old man's eyes fly open.

Bursting into view from around the bend surges a rangy, gray-brown leader. He and the team that follows are certainly no phantoms. Here he comes, the spirited animal driving his team hard, his ground-eating strides closing the distance toward the old man.

"Hot Foot! On by!" The long striding husky leads his team on by and the old man's attention switches to the driver. He sees a young stranger, perhaps somewhere in his late 20s. There is a friendly, but determined glint in his eye. The old man and the young driver lock gazes, wave and connect for a moment.

"Who are you, son?" cries out the old timer to the receding man on the sled. As his team disappears behind a low hill, the driver turns slightly on his runner tails. Over his shoulder he cups a glove to his mouth and calls back, "Wilmarth!"

The Iditarod lives! Behind the unquenchable faith and relentless drive of Joe Redington, a simple, yet remarkable country visionary, the old trail has been reborn, raised to new vitality, glory and fame. The trail-breaking running of the Iditarod Trail International Championship Sled Dog Race, is underway, the longest, richest, most grueling sled-dog race in history. Intrepid men, including active miner, Dick Wilmarth of Red Devil, Alaska, with his great Lime Village leader, Hot Foot, are on the trail in quest of adventure and $50,000 in prize money.

Rod Perry: *That no road was ever built over the old trail's route and that the country it traverses remains largely raw wilderness has preserved its primitive character and colorful, gold-rush luster through the decades of abandonment as if the trail has had an appointment with destiny.*

To the trail's romantic allure may be attributed one of the main reasons the Iditarod would one day live again. A half century after heavy trail use died out, in a "man-and-team-against-the-wilderness" setting, the old path experiences a glorious rebirth. From its long slumber it awakes to hear the barely audible hiss of runners and the creaking of sled joints, it feels the staccato footfall and listens to the panting of trotting huskies. The world's longest, most grueling sled-dog race is being held over its spectacular course, capturing international attention.

In future years, Ian Woolridge of the London Daily Mail will coin the phrase to describe the event, "The Last Great Race on Earth®." Nothing else will so universally be acclaimed to epitomize the Spirit of Alaska. It will gain such international recognition that if questioned, "what comes to mind first when you think of Alaska?" more people around the world would answer, "the Iditarod!" than anything else. Eventually, the direct and indirect economic benefits of the Iditarod Race to Alaskans, not to mention the value of its intangibles, will surpass in worth all of the gold ever panned, sluiced and dredged out of Iditarod during its mining glory

So, trailmate, not so fast with unharnessing our animals. My zest for the trail is undiminished. I still hunger for the view over the next ridge and exult in the feel of the team's power coming back to me through the sled. The dogs are hitting their tugs, anxious to be gone. The pull of the trail is just too magnetic to resist. I need a traveling companion. . . .
Old friend, will you come?

Preview to Volume II

---◆---

TRAILBREAKERS
PIONEERING ALASKA'S IDITAROD

Volume II
Founding the Last Great Race on Earth®

AFTER LAYING DORMANT for a half century, the old trail is revived with an epic adventure. A great sled dog race courses over its thousand-plus miles.

Race pioneer and historian, Rod Perry has written *Volume II* in two major parts:

In *Part 1*, he chronicles the tries, trials and tribulations of legendary race founder, Joe Redington as the visionary man struggles amid apathy, disbelief, ridicule and open opposition to finally prevail to get the event off 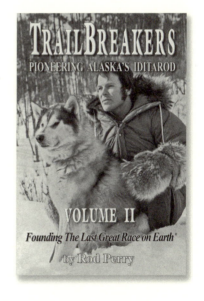 the ground and eventually imbed it into the core of Alaska's culture. Rod tells heretofore untold tales of the founding, known only to a very few Redington family members and other old race insiders closest to Joe (such as how the major part of the purse for the trailblazing race was secured through blackmail of a very prominent Alaskan!)

Part 2 details the incredible story of the preposterously crazy, wild and wooly, audacious, glorious first Iditarod Trail Race. There's never been another remotely like it. The story is told as only one who ran it, and one of Rod's talent as a raconteur can.

Even many of Rod's race preparations are outrageous, such as the revelation that one of his mentors is none other than the fabled old sourdough who had "dispatched" his first wife, cremated her body in the cabin stove then disposed of her ashes down a hole in the ice of Lake Louise!

During the race itself, the trail-breaking pioneers experienced incredible adventures:

- Two men lost for more than a week and nearly starving before making their way back to civilization—and all the while, race officials not even aware they were missing!

- One member of a two-man team (driver tandems were welcomed on the first race) too badly injured to transport on a sled, had to be abandoned by all of the drivers bringing up the tail end of the race until no one else was coming. His fate was dependant upon those drivers making it through to the next distant checkpoint in hopes that primitive communication there would be able to connect to the outside world and summon help.

- An official and two competitors drunk most of the way.

- A man allowed into the race without paying an entry fee or sending out supplies, making his way across the course by raiding food drops of other racers—mainly Rod's.

Race fans acquainted with today's highly structured event can hardly imagine the rag-tag disorganization and wild craziness.

The core of *Part 2* features the two-installment article published in the March and April 1974 issues of *Alaska Magazine*, the longest two-part article in the history of the publication and the first article on the Iditarod to ever hit the international periodical press.

As well, *Part 2* tells the story of Dick Wilmarth, the gold miner who came out of nowhere to win the first race, his only prior experience running dogs having been one winter on a trapline, and that 10 years before. As of March 2009, of the hundreds of finishers who have driven their dog teams across Alaska to cross the finish line on Nome's Front Street, Dick Wilmarth was the first, the trailbreaker of race era trailbreakers.

Rod holds what he believes to be the only extant recordings of all of the radio reports of the first race, taped by the late Ann Sisson who sat dutifully by the radio with her old cassette recorder for over a month in 1973. Many of the reports are worked into *Part 2*.

Following *Part 2* is a section on "*Myths, Misconceptions and Misleading Bunk.*" Rod corrects untruths and skewed information that has been repeated so often by so many for so long that much of it has become entrenched in race lore as unquestioned fact. Indeed, some of the inaccuracies have worked so well to add romantic color and fit so well with race promotions they seem better than fact. A few of the inaccuracies have taken on a stature of that elevates them beyond mere legend. Indeed, some have grown to the point of being held virtually sacred by unknowing race fans, all because the media endlessly repeats the errors, concoctions and embellishments handed down by earlier fabricators.

Some might view Rod's unveiling of the truth as outright heresy.

Rod, feeling strongly that history should strive for accuracy says, "So be it!

Books by Rod Perry may be purchased at
www.rodperry.com

Golden Time Line

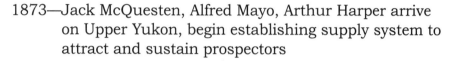

1873—Jack McQuesten, Alfred Mayo, Arthur Harper arrive on Upper Yukon, begin establishing supply system to attract and sustain prospectors

1875—George Holt becomes first white prospector to find and cross Chilkoot Pass, begins era of seasonal prospecting expeditions in from Alaska Coast

1882—Prospectors begin to stay year-around on upper Yukon

1896—Klondike Gold discovered, late August. Nearby miners stampede, stake all of Bonanza Creek and El Dorado Creek bottoms within days

1897—Rush to the Klondike begins seven months after main creek bottoms taken

1898—Great Klondike Gold Rush: major part occurs almost two years after strike

1898—Nome Gold Strike: discovery of upland placers

1898—White Pass and Yukon Railroad (WP&YR) begins at Skagway

1899—WP&YR broaches mountains, establishes temporary railhead in interior

1899—Golden Sands of Nome discovered

1899—U.S. Mail contracts with dog drivers to send winter mail to Nome over WP&YR and down Yukon River Trail

1900—WP&YR finishes railroad to Whitehorse, Yukon Territory

1902—Fairbanks Gold Strike

1902—WP&YR builds Overland Trail, Whitehorse to Dawson

1902–3—Fairbanks develops connecting trail to Gakona to join Valdez-Eagle Trail. U.S. Mail contract for Nome's winter mail soon switches to this "All American" route

1903—Alaska Central Railroad construction begins in Seward, bound for Fairbanks

1904—Abraham Appel establishes post on Kuskokwim at Takotna River mouth

1905—Alfred Lowell and son-in-law "Colonel" Harry Revell contract to carry U.S. Mail by dog team to communities around east side of Cook Inlet and Susitna Valley

1906—Ganes Creek gold strike begins five years of Inland Empire discoveries

1907—Alaska Central Railroad goes bankrupt with 52 miles of track, 72 miles of roadbed and approximately 150 miles of surveyor's pack trail completed

1907—Major Wilds Richardson of Alaska Road Commission (ARC) upgrades Valdez – Fairbanks dog-team and pack trail to winter-sledge and summer-wagon road

1907—20 miners from McGrath area travel over trailless wilderness, averaging a month to reach Susitna Station. All straggle in, their condition described as "pitiful"

1908—Colonel Walter Goodwin of ARC with a crew of four scout feasibility of proposed Seward-to-Nome Mail Trail early in year. Become first to travel entire route

1908—Girdwood-to-Bird Creek Trail: mid-year construction effort to replace Crow Pass with easier, safer trails toward Upper Cook Inlet

1908—Iditarod Gold Strike, Christmas Day. No word of late '08 discovery gets out as miners remain in remote location until ice-out

1908—Passage over route of future Iditarod Trail still infrequent. Desolate wilderness between McGrath and Susitna Station lacks trail and lack of resupply sources continue to thwart would-be travelers

1909—Iditarod Gold Rush finally begins in mid '09 when, one-half year after discovery, miners leave site to record claims

1909—Alaska Central Railroad, during reorganization under receivership, extends rails to Girdwood and primitive roadbed another 40 miles, allowing access to Indian Pass

1909—Even after Iditarod Gold Rush creates powerful pull, lack of trail from Su Station to McGrath keeps travel infrequent over future route of Iditarod Trail

1909—U.S. Mail reaching Iditarod and Nome comes through Fairbanks until 1914

1910—Bob Griffis contracts to bring 700 pounds of gold out of Iditarod. With no trail yet from McGrath to Susitna Station, struggles more than five weeks to reach Seward

1910—Still no trail from Susitna Station over desolate Alaska Range stretch of Iditarod Trail, still hardly traveled even with last great gold rush at peak

1910–11—Walter Goodwin from Nome with nine men, 42 dogs, and Anton Eide, from Seward with similar crew, construct the Iditarod trail, first-ever defined trail over route

1911—Late winter-spring, still no great use of new Su Station-McGrath stretch. It's cut, but daunting. Mushers must

carry everything with them to supply their trip, start
to finish

1911—Entrepreneurs hurry to use last of winter trail, then
summer building conditions to establish roadhouses
Susitna Station to Iditarod; finally everything in place
for traffic

1911—Iditarod Trail really begins to be the Iditarod
Trail as most think of it. Dog team and foot travel
extremely heavy

1914—"Colonel" Harry Revell captures contract to take
Iditarod and Nome mail from Seward

1915—U.S. government takes over building railroad,
Anchorage becomes construction headquarters.
Mail drivers pick up mail farther inland from trains
carrying it from Seward

1917—Last-ever dog-team mail delivery out of Anchorage
leaves in late March

1918—Iditarod traffic and mail decrease to point Colonel
Revell gives up mail contract.

1922—Alaska Railroad reaches Alaska Interior, rendering
need to cross Alaska Range by dog team obsolete. Use
of old route to Iditarod via Rainy Pass largely ceases.
North of Range, Nenana becomes new trailhead, trail
leads through Minchumina, Telida, Nikolai

1924—Pioneer aviator Carl Ben Eielson, makes first mail run
by air in Alaska

Late 1920s—Dog-team mail along Iditarod Trail phases out.
Teams continue to be heavily used across Alaska
Bush for travel, transport, trapping and racing

More About the Author

———◆———

GROWING UP ON THE OREGON COAST, Rod had a father whose compelling descriptions summed with his avid reading about the North to inspire his enthusiasm for life in Alaska. In 1963, just five years after the territory became the forty-ninth state, he first came to southeastern Alaska to work with the Alaska Department of Fish and Game. After returning to Oregon State University to finish a Bachelor of Science degree in wildlife management, Rod and his brother, Alan, moved to Alaska permanently.

During his first years in Alaska, he helped coach the wrestling team at Dimond High School in Anchorage with Larry Kaniut, who would go on to become the well-known author of *Alaska Bear Tales I and II, Some Bears Kill, Bear Tales for the Ages, Danger Stalks the Land* and other popular books. Rod and Alan both won Alaska freestyle (Olympic-style) wrestling championships in their respective weight classes in 1968 and 1969.

On the Kenai Peninsula, fabled then as supporting one of the greatest moose populations in the North, Rod served for a time on a moose research project. Though he was highly interested in the work, his creative nature, thirst for adventure and bent toward independence made agency work too confining. Additionally, a big part of his reason for moving north had been his vision to produce his own outdoor adventure motion pictures.

In 1969 Rod began assembling footage that would become part of his major motion picture, *Sourdough*. It depicts the story of a venerable old prospector and trapper, a member of a vanishing breed attempting to carry on a traditional northern wilderness lifestyle amidst a passing old-time Alaska. Rod's father Gilbert Perry, (pictured on the cover of this book), starred as the old sourdough. With final production help from Bob Pendleton, George Lukens and Martin Spinelli of Anchorage's Pendleton Productions plus Hollywood's Albert S. Ruddy Corp. (which produced *The Godfather* and *The Longest Yard,* among others) *Sourdough* swept around the globe in 1977–78. To this day more viewers worldwide have seen it than any other motion picture ever filmed in Alaska, including features made in Alaska by major Hollywood companies.

During the years of filming *Sourdough* Rod took time out each season to guide sheep hunters in the Wrangell Mountains with master guide, Keith Johnson. He also managed to work in a lot of his own hunting. On one memorable marathon, Rod, his brother, Alan, and their friend John Lindeman made a 120-mile-long backpack hunt for sheep. That same fall he continued to take friends in quest of moose until he and six others had their winter meat supply.

Needing a dog team as part of his motion picture cast led Rod to assemble a few huskies, which he boarded with friends, Mike and Carolyn Lee. On one fateful weekend driving dogs at the Lees, Rod met dog musher, Joe Redington. The man set Rod's imagination afire. Joe said he was planning a sled-dog race of epic proportions to be named The Iditarod Trail International Championship Sled Dog Race. Rod did not see how he could prepare and compete while in the thick of filming *Sourdough* but somehow, some way, he just had to go.

The idea of staging an event of such a size, cost and difficulty drew endless public ridicule and scorn, especially from Anchorage-area sprint mushers. As a result, although the Anchorage bowl held half of the state's total population, only one local driver—Rod—was interested enough or had enough faith in the Iditarod to compete in the first race. The media, therefore, focused more attention on him than might be expected for a seventeenth-place finisher. Drawing even more of the home-town air time and ink than Rod, however, was his big, Malamute-Siberian lead dog, a real character named Fat Albert. Anchorage media soon made the colorful dog a local celebrity.

After completing the historic first Iditarod in 1973, and with the snows hardly melting from the trail, Rod chronicled his and Fat Albert's wild, primitive, trail-breaking experiences for *Alaska Magazine* in what editor Ed Fortier said was the longest two-part article ever to appear in that journal. The article was otherwise historic in that it was the first-ever feature-length piece on the Iditarod Trail Race to hit the international periodical press. One result was that Fat Albert's celebrity status began to spread beyond Alaska's border.

The following year, the *National Observer* (a publication noted for journalistic excellence and a readership among the country's moneyed intelligentsia) ran twelve straight weeks of Fat Albert and Rod Perry news. The *Observer* was the weekly news magazine companion to *The Wall Street Journal,* and several weeks, the *Journal* itself printed the coverage. That put the race before the eyes of the nation's foremost business and political leaders. It was reported that over 160 newspapers around the country ran some, if not all of the articles. The *Observer* staff stated that the series drew more reader response than anything else in the history of their publication, including their coverage of the Kennedy assassination and Watergate.

By the third year of the contest, *Sports Illustrated* took the race to its millions. Associate editor Coles Phinizy opined that in the short history of the Iditarod, the event had already established its Babe Ruth—but that the figure was not a man, but a dog named Fat Albert. Phinizy devoted a significant share of the feature to Rod's big leader. *Reader's Digest* picked up the *Sports Illustrated* article, further extending the legacy of Fat Albert.

With all of the vast coverage, Fat Albert became the most well-known sled dog since Balto, the lead dog famed for the

Rod Perry with Fat Albert

1925 Nome Serum Run. Fat Albert publicity on the pages of some of the most widely read newspapers and magazines in the United States played a significant part in jump-starting the Iditarod in the international consciousness.

345

Then Cecil Andrus, Secretary of the Interior under President Jimmy Carter, appointed Rod to the original Iditarod National Historic Trail Advisory Council. In 1980, personally worried that the new agency trail administrators might not be "doggy" enough, Rod outfitted and led the top three local officials to McGrath by dog team.

Rod and his brother, Alan, ran the first six races, three apiece, placing in the money each time. Rod has often lamented that his two biggest undertakings, *Sourdough* and the Iditarod, overlapped. *Sourdough* would have been better without the Iditarod to divert his energies and visa versa. But Rod states emphatically that he would not have given up either for the world.

Away from the spotlight, usually on his own, Rod has promoted the race in every way he could. As an example, he designed and produced the large and colorful Anchorage–Nome Iditarod Mushers patch. It is one of the world's most famous, exclusive and coveted patches, and one that, properly, may be worn only by drivers who have officially completed the great race. Using a picture taken of him and his team approaching Nome on the first Iditarod for a model, Rod became "the musher on the patch."

In order to run the 1977 Iditarod, it was necessary for Rod to drive his team some 175 miles through largely trackless wilderness from his training headquarters at remote Lake Minchumina. On the way out he encountered trapper Leroy Shank, beginning a long friendship. As Rod's party stayed at Leroy's remote cabin overnight, a dream was kindled within the trapper to run his trapline by dog team. Driving dogs on his trapline led Leroy to driving dogs on the Iditarod, which finally led to him spawning the idea for the North's other epic sled dog race, the Yukon Quest. That race runs a 1,000 miles between Fairbanks, Alaska and Whitehorse, Yukon Territory.

Leroy invited Rod to stay at his Fairbanks home the winter of 1983–84 and help him, his friend, Roger Williams and the support group they had assembled get the Yukon Quest off the ground. Leroy, Roger and Rod worked 16-hour days, seven days a week, all winter long on the project. Early on, the three added Bud Smythe to form a quartet to drive to Whitehorse. There they spent four days breaking the news of Leroy's plan to Canadian mushers, government officials and the public, convincing them of the Yukon Quest's tremendous potential and helping them get an official structure started.

On their journey to Whitehorse and back the four discussed and argued race philosophies and rules. A number of the rules that became Yukon Quest cornerstones and characterize the race, particularly during its early years, were either of Rod's creation or carried his input.

Following his early Iditarod years, Rod fished commercially for everything from razor clams, shrimp and king crab to herring, halibut and salmon. Most prominently, he owned and operated a Bristol Bay salmon drift gillnet business for many years with his partner, Reverend Keith Lauwers, one of Alaska's most well-known and beloved ministers.

Besides big-game guiding, working on moose research, commercial fishing, and running the Iditarod, Rod humorously supposes that he can lay claim to having done just about everything else on the classic Real Alaskan list. He has survived several bear charges, his closest call being the encounter at three paces in a dense thicket with a snarling sow with cubs guarding a kill. He has lived in the Alaska Bush, some of that time in Eskimo villages where he was honored with an Eskimo given name, Bopik. Rod even developed a taste for Native delicacies such as muktuk (whale skin with blubber attached) and oshock (walrus flipper buried in the frozen ground for a year to ferment.) Rod helped build three log cabins. He served nearly two decades with the Alaska Department of Fish and Game.

While Rod does lack a couple of musts on most people's short list of necessary Real Alaskan accomplishments, he laughingly boasts others that, though unusual and bizarre, should more than make up for the omissions. For instance, Rod has never been a bush pilot. But how many bush pilots can truthfully claim to have ridden a wild moose? (Brother Alan, later rode one, too.) Nor has he climbed Mount McKinley (although, with their dog teams, Rod and his old pal Ron Aldrich helped veteran freighter Dennis Kogl haul a climbing team's gear and supplies for a Mount McKinley assent through McGonnigal Pass to a high ridge above the Muldrow Glacier.) On the other hand, how many McKinley climbers can truthfully boast to have sucked milk straight from a moose's udder? Rod has done that, not once, but twice! (He says the first time was spurred by curiosity, the second by hunger.)

For some 25 years Rod's old wrestling-coach friend, author Larry Kaniut, prodded him to write a book. His knowledge of gold-rush history and intimate familiarity with the details of the founding of the Iditarod Trail Sled Dog Race made producing this two-volume work second-nature to Rod. How the original gold rush trail came to be—*Volume I*, and how the modern race was established—*Volume II*, came as readily as driving his dog team over a well-broken trail.

Rod and his wife, Karen, have raised and home-schooled a family of five children, Jordan, Ethan, Levi, Laura and Gabriel. They live in Chugiak, Alaska.

Resources and Recommended Readings

———◆———

Israel C. Russell, National Geographic Society

An Informal Background of Mushing in Alaska, the Alaska Trail System, and *the Iditarod Trail* by Don Bowers

Shadows on the Koyukuk by Sydney Huntington as told to Jim Reardon

Two years in the Klondike and Alaskan Gold-fields by William B. Haskell

Alaska Department of Natural Resources, Division of Parks and Outdoor Recreation. *Alaska State Trails Program.* Online at http://dnr.alaska.gov/parks/aktrails/ats/idita/ iditarod2.htm

Bowers, Don. *An Informal Background of Mushing in Alaska, the Alaska Trail System, and the Iditarod Trail.* Mike Zaidlicz, Bureau of Land Management, and Joan Dale and Rolfe Buzzelle, Alaska Office of History and Archaeology, contributers. Online at http://backstage-iditarod.blogspot. com/2008/06/don-bowers-history-of-iditarod-trail.html

Brooks, Alfred Hulse. *Blazing Alaska's Trails.* Fairbanks: University of Alaska Press, 1953 (2nd Ed. 1973).

Forselles, Charles. Edward Pratt, ed. *Count of Alaska: A Stirring Saga of the Great Alaskan Gold Rush: A Biography.* Anchorage, AK: Alaskakrafts Publishing, 1993.

Hamilton, W. R. *The Yukon Story.* Vancouver, B.C., Canada: Mitchell Press, 1967.

Haskell, William B. *Two Years in the Klondike and Alaska Gold Fields.* Hartford, Connecticut: Harford Publishing Co., 1898.

Heller, Herbert L., ed. *Sourdough Sagas.* Cleveland, Ohio: World Publishing, 1966.

Huntington, Sidney. Jim Reardon, trans. *Shadows on the Koyukuk: An Alaskan Native's Life along the River as told to Jim Reardon.* Anchorage, AK, and Portland, OR: Alaska Northwest Books, 1993.

Iditarod National Historic Trail Alliance. *Iditarod National Historic Trail.* Online at www.iditarodnationalhistorictrail.org.

Martinsen, Ella Lung with Edward Burchall Lung. *Black Sand and Gold.* Portland, OR: Binford & Mort Publishing, 1976.

Minter, Roy. *The White Pass Gateway to the Klondike.* Anchorage, AK: University of Alaska Press, 1987.

Russell, Israel C. "Timberlines." *National Geographic Magazine 14* (February 1903). 80–81

Russell, Israel C. "An Expedition to Mount St. Elias, Alaska." *National Geographic Magazine 3* (May 1891). 55–204.

Russell, Israel C. "Second Expedition to Mount Saint Elias, in 1891." *Thirteenth Annual Report of the United States Geological Survey 1891–'92.* Washington, D.C. : Government Printing Office, 1893.

Russell, Israel C. "A Journey up the Yukon River." *Bulletin of the American Geological Society 27, No.2* (1895). 143–160.

Russell, Israel C. *North America.* New York and London: D. Appleton and Company, 1904.

Herbert L. Heller, editor *Sourdough Sagas.* Cleveland World Publishing Company, 1966 U.S. Dept. of the Interior, Bureau of Land Management. Iditarod National Historic Trail. Online at http://www.blm.gov/ak/st/en/prog/sa/iditarod.html.

Walden, Arthur T, [Treadwell]. *A Dog Puncher on the Yukon.* Rpt. Wolf Creek Books, Inc., 2005; Houghton Mifflin, 1928.

Wright, Allen A. *Prelude to Bonanza : The Discovery and Exploration of the Yukon.* Sidney, B.C., Canada: Gray's Publishing, 1976.

Also, be sure to visit the Anchorage Field Office of the Alaska Bureau of Land Management's Iditarod National Historic Trail. It's a trip well worth making.

Caption Merrill and Alma Leonhardt visit Anchorage, 1918